AF581265

No Body Armor

Donald R. White

The Author greatly appreciates the assistance of noted Vietnam War Historian Bernie Weisz in the writing of this narrative. Bernie Weisz is also a master of the English language and book reviewing.

ISBN: 978-1-4834-0049-5 (sc)
ISBN: 978-1-4834-0227-7 (hc)
ISBN: 978-1-4834-0048-8 (e)

Library of Congress Control Number: 2013911658

Lulu Publishing Services rev. date: 8/26/2013

TABLE OF CONTENTS

— Chapter One —

Background

St. Matthew 7:13

Enter ye in at the strait gate,
for wide is the gate and broad the way
that leads us to destruction.

On the beautiful afternoon of May 27th 1955 I left the Civic Auditorium at Ardmore, Oklahoma. I had just graduated from High School. I stepped outside at about seven pm. I looked up and saw many swallows and swifts flying around, in the warm spring air. I heard the church bells ringing at the Methodist Church, across the street. I was young and of good heart. I was your typical young man with no anger for any living soul. I had no clue to what lay just down the road. The reader should be forewarned that this book ends in stark reality and if your senses are tender perhaps you should proceed no further. In the next fourteen years I had crossed the boundaries that bound humanity to a safe and sane course and become a stark realist, with little remorse for the violent actions that my vocation dictated. Nevertheless my life was one that most would think quite normal for the 50s. Bill Haley and the comets were really roaring and rock & roll was here to stay. Elvis was a young kid just about to make his move. I laughed and loved life and worked hard in the tire business. During school I had a few fistfights like many young men do at that time of life. James Dean was king and your collar was up, pants low, and a ducktail was what was happening. You had to be cool and tough, without really knowing what tough was all about. I started out with a 1939 Buick that I bought on a salvage yard for ten dollars, and fixed up to run. One day I saw some girls I barely knew walking down the street and to show off I speeded up and hit a drainage dip. Both my hood and turtle back flew up and one of the doors came open. As I sped off, I looked in the rear view mirror and the girls were lying on the sidewalk convulsed with laughter, it was time for another car, which was a 1946 Chevy. Previously I had joined the Oklahoma National guard in 1954.I liked the guard we had weekly meetings and an occasional weekend at the firing range. We fired the M-1 Rifle and other light infantry weapons. Summer camps were two weeks long at fort hood, Texas. After two years I made sergeant E-5 and got the big head. In 1957, I had changed to a 1952 ford and was working in automobile parts. That was the year I married a young Lady and it was a mistake for both of us. I soon became a divorced man and joined the crowd. In 1958, I was the shop foreman of the Montgomery Ward tire shop at the exalted salary of fifty dollars per week. There were major changes in an otherwise normal life that year.

As 1958 passed, I tired of menial jobs. In my generation there were few scholarships and student loans for higher education. My parents were lower income but great parents. My father was in the army in WW1 and the navy in WWII. I decided to join the army, which I did on August 1, 1958. Twenty years and a month later I retired. I was infantry all the way and if I did it again would do the same. I came down with strep throat in airborne school so that took care of that. After basic and advanced infantry training I was sent to the 25th Division in Hawaii. I got off the boat on December 24, 1958 and pulled my first police call on New Year's Day 1959. The years went by slowly and after twenty four months in Hawaii I went to the sixth Infantry at Ft Hood, Texas. While there, I married my wonderful wife of fifty years on October 19, 1962. I had received two promotions previous to buck Sergeant E-5 and then to Staff Sergeant E-6. I was on leave, and had been married three days when the phone rang at 0330 in the morning. It was the 1st Sergeant and he said, return to the unit quickly. It was the Cuban Missile Crisis, and at six pm the next day I loaded our armored vehicles on railroad flat cars at the railhead. We were gone from Ft. Hood from October 23rd until December 15th having been fully armed and waiting at the Hollywood race track just north of Miami. In October 1963, I was sent to the 1st Battalion 27th infantry at Scofield Barracks on Oahu. I was back in the 25th and preparations for Vietnam. The Honolulu Advertiser (local newspaper) and a famous one, had picked up rumors that we were going to go to Vietnam. The army always caused a man extra stress, but for the unit it certainly upped the feelings of anxiety. We began to have practice alerts where we made a complete load out of equipment and even loaded trucks and proceeded to an assembly area down behind wheeler field of Pearl Harbor Fame. We were all the way to the assembly area before being told it was only practice. I was the C Company Weapons platoon sergeant and as such was also a trained forward observer and assistant to the platoon leader. We went through the jungle training school and survival school twice. We began to run field exercises on summit trail along the top of the mountain chain on the east side of Oahu (windward). One field problem on the trail, lasted seventeen days and it rained every day. I had been selected to go through an extensive weapons test also that lasted twenty two days. Later on in the war this was of great benefit to me. We test fired hundreds of rounds from two assault rifles /the M-16 and stoner/. We also fired the M-14 against the assault rifles. The M-14 was great, and was lighter than the old M-1 and loaded more ammo. The M-14 would be a great weapon for the open areas of Europe. I felt like stoner was a better weapon than the M-16. The M-16 had difficulty with accuracy past fifty meters. Today's M-16's have a much better barrel giving far better performance. However for the Vietnam jungle, the M-16 was great because of the very short range that we met the enemy at. With so much point blank action taking place the M-16's hitting power and rate of fire were superb.

There were actually two Vietnam wars. The First Vietnam took place at MACV headquarters in Saigon. There, Officers and Enlisted wore khaki and tropical worsted uniforms with their ribbons. These people were nice and clean and lived the best of a tough war. At MACV /military assistance command Vietnam/ the press conferences were held, and it was here that war correspondent's from many nations assembled. They tried to shoot holes, in the briefing the American public information officer gave them in the daily situation rundown. The correspondent's, mostly American, referred to the press conference as the Saigon Follies. The American press has a special responsibility for the American people turning against their soldiers. The second Vietnam war was in a place called Nam. In Nam, men seldom smiled or laughed. Most conversations were hushed and serious. In Nam, everyone was tired, dirty, and dangerous. The long black train ran every day in NAM. I operated in Nam and was in Saigon one day passing through. In Nam we were first armed with the M-14 rifle. It had a selector and could be fired on full Auto. It fired the 7.62 NATO cartridge and was great for open field warfare. In Nam only the Saigon plains area in 111 Corp had much open area, and was mostly rice fields. In February 1966 at Cu Chi we were issued the M-16 assault rifle. The much maligned M-16 was a very light weapon with a high rate of fire. The M-16 fired a small cartridge, in the 223-caliber range. When first used in Nam it had a few malfunctions. This was caused by magazine springs mashed to tightly. We had twenty or thirty round magazines, if the twenty was loaded with eighteen and the thirty loaded with twenty eight the rifle functioned just fine. It was quick and easy to tear down and clean, which I required of my men each day, situation permitting. The M-16 slug had super velocity and tumbled, when it hit an enemy soldier it resulted in a quick kill, in most cases. I have seen enemy KIA hit in the head, with the inside of their cranium shining. I said it was a long black train. Every man except the M-60 gunners carried twenty two magazines. We also carried six Fragmentation grenades a piece, that were absolutely devastating. American rifle platoons were also armed with the Claymore command detonated anti personnel mine. In my platoon's we carried twenty two, even though we seldom had twenty men, being always at near half strength. The TO&E called for forty four enlisted men and one officer. I was a platoon leader more often than not, because of casualties. We had one M-79 grenade launcher in each squad. The M-79 was an effective weapon, very accurate out to fifty yards. The only drawback, was a small killing radius. In addition, I had most of my men carrying the M-72 Law, an anti tank weapon that was a bunker buster. Normally, we also had two M-60's and I had big troops for gunners. We carried as much m60 ammo as humanly possible. The M-60 was a very good machine gun, that fired the 7.62 NATO cartridge. Our enemies, the hard core black uniformed Viet Cong and the well-trained khaki uniformed NVA, carried the AK-47, a very deadly weapon. There has been much discussion comparing the M16 and the AK-47. They were both high velocity DEATH, that were both equals, except the AK-47 was better in bamboo. The AK-47 cartridge was a 7.62 caliber and would cut bamboo whereas the M-16 would ricochet off. The enemy outnumbered us in many point blank combats, but never had more than five or six magazines a piece, as was verified by body count. In addition their grenades had been out there a long time and some of them malfunctioned. They carried the standard communist bloc machine guns and Chinese Claymores, both deadly but we always had more and better munitions. Some of the VC hardcore were skillful and brave. The NVA were better trained, armed and led, than the VC. The VC, being guerrillas, were mostly recruited in South Vietnam. In addition, the RPG /rocket propelled grenade/ was a deadly weapon for both vehicles and personnel and was used by both VC and NVA.

The late Howard University Professor Barnard Fall wrote two great books about the war. He stated that the terrain was the most awful that Infantry had ever experienced. The Books were ***"Street Without Joy"*** and ***"Hell in a Very Small Place(1)"***. The American Army and Marine infantry went everywhere, and many places the French in the first war, never went. To do this the armed forces developed special uniforms called jungle fatigues. These uniforms were probably the best that could have been developed. When wet, they dried quickly. They were a light green and blended in with the Woods or if you prefer jungle. The Special Forces said a man in a tiger suit is a man in a tiger suit, but the light green works. We had large rucksacks and two canteens, and water is heavy. We had a first aid pouch and in addition, if the supply system was working, carried three meals of combat rations, many very old. Some of the combat rations were uneatable and sometimes we had one meal of LRP /long range patrol/ rations. They were much better, but in the infantry units I was in, we had them only once in thirty or forty days. We carried salt pills and malaria tablets. We also carried Halazone tablets to kill the pathogens in the water. More often than not, we had to drink creek water. Mostly we slept in the jungle in ambush and lying on the ground. The rucksack load also included an M-72 law per man and a Claymore mine. My load was heavier, as I carried the platoon's extra three bandoliers of M-16 ammunition and everyone carried at least one belt of M-60 machine gun ammo. Then add to all that, your individual weapon and grenades, and the RTO carried an Anprc25 radio. The load totaled a good sixty or seventy pounds per man. There it is, and it was not a war for fat boys. The temperature was always near 100 and humidity mostly Maximum. It was sometimes cooler in the monsoon but chilly at night in the highlands with a wet uniform on. The enemy had black pajamas for the VC and heavy khaki for the NVA. Why the communist bloc could not come up with better and cooler uniforms, I don't know. The enemy's load was much less than ours. There were several factors that caused it. Their food was rice in a sock around their neck. Some had canteens, and as they were acclimated, they didn't need Halazone. They had no salt, but sometimes had malaria tabs. They carried the AK-47 or weapons captured from the South Vietnamese, M-16s or M-1 rifles with their machine guns and claymore mines. One big factor, both good and bad for them was they had far less ammo and grenades than us. Unlike us, they lived underground in miles of tunnels and deep bunkers. The triple canopy and heavy jungle and bamboo added to the tunnels and bunkers, negated the effect of our air and artillery support to a definable degree. Our Army units carried NO flak jackets and NO body armor of any kind, except flak jackets on firebases. Some US Army mechanized infantry battalions had flak jackets. The NVA and VC like us had no body armor. In WWII the 90th Infantry Division had more days in combat than any other US Division: 308. The average infantry soldier in NAM had 365 days the tour length. General S.L.A. Marshall in his book ***"Men Against Fire(2)"*** determined not more than 30% of WWII US Infantry soldiers fired their weapons. Steven Ambrose's fine book, CITIZEN SOLDIERS (3) stated in WW11 Infantry units, only 11% fired their weapons. General S.L.A. Marshall stated in Men Against Fire(2) almost 100% US infantry in Vietnam fired their weapons, while engaged in battle.

There have been many young soldiers who have stated the manuals /the book/ were useless. These young troops meant well, but they were incorrect. The tactical manuals that lay out basic fire and maneuver technique are actually just guides and not regulations. They represent the combined knowledge of American fighting men, gained in many wars. The three standard maneuvers for light infantry units are frontal attack/fire teams leap frog/ or maneuver right or left. Light infantry is infantry on foot, and not mounted or moving in M-113 armored personnel carriers with fifty caliber machine guns. All the units I was in were light infantry on foot. On only two occasions were we mounted on the M-113. The basic scene was in an encounter battle, as many battles were in NAM, or to be more formal a recon in force. The recon in force was advancing in several units in supporting distance to locate the enemy. We first laid down a base of fire and attempted to gain fire superiority and use our indirect support /mortar, artillery, or air support/ if possible. Base of fire better defined, is with our machine guns and rifles, try to pin down the enemy. This gives, a leader a chance to locate the enemy and decide if they are experienced or FNGs, and make a tactical decision. The size of the enemy force, their firing characteristics, and the terrain can help one determine which of the three basic maneuvers to use. I always avoided the frontal attack unless the enemy force was small and not cohesive, and not located in a strong built up position. I have never seen a Communist tactical manual, but believe, their manuals were basically like the Soviets WWII manuals. I think the Soviets were almost word for word, like the WWII German infantry manual which was like ours, but called for an initial frontal attack. If the defenders position be breeched, then maneuver on their flank to their rear. In addition to our own weapons plus all the indirect support we could get, we also used the M-72 law against enemy bunkers with devastating effect. I always knew, if the enemy's fire was heavy and steady, they were veteran troop's well lead. However if they fired only on full auto and seemed wild firing over our heads, I knew they were new and not well lead. When that happened, I knew we could be more aggressive. Leaving a strong base of covering fire if the terrain permits, one can then lead at least two squads around the left or right of the enemy's flank. Once you have their flank, attack it. Just remember if you get in their rear, your base of fire must cease-fire. Terrain is important to tactical decisions. In the war, I led one maneuver left through a B52 bomb crater to take out an NVA Bunker. Early on in 1966, I took out a VC bunker, with a right maneuver, through smoke and with the enemy pinned down. In the last few pages I have given the order of battle as far as weapons, equipment and ordnance are concerned.

The Vietnam War had far more justification than our two military ops today. Soviet premier Khrushchev said, they would bury us. Starting in

1945, the soviets took East Germany, Poland, Latvia, Lithuania, Estonia, Bulgaria, Hungary, Yugoslavia, Albania, Rumania, Czechoslovakia, China, North Vietnam, North Korea and Cuba and almost France. All were taken by force and fear. When they started through South East Asia, folks in the defense and state departments and the White House saw the handwriting on the wall. Our Vietnam effort was only to buy time for South Vietnam to grow strong. We certainly did that.

There have been several General Officer opinions as to buying time for South Vietnam and even winning. The first MACV Commander, General William Westmorland advocated building the South Vietnamese forces, while we engaged, weakened, and destroyed the main force of the VC and NVA. Westmorland wanted to do this in ever larger search & destroy missions in the border areas. This was to take place after the evacuation of the civilians, giving us a free fire zone. Civilians were to be located far from the borders in new hamlets guarded by South Vietnamese forces. This initiated the bloody battles of 1965, 1966, and 1967, and until the summer 1968, and included Tet 68. In early June 1968, Creighton Abrams, one of Patton's WWII Officers, took command of MACV and Westmorland went to the Pentagon to be army chief of Staff. Abrams initiated a new strategy in the hopes of reducing casualties, and still battering the enemy forces far from the civilians. Abrams strategy had the marines in small units in 1st Corps on the border with North Vietnam. The Marines covered the north boundary and for a distance down the west side of South Vietnam on the border with Laos. To the Marine's south the Army's fourth infantry division operated on the border with Cambodia and Laos The fourth infantry division, defended the border far south into 111 Corps area. The bulk of our forces in the Saigon area and delta, linked up with the fourth division on the Cambodian border. Abrams kept a large American force in the interior for reinforcement,if necessary. If any of the border units made heavy contact, then large reinforcements would be sent by MACV. Abrams saw this as security for South Vietnam's civilians, while the South Vietnamese government, WON hearts and minds. Meanwhile in the border areas, we would inflict a heavy defeat of the enemy main forces. This was called village security, which was the heart of Marine general Lew Walt's strategy. The Marines, whose fame is well deserved, had a fine general to lead them. General Walt differed from Westmorland and Abram's, in that he wanted to avoid further border battles, where previous heavy combat had ensued, without total victory. General Walt thought that by engaging the enemy nearer our bases, our firepower and air support would be enhanced, and we would win. The fact that the villages would be heavily guarded by the Marines should allow hearts and minds to be won. Meantime, we would destroy the enemy and allow the South Vietnamese to win the people and finish the war. This was a form of Vietnamization before Nixon-Kissinger. I am only a little old sergeant, but I think that any war with partially open borders and sanctuary is going to be very, very tough to win. All three General's were some of America's best and they did their best with a tough proposition. It was a war where we won all the battles, and had a 10 to 1 kill ratio, and still not victory.

In this war, all the infantry fighting was virtually point blank. Casualties in the period from fall 1965 until late summer 1969, had been heavy. Our killed in action, ran from 100 plus to 800 per WEEK in this time. A case in point: in the week of WOODSTOCK, 109 American fighting men were killed. Any counter insurgency war with conventional close quarter's infantry fighting can be extremely difficult to win, when the enemy can fall back over the borders and rebuild. You can see this in today's military operations. In the 1970 Cambodian incursion, the United States and South Vietnam, were compelled to pull out before the NVA could really be hurt by American leftist opposition. It makes me roar with laughter when I see today's chicken hawks blowing about their patriotism.

In his book ***"A Better War(4)"*** Lewis Sorley states by late 1970 the war was won (page 217). The VC was almost wiped out and the heavily battered NVA, had pulled out to the border areas and Cambodia and Laos. At that time, ninety per cent of the population was secured by the South Vietnamese forces and Government. President Nixon was elected on a promise to end the war. After Nixon's Vietnamization and our pull out, the South Vietnamese stood alone. After Nixon's fall and Gerald Ford becoming president, the democratic controlled congress, cut off aid to South Vietnam. This, despite Nixon's solemn promise that the US would always support the South Vietnamese armed forces and Government. The American left had finally won. In the 1970's, a former South Vietnamese officer told me, at the time of the final North Vietnamese offensive, that the South Vietnamese army had only eight rounds per artillery piece. In the writing of this narrative, I had the use of the maps I used in Vietnam. They helped me in my rendition, matching my memory in detail. History does not have many worse stabs in the back, then our abandonment of South Vietnam.

— Chapter Two —

First Rendezvous

I have a rendezvous with death
At midnight in some flaming town
When spring trips north again this year
And I to my pledged word am true
I shall not fail that rendezvous
—Alan Seeger WWI, 1916 killed in action

When my turn came, I followed my platoon as the Lieutenant led them over the rail on the net to load the Landing scow. In this truth of sorrow and bloodshed I have decided to omit the names of the killed in action. I do this, so family all these years later, would not be subjected to another round of heartbreak. It has been forty four years since my last deadly violence, and I could not remember all the names any way. The names I will use are those of my men, who I have been in contact with for years. We were loaded with our complete basic load of ammo. We landed at Vung tau, a former French army resort near Bien Hoa. I was the weapons platoon sergeant of C Company 1st BN, 27th Infantry Wolfhounds, 25th Infantry Division. None could be sure of what lay just down the road.

When the scow ran up on the beach. We in full battle gear and also carrying heavy duffel bags, walked off on the white sand. There was a large delegation carrying signs reading "Welcome US Fighters against communist aggression." They were all young woman wearing the white Ao Dai It was a lovely white outfit that many woman wore around the large population centers. The Vietnamese women, who lived in the countryside usually wore muddy dirty black pajamas. You could hardly tell women and men apart. Most people in the countryside had badly stained teeth ,from chewing betel nut. The reception on the beach was far better than any reception in the US. We loaded into 2 ½ ton trucks for a motor convoy ride somewhere. There was a Tank at the front as the point and an armored rear guard. There were several Huey D model Gunships overhead. The day was bright sunshine and very hot. Late December and early January was in the middle of the dry season. Everything went smoothly and we went down main street in Ben Hoa. There were hundreds of little boys running alongside, begging for cigarettes or candy. After a few more minutes we arrived at a hill with an ugly red brick building located there. I was told, it was referred to as the college. A Battalion from the 173rd Airborne had the area secured in a large perimeter, well dug in. When we were unloaded, the Company Commander put us in a perimeter inside the 173rd. In a quick meeting all the leaders were informed that the 173rd was going to keep us safe and indoctrinate us. When the meeting was over, we started to dig in. The dry ground was like concrete and it took awhile. A 173rd 1st Sergeant walked through our area when we were finished and said very little, but seemed pleased. The troops from the airborne unit were young but looked thirty or better. They looked very tough and very tired, there was little talking. In late evening we were served a hot meal from a mess hall set up in the middle of the perimeter. The mess hall was heavily sand bagged. I heard someone say; "Where in hell is the war?" Just after dark we found out. I noticed when the convoy turned into the perimeter that there was a South Vietnamese perimeter down the road, and heavily fortified. It was dark and no moon when all hell broke loose. The VC hit the South Vietnamese hard with a mortar barrage and a ground attack. The Arvin /Army republic South Vietnam/ unit held out okay but the whole world lit up. I had put up my poncho over my hole and a fifty caliber slug hit it and tore all to pieces. The fifty round missed me, but not by far. This was just the first of thousand's of pieces of communist lead that almost got me. I was glad I didn't feel any great fear. I heard some 173 troops saying; "better them than us." About midnight the fighting quieted down, after Puff the Magic Dragon showed up and inundated the terrain around the Arvin outpost with thousands of fifty caliber rounds. The hill we were on, showed us the lights of Saigon. After midnight, there was a big mortar attack on the capital. The town lights slowly went out. You could plainly see the defensive perimeter from the tracers and heavy firing. I gradually settled down and went to sleep for an hour or so. Being inside the 173rd, we had no security responsibilities. Well so much for day 1 of 531 that had drawn to a close. As the Lord said; "The evil thereof was enough for the day."

The next day began at 0530 when 173 had stand to. The 173rd no doubt had a fifty percent security set up the rest of the night, after the firefight down the road. The fifty percent tactic means every other man awake at all times. In such situations the platoon sergeant would be awake until midnight and the platoon leader, the rest of the night. That night I dosed fitfully, maybe 2 hours lying on my poncho liner and what was left of my poncho. If the reader is not familiar with military time,

0530 is 5 and ½ hours since midnight. That is normally thought of as the twenty four hour clock. We had cold combat rations for breakfast and washed it down with cold water. At eight am, the Company Commander sent for me. The Captain told me to get my gear and go down to a two and 1/2 ton truck, Army slang, deuce and a half. He also added, I was going with the Battalion advance party to a place known as Cu Chi. He told me that I would be given C Company's position at Cu Chi and be ready to guide the company into position when they got there. At that time, we still carried the M-14 and were not issued the M-16 until about a month later. We also were still wearing the normal army fatigues, not being issued jungle fatigues until about the same time we got the M-16. In Vietnam, troops were moved by helicopter more than road transport, as ambushes and mines and booby traps were everywhere. In this instance, the entire Battalion's equipment excluding the gear each trooper had, was being moved to Cu Chi and that required a truck convoy. The convoy again was heavily guarded with Tank's and Gunship's. We left about 0830 and got to Cu Chi village about 1800. The trip was uneventful on highway one, a French built road that at one time was black top, and now was in bad shape. I will always remember Cu Chi for several reasons; one was an ESSO gas station in town. At Cu Chi, we turned a hard north east on a dirt road, hardly more than a trail. This road would soon be a street without joy. After about two miles, we pulled off to the left side into a huge open rice paddy that was dry and very hard to dig in. I was told rice pddies such as this had been there for a thousand years. The 1st Infantry Division /Big Red One/ was in position there with only one Brigade in a huge perimeter. They had not gone in deep, just a fighting position and their mission was to familiarize our unit. Our unit in total was the Second Brigade of the 25th Infantry Division /Tropic Lighting/. We had three infantry battalions and a mechanized infantry Battalion in the brigade. The brigade would be there in several days to dig in. I don't know which was the hardest ground to dig: that old rice paddy or the pimple hill at the College. Cu Chi was in the middle of 111 Corps tactical operations area, and was very flat. That small hill at the college and the Nui Ba Dinh were the only high ground I ever saw in the area from Saigon to the Cambodian Border. The Nui Ba Dinh /black virgin Mountain/ in Vietnamese, was NW of Cu Chi at Tay Ninh city. It was twenty eight miles to Cu Chi from Siagon. Myself and the rest of the 1st Battalion 27th Infantry advance party dug in, at the area we were taken to. It was quite when we got there but very soon after dark it began. We had a mortar attack but none of our group was hit. The mortar attack lasted three or four minutes, they over shot our position by about fifty yards. They always fired quickly and moved because our counter battery would zero in their area quickly. In the next two months I counted sixteen mortar attacks I went through. Just after midnight Red One sprang an Ambush out to our front and killed three VC. At daylight the patrol brought in the 3 dead VC and laid their bodies on the ground.

The three dead VC really brought home to the advance party troops with me the reality of it all. I was fortunate in that I have always been able to accept reality and knew what was coming. A red one platoon sergeant showed me his original helmet. The helmet had a hole in the side and scratches where the slug had gone around in a circle inside. Then it must have come out and off in a tangent. He only had skinned places on his forehead. He was a lucky guy and sometimes strange things just happen. In the afternoon the Battalion started coming in by chopper. On toward evening I showed the Captain and the platoon leaders the limits of our position. The company started digging in like quick. Since I had my hole dug, the CO wanted me to take him and the XO to the right limit to link up with the company going in on our right. On the short walk back, a sniper opened up on us from our right out in the timber. We were digging in just behind the red one positions. The Red One Company to our front opened up but after a few shots they ceased fire. The sniper probably dropped down in a hole and into a tunnel. The undergrowth was so heavy in the tree line and everywhere I fought in South Vietnam that bunkers and tunnels were hard to see. When we started moving again the sniper opened up again. He must have fired at least twenty rounds and as we had cover never hit anyone. From that day forward I kept in mind the incident. This was a learning experience. When you're under fire if the rounds zing they are high, if they pop they are hitting all around you. The only time you could not determine that was if the fire was so heavy leaves and small limbs were falling all around you. We went in country only about fifteen men short of our 144 and six Officers. Never again in the war would I be in a company anywhere near that size. For the next several days red one gave us some excellent instruction on local mines and booby traps. They also took us outside the wire on patrols and ambushes. In the practice operations, we made little contact but one or two VC were killed. In a few days red one pulled out and it was our baby. We received an intelligence briefing that several miles to our front was a VC hard core Battalion. They were in a fortified village in deep bamboo, and surrounded with tunnels and booby traps. Most enemy booby traps ranged from a hole in the ground with bamboo stakes /Punji stakes/ sharpened sticking up and with buffalo crap on the tips, and all the way up to dud artillery shells or bomb's rigged with fuses. One of the most surprising things I saw was an M-48 tank with the engine blown clean out of it from an anti tank mine. Nam was a place where Death came everyday in many different forms. We had orders that we would keep two platoons out everyday, sweeping our front near the wire. One platoon would stay behind the wire to finish our fortifications. We made contact everyday but most of it snipers. We also began construction of tents with wood floors and sandbagged walls for troops to sleep when needed. There was never much sleeping. I was twenty eight years old and was surprised at how many sleepless nights I could go and still function. For years after Nam I had bad sleep problems. We lost our first KIA,on our third night without red one.

Soon after the departure of red one the long black train got in motion. It was necessary to hold in check the enemy, while we finished our part of the bunker line. The concertina and razor wire were already in. On most nights the company Commander put out squad sized ambushes in front of the flank platoons. They were first platoon on the left third platoon on the right and second platoon in the middle. My platoon, the weapons platoon with three 81-MM mortars was in the middle by the command group behind second platoon about 25 yards. We had the mortars set up in sand bag emplacements and our bunkers alongside. The fire direction center was in a bunker in the middle. Just after red one, left my platoon leader was pulled out of the unit. I was never informed why and didn't care. I was now the acting platoon leader and remained so for months. The weapons platoon leader was responsible for supporting Mortar fire. If we had no artillery control party, as was sometimes the case, I took care of that to. I was positioned in the company area in the base perimeter and did not go on night ambushes. When we left base camp perimeter /Cu Chi/ moving on search& destroy missions, I was following just behind the company command group, usually in the middle of the battle formation. After the first month and we had secured Cu Chi, we were out on search & destroy type missions most of the time.

On the third night after red one left us the second platoon night LP /listening Post/ between the night ambushes and much closer in got hit. This same set up had been in use for three nights in a row. Doing the same thing in any type infantry war is always dangerous. The VC, in the heavy jungle type terrain to our front were well hidden and caught any mistakes on our part. They hit the LP with an RPG /rocket propelled grenade/ and a heavy firefight ensued. I marked center sector just 50 yards ahead of the LP. We fired a 3 round HE mission, it had to be on top of or close to the VC. HE was a very effective high explosive shrapnel round with a fifty yards killing radius. The RPG had taken off the right arm of one of our guys. The VC were in force maybe twenty five or thirty and had silently moved between the ambush locations. The Company Commander quickly ordered second platoon, on line forward to the relief of the LP. Both flank platoon's laid down a base of fire to cover. Normally at night we would rather use our Claymore's, as they are super bad and don't give away your position. In this situation it was necessary to be careful, as it was DARK as the Devils Heart and we had troop's out there. The second platoon reached the LP as the Company CO ordered another mortar salvo. The VC bugged out and the woods and bamboo were deathly quiet. The second platoon swiftly brought in the wounded man. The LP was reinforced but set up closer to the bunker line. The company medic had already called for a dust-off to pick up our troop.

He was in shock and bleeding badly even though the medic had used a tourniquet and treated for shock. He died just as the dust-off circled. Dust-off is Nam speak for a Medevac Chopper.

The next morning at daylight we prepared to sweep the battle area. Just our bad luck, Battalion sent a reporter from the Honolulu Advertiser out to us as we had just had a heavy contact. In addition no artillery control party had shown up even though one was supposed to always be with us. The CO said; "White: you're going with us and stay by me as we have no arty party." The CO put the three rifle platoon's on line with a squad left to cover the bunker line. The flank platoon's bent back a fire team to cover each flank. Not a good formation in heavy undergrowth but the best the CO could do. That meant our flanks were almost wide open. I left the next senior NCO in my platoon in charge. My RTO /radio man/, was right behind me with orders to hand me the handset instantly if need be. We moved forward slowly.

The day was just getting hot and was still with no wind. On our way forward we picked up the two night ambushes. The newsman walked just ahead of me with the CO. He finally got told to keep his voice down. When we came to the spot the LP occupied we paused. I had been following us on my map but in the flat heavy jungle there were no landmarks to locate off of. I had to estimate how far we had come to know a coordinate for our position. The CO, knowing a large force could be waiting for us just ahead in bunkers and hard to see, wanted to be careful. The CO said; "White: here is our position." I saw he had underestimated how far we had come. In that type of terrain we were following a compass azimuth. The Newsman was standing there and I didn't want to nay say the CO in front of him. In all the long war ahead I NEVER made that mistake again. The Captain said, "White get some artillery about 100 meters ahead of us". I called for artillery. I can't remember call signs accurately after this period of time. I asked for fire mission, mark center sector, azimuth 295, /we were moving NW/ and gave them the Captains coordinates. I requested white phosphorus which makes white smoke and can be seen a long way to adjust from. A long way in that terrain is maybe 150 meters when the smoke gets high. In a few seconds they gave me:" on the way". Luckily, I didn't tell the CO on the way. I waited for it finally looking to the rear, and seeing its smoke. It was at least 150 behind us. I knew he underestimated how far we came. Quickly I called back," add 750," I wasn't taking chances with our guy's lives. I heard some troop in the FDC say, "WHAT add 750" then back behind I heard another voice say; "That's right, Damn it, shoot it, he is out there and you are safe in here". In a few moments I heard:" on the way" it came quickly and my heart was glad when it detonated about 150 or better in front of us. The Captain said; "Good job White, Now give me a six." It was HE 105mm with a 50-yard killing radius. I gave them, "fire for effect six rounds HE". The rounds came in accurately and the CO said, "Good job, White." I stopped sweating so much. The Battalion CO called and said, "hold up where you are for a recon chopper". We quickly formed a Perimeter.

The LOH /Light Observation Helicopter/ came in quickly circling the area slowly. They drew no fire and left us. The Battalion CO called and said" OK but move slowly". I heard the Captain say under his breath" "You're damn right, slowly!" and quietly to the other platoon leaders:" get your points out and we move and slow". We went back to the same battle formation and moved out. Lots of nineteen year old guys getting older fast out there. We still had the M-14 rifles and they made moving in heavy bamboo and buffalo grass hard. The big tall rubber tree's towered over us. Everything was so quiet and still except for the noise we made in that crap. I bet the Advertiser Newsman was wishing to hell he was in Honolulu. Quickly, we came to the VC position of the night before. There was a damaged AK-47 lying there. I saw the black spots where my mortar rounds had come in. All that was left was five or ten large blood spots and blood trails leading away from the area. In another short distance was the spot of my artillery shoot. We moved through everything quietly, and in just a few minutes, all hell broke loose. We had a very tough fire fight on our hands. The VC were hard to see, in the undergrowth and in their bunkers. The Co yelled; "Arty!" I called red leg FDC, yelling over the sound of the shooting and said, "From last concentration add 200 white phosphorus." It came quick and was about fifty or seventy five meter's in front. I called, "for twelve rounds HE for effect". It came quickly and was just where we wanted it. Our men were fighting hard and the firing was heavy. We moved forward and the VC fell back. I only actually saw a very few in the undergrowth. No telling how many disappeared in bunkers and tunnels. We advanced through what had been their position and grenaded all their bunkers. It seemed a miracle we only had five men wounded. I counted three dead VC and several pieces of bodies where the artillery came in. One of our men vomited and I felt ninety years old. We halted again and formed a perimeter, the Captain wanted to search the bunkers and tunnels.

About 1200 (noon) the Captain decided to fall back to our bunker line. Before we could move disaster struck. We had stayed to long in the same place which was always a mistake in Nam. We were moving from a perimeter to our battle formation and our men were too close to each other. Several VC mortar rounds came in and we had six young men killed instantly. There were also another fifteen wounded lightly. One of the badly wounded died saying over and over; "I can't breathe." I was to hear that so many times over the next few years. I fought to control myself, as I was wild with hate and battle fury, yet unsure whom to hate. Quickly we formed another perimeter and had to stay in the same position. It was clear enough there for a Dust-off to hover. We got several of the worst wounded off to safety with our medics doing all they could. The rest we carried with us until we were close to the bunker line, then an armored personnel carrier M-113 Medic Track came to us and got the rest of the wounded.

Just after we reentered the bunker line, one of the platoon leaders sought me out. I could see he was terribly shocked as five of the KIA's had been from his platoon. He said,"White, did you know I called a fire mission from the mortar section?" I said, "No, I had my radio on red leg because we didn't have an artillery FO party." It was standard operating procedure for each rifle platoon to have a mortar section FO with them so they could independently request mortar support. Apparently impact from the mortars was at the same time or close to the impact that killed the seven. I was as horribly shocked as he was. We were still new FNG's and trying to learn fast. We both went quickly to the mortar fire direction center. When the rest of my platoon saw us, they looked surprised, wondering what was up. We sat side by side, as I took the M-16 Plotting Board and worked the entire data for his fire mission. The impact the mortar's had, if there were no bad powder bags, would be close indeed to the point where the men were killed. One big problem was that none of the company officers or me could be sure of our pinpoint location because of the flat terrain and short visibility. We had a tense meeting with all platoon leaders. The First Sergeant and I went over the firing data for everyone. The shrapnel had already been sent by helicopter to MACV for the shrapnel analysis experts to examine. The decision was made by the Company Commander to wait for the report before any type action was taken. I asked my FO about the mission, and did he see impact? He replied quietly; "Yes, it was about 50 or 75 to the front." He seemed earnest and truthful and had always been a good man. We were new troop's and had already lost eight killed in a few days. In a short time, we wouldn't have been surprised at the loss of eight in a few days. Thank god the analysis came to us in three days and it was communist bloc steel, commonly seen from a Chinese 82-MM Mortar. It was a great relief for everyone. The Honolulu Advertiser reporter wasted no time getting the hell back to Hawaii.

In the next few days we were issued the M-16 rifles and ammo plus twenty two magazines apiece. We also received our jungle fatigues consisting of two sets. Since I had test fired the M-16 in the SAWS weapons test at Scofield eighteen month's previous, there was no problem with disassembly and cleaning and reassembly for my platoon. I believe I was the only man in the company who had fired one. That presented no familiarization problem for the company. The action in Nam was always so close that many times we fired full auto at the enemy location. This made using the weapon simple and was the reason the weapon was manufactured like it was. We received information that in other units the M-16 had some failures to chamber after firing a round. That was solved by only loading eighteen in a twenty round magazine thus the spring was not mashed so tight. I never had much trouble with the M-16, and when fired at an enemy up close it was devastating. This was why assault rifles were designed. In all the war to come, I never killed a VC or NVA more than a few yards away.

During the time that we received our M-16's and jungle fatigues, we also had a very short stand down to finish our company area behind the bunker line. Everything was done except replacing the tops of our semi permanent tents with tin. In the time of the French Rule of Indochina, many villages had been built using tin. Probably our arrival in the Cu Chi area started a huge inflation and economic boom for the local Vietnamese. Our need for tin caused one of the few amusing incidents I was involved in. We had no supply channel for tin, so Company Commanders were told to fend for themselves. The Company CO decided to send the supply sergeant to Cu Chi village, two miles down the road to buy tin. We all chipped in and he had over seventy dollar's, which should have been enough. The exchange rate was 118 Piaster's to the Dollar. The supply sergeant came back with eleven pieces. This was about ten per cent what was needed. The Company CO was furious, and knew we had been scammed. Unfortunately, one of the company officers just remembered that Sergeant White had done some scrounging at Scofield Barracks in 1965, that saved an outgoing company commander from having to pay for forty six missing sheet's in the company inventory. I was given eighty dollar's which was all we could come up with and told to handle it. We needed at least seventy more pieces. I took a two and 1/5 ton Truck and a Jeep and seven men. There was a fifty caliber machine gun mounted on the truck and an M-60 on the jeep. We of course had our individual weapon's and grenade's as well. The road to Cu Chi was still dangerous, as it probably was the entire war. I was told to go to the local bar and ask for the Momma San .When we walked in, she was talking to a GI at the bar. When I could, I said, "Mamma San I need to buy tin". She asked my name in Pigeon English and I answered: "Sgt White." She said, "SAGEE WHA you and your men step up to the bar and have a beer". We all had a Beer; it was "Bomadebom 29," and an Advisory team Sergeant had told me that dead rats floated in the vats at Saigon. The beer was powerful and shot to my head fast. I waited and waited; she kept talking to the GI. I finally told my men; "let's go". We went outside, there were seven or eight Vietnamese men standing around a huge pile of Tin.

I pointed at one who looked like he might be the man in charge. Then I pointed to the Tin and then our truck. He understood, and then I held up both hands and flashed all ten fingers up and down ten times. They started loading the Tin. There was still no Mamma San. When the truck was full and I do mean full, I took the money out of my pocket and threw it on the ground. The slicky boy's started a huge brawl over the money. They were wrestling on the ground for it. A huge dust cloud came up. I looked at my men and said; "LET'S GO". We started back down through town to turn on the road to the perimeter. One of my men yelled in my ear, "Look behind us". I looked; Mamma San was running after us as we were driving slowly. She was yelling; "Sagee Wha! Sagee Wha! You number 10 GI! You sombeech! You come Cu Chi no mo!" We had more than enough tin, and Sagee Wha has no come to Cu Chi village no mo.

— Chapter Three —

To Reap

He that observeth the wind shall not sow;
And he that regardeth the clouds shall not reap.
Ecclesiastes 11:4

On a hot February day in 1966, a small detail of combat engineers, eight in number went out the heavily guarded main entrance of the Cu Chi perimeter. They were in a ¾ ton truck. Before day's end, they were all dead on the road to Cu Chi village. Whoever sent them to check the road for mines, made a bad mistake to send them without proper security. This was the same road I had used just three days previous to get tin. However I was moving swiftly, and had two machine guns of which one was a fifty caliber. The Brigade Commander apparently decided it was time to do away with too much caution. An LOH Chopper sighted sixteen Viet Cong moving through the trees a mile east of the road. The VC were heading toward and old laterite pit. Moving quickly the fifth Mechanized Infantry had a company surrounding the VC, a tank platoon was moving with the fifth mechanized unit. In one very short minute all sixteen Viet Cong were killed. The bodies were placed on the tank's and dumped in the main street of Cu chi village. This event, plus the heavy fighting we had been involved in near the fortified village, led to a new more aggressive approach.

We received orders for a two Battalion operation from our bunker line to take out the VC Village. The first & second battalions of the 27th Infantry carried in M-113 armored personnel carriers would make the strike. My unit C Company 1/27th Infantry of the 25th Infantry Division was the right flank company of our Battalion and linked up with the 2/27th on our right. Just before the M-113's loaded us up, a sad event happened in the company just to our right. The artillery had been pounding the village and must have had a short 155 MM round. The shell hit a platoon sergeant in the company to our right. It was a bad scene, and very little of his body parts could be found. There are friendly fire accidents in all wars. This one was extra bad, one of the reasons I gave the warning earlier in my Narrative. This caused a delay in the jump off. We did leave the start line an hour later. In our movement to contact, the artillery kept pounding the VC and there were several airstrikes with napalm and bombs. When we hit the village the enemy was underground and running for their lives. We received small arms fire probably as a delaying action. We grenaded every bunker and tunnel and kept moving forward with the M-113's in front. There was a sizable body count, I don't remember just how many.

In the two Battalion operation just concluded both battalions all together only had ten or twelve wounded and no KIA's. That was unusual for a Nam action and raised morale among the troops. I rode in the same M-113 with the Company Commander. We had an artillery liaison party. I kept our mortar section firing just ahead of our advancing line. This operation was the next to last one of my war in armored personnel carriers. That night after the operation, the VC fired a sizable mortar attack into the perimeter. They just wanted us to know that they were still around. Several days later, we went on our first helicopter air assault operation. The operation was against a large village, fifteen miles south west of the Cu Chi perimeter. The village was controlled by a hard core VC Battalion, according to intelligence. The landing zone was outside the village on the west side. When we made our approach, gunship's were running a daisy chain at tree top level firing rockets. I could see many Vietnamese running away from the Village. We had strict orders to keep gunship's and all other supporting fires away from the Village. Sometimes fighting in Vietnam was almost like having one arm tied behind your back. On the way in I watched tracers floating slowly toward us. When they got close to the bird they passed with a zip. When a bird was hit it sounded like a hammer. The bird hovered three or four feet off the ground and we jumped out and ran under fire to the wood line. In this operation, for a tryout we carried one 81MM Mortar and twenty rounds. If the company got pinned down, I would quickly set up and pump out a few rounds quickly at the enemy position. In all the heavy fighting coming very soon, I never had a good chance to try it. We formed up in skirmishers and swept the Village, the VC had bugged out. This was an occurrence that happens many times in counter guerrilla operations. There was no attempt to land the platoon's in blocking positions that would give us an encirclement. That is always hard to do in guerrilla war. The idea was to flush the VC out and know that the gunships would hit them hard. If we had pinned them down, civilians would have been killed in the crossfire, as they would not have left the Village. Sometimes the Viet Cong would use the civilians as human shields. The enemy depended on fear and brutality to win hearts and minds. As it was, the gunships killed three or four VC. We had no casualty's and were now looking at a fifteen mile hump to the perimeter.

We followed an old French road impassable to vehicles. We stayed in the brush at the side of the old road about fifty meters out. We had a strong point and flankers out. The day was hot and still as the Nam always was. After about an hour there was a loud explosion to our front. We deployed for close combat quickly. We moved on very cautiously and found an old man and woman lying at the side of the road. They had stepped on a VC mine. They were both dying; the poor old woman was vomiting blood and the old man had the death rattle. We called for a dustoff and formed a perimeter. The Medic did what he could. They were both dead before the chopper got there.

In counter guerrilla war such as we fought in Vietnam, when civilians were killed and their bodies found by US troops, we followed our SOP. Our SOP was to give notice up to the Chain of Command to the nearest US Advisory group. In turn the South Vietnamese District Chief would see to the collection of the bodies and proper notification of family. When the two old people had died we moved immediately as the day was getting late and we did not want to be a sitting target. Tactical considerations dictated leaving bodies of dead noncombatants to be secured by their families. We also left the bodies of dead enemy soldiers where they lay in most cases; to do otherwise increased the danger to our troop's. We moved quickly on down the dim road. When we were within five miles of Cu Chi perimeter we began drawing fire from all directions. Most of it was high and inaccurate; we returned fire when there was a target. When we approached the perimeter wire, the action died away.

Word came down the chain that we now had a secure situation in the base perimeter area. We now began to prepare for airmobile operations further away from the base. This meant we would soon operate in the border areas and in such places as the "Plain of Reeds". In addition we were going to operate in the rubber plantation areas such as the "Phil Hoel": and the" Michelin". When our mission called for operating out of a company patrol base, the weapons platoon would stay in the perimeter to handle the mortars. When the entire company was moving in a search & destroy mode the weapons platoon would be a fourth rifle platoon. I was still without a platoon leader so I continued to be acting platoon leader. This period of adjustment took just a few days. During this short time there were two happenings that were noteworthy.

The Battalion continued to operate platoon size patrols and ambushes to our front in both day and night. One day I was at the Company Command Post and heard a firefight began on the Battalion radio frequency. One of another company's platoons encountered a sizable force of Viet Cong within a few hundred yards of a Village. The platoon leader called for artillery support. The request was put on hold while air clearance was obtained. The fight was too close to the Village. I looked at my watch; it was 13 minutes before artillery was cleared to fire. During that time we had five wounded. In Vietnam we tried very hard to avoid civilian casualties. As the war continued our forces and the South Vietnamese moved the vast majority of the civilians to new life hamlets over near the coast. This gave us free fire zones in all the border areas.

Free fire zones are not perfect, but war is a symptom of an imperfect world. The Nam was always a dark valley of violence and killing. Not long after our return from our first air mobile op, we conducted a company sized sweep out 1000 meters or so and back without contact. I of course, was with the company command group. When we returned the Captain had the latest info waiting on him. Apparently a big operation was in the offing. This operation was to the Phil Hoel Plantation area. I had heard rumors that Red One had got in a really bad scene there. I also found out that my order for new batteries for our PRC-25 radios had not come in. That really pissed me off, and I wound up getting in an argument with the Company Executive Officer. When enlisted men argue with officers, they get the short end of the stick. Why would I remember such a mundane event 46 years later? When I returned to the mortar section something happened that has always bothered me deeply. The Vietnam War has always been like a monster running just behind me in the darkness. I was hot and tired and taking my gear off at my bunker. My platoon had Staff Sergeant E-6 who was next to me in rank. I always left him to control the platoon when I was on an operation with the Company Commander. This happened on company sweeps near the base camp and in range of the mortars. He was a Hispanic, from Arizona or New Mexico. I thought very highly of him and I never met a soldier who I had more confidence in. He was a real good guy with a family and he came to me with a request. A Hispanic buddy of his in one of the rifle platoons was going out at dark leading an ambush. He said; "Sgt White, I haven't seen much action as most of our heavy contact has been near the perimeter and I am always with the tubes. I would like to go out with my buddy from third platoon tonight." I was never a platoon sergeant who was overly friendly with my men. In this case I was very tired, aggravated and hot. I snapped at him; "Hell no, you know that's an improper request". I went on, "your duty is with this platoon not third platoon". His friend, another staff sergeant walked up at that time and supported his request. My man asked again and told me he felt guilty because he had stayed in so much. I said, "Hell, we still have 10 months to go and you're going to see a lot of action, I don't want to hear about it again." Still after about fifteen minutes he came to me again almost pleading. I finally relented, saying, "okay, just go on out there and get yourself killed," and walked away. As God is my witness, I just wished later I had been a prick a little longer. The ambush made contact and it was heavy. This was about 0100 and we fired in their support for over an hour. There were several Viet Cong killed and our guys had one KIA. I spent hours in self-hate when I got the word. That's right, it was him and he was such a fine good man and a father. He was the first man killed in a unit controlled by me. The long black train was running and there would be many more.

In infantry war there are many hazards and also much heartbreak. Somewhere near the first of March 1966 and our first rubber plantation operation, a real zinger came through the mail. We received mail several times a week depending on the tactical situation. One hot afternoon a resupply bird came in and brought us the mail and beer. Sometimes cruel happenings came with the mail. I remember one troop who got divorce papers with the mail and someone laughed and the battle started. It is a bad situation when one remembers 80 or 90 men are sitting around with fully loaded weapons. We had "Dear John" letters come in every so often. That's really disgusting when the troop's are laying it on the line for their country. On that afternoon, I had a letter from my wife and was leaning against a bunker reading it. One of the rifle platoons was positioned just twenty or twenty five yards in front of me. I heard an anguished cry and a young troop jumped up and jerked his pistol out. His platoon sergeant acting quickly, grabbed him trying to get the weapon out of his hand. Several more troops jumped in to help. The pistol went off, and the bullet took a big piece of the platoon sergeants ear with it. The young soldier was put on a bird, tied with rope and an armed guard. He was apparently sent to the field hospital at Binh Hoa. Some months later on a bad afternoon we took a bird just before dark. One replacement got off: it was him. His face was as white as when I saw him last. He was killed three days later. Poor kid just could not get his mind on the war.

In early March 1966 we loaded out for the rubber plantation. This location was on the north side of Highway One about halfway to the Tay Ninh Combat Base. This was the first time out of Hau Nghia province. The plantation was known to have a heavily fortified tunnel and bunker complex occupied by large forces of Viet Cong. We were told that in addition there might be an NVA Company with them. They were armed as usual with AK- 47's and a smattering of American weapons either captured or stolen from the South Vietnamese. We were told to expect heavy mortar fire and it was possible there might be some NVA artillery carried by Elephants. I saw that many times later in the war in the highlands. It was possible to sometimes run across a tiger, a baboon and even a rare wild elephant. However; there always seemed to be very few animals or birds and only around villages. The plantation had thousands of rubber trees planted in long rows. It was necessary for an American unit to move on line down the rows so only one troop would be moving in each gap between the trees. If we moved across the rows, one enemy machine gun sitting at the end of the row could flank the entire company and shoot through everyone at once. I am referring to skirmishers as our battle formation and not single file.

When I first saw the plantation; it was what I expected. The trees were tall and dark, the undergrowth was at least sparse except by the river on the west side. We moved in slowly, everything was still and dark. We made the only sounds as we moved and there were trillions of large red ants. Every time I brushed against a limb several of the ants fell on my neck. When I mashed the first one it made a loud pop. I thought, "Four more and I will be an ace." I made ace many times before that operation was over. Since we were far away from Cu Chi we took weapons platoon as a fourth rifle platoon, and I was still the acting platoon leader. The Company Commander had three platoon's on line as skirmishers and my platoon following the command group and covering the rear. At that time we were down to around ninety men total. Since we came to the war two and one half months before we had lost about fifteen killed and almost thirty wounded. We went in with about 130 enlisted and 5 officers and we had not received enough replacements to make up for the losses. An American rifle company at that time should have had 144 enlisted and five officer's, if memory serves me well. Much heavier casualties were ahead. We continued moving forward slowly, everyone tense and of course quiet. Infantry moving in such conditions in Nam, relied on hand signals whenever possible. Normally the Nam woods are very quiet except for a tree lizard that makes a familiar sound. When that sound stops, get your M-16 off safety. I and my men and everyone else kept their right thumb on the safety. In Nam if you fire first, then there is a good chance you will fire last, which means you're still alive. Suddenly the woods opened slightly and we came to a drainage ditch. I felt that darkly depressed feeling so associated with violence.

We soon got our first look at the VC. They were dug in and in a heavily fortified position. They were waiting for us and probably had scouts moving ahead of us. They opened up on us with everything they had. By sheer luck, we had seen them seconds before and dove into the ditch, firing as we did. For a short time we shot it out at point blank. We had some losses but not yet heavy. There was no doubt the VC were hurt. The Company CO was trying to figure out how many there were as he was talking to Battalion. Our artillery liaison was calling for fire. I had my men at the back of the ditch with every fourth man watching the rear. Then a Viet Cong ran up on the company's left flank and fired an entire AK magazine right through the middle of us. There was no one hit by some odd chance. We filled the space he had been in seconds before with bullets. We had a tank platoon following behind us and they quickly came up. Our battle tactics had the tanks in the right position. It was one of the few times I was around tanks in a big firefight. In areas of low visibility, the infantry leads the armor to guard against anti tank guns. The tanks opened up on the VC position with their main armament.

After the tanks fired their volley, at the Captains order, we moved forward with the tanks. The enemy fire lightened up, but one of our men was hit and fell in a small opening, perhaps a bomb crater. I was the leader closest to him and taking one of my men with me, ran to him and dragged him to cover. We continued forward and carried the enemy position. The enemy had gone underground and kept sniping at us from their tunnel openings and bunkers. I discovered later my helmet had been shot away. Our troops were brave as American fighting men always are. We were still moving forward with the tanks. A VC in a bunker shot at me, no doubt because my radio man /RTO/ behind me identified me as a leader. The shot grazed an assistant machine gunner just to my left front. The bullet hit his machine gun ammunition causing the tracers to light up like fireworks. We were all on the ground at that point. The platoon sergeant in the rifle platoon to my left shouted VC and threw a white smoke grenade to mark the bunker. The bunker was only perhaps ten yards to our front. The Company CO looked over his right shoulder and said; "White get that bunker". I pushed out several of my men to the right and pointed where I wanted them to fire and yelled, "cover me". The bunker was just a blob of white smoke in the gloom. I told my men to fire and jumped up to circle to the right rear of the bunker. I could hear the pops around me as AK slugs passed by. When I got to the side aperture /opening/ I emptied a twenty round Magazine, /loaded with eighteen/ into the bunker and dropped down at its side and reloaded. Then I stuck the M-16 barrel in and looked in. The VC never knew what hit him. He was armed with an M-1 Rifle from WW11 days. The South Vietnamese were armed with M-16's at that time. It probably came from a dead South Vietnamese or the VC was a deserter. This was my first killing with a personal weapon and there would be more. I felt nothing and had no idea how much damage I had done to the enemy with the artillery and mortar missions, I had called back through the months.

I reached into the bunker and got the M-1, holding it up for the troops to see. The first sergeant, a Korean War infantry vet yelled, "let me see that Whitey, I haven't seen one since Korea". He was immediately hit in his right leg above the knee. I liked him very much and he was a top soldier. Now we had several wounded including the first sergeant, at that point yet none had been killed. I had lost track of time but believe it was mid to late afternoon. It had been a long shoot out and our men had fought well, as usual. The enemy's fire died away and we knew they were trying to move away from us, going underground. The CO set up a perimeter and gave orders to grenade the bunkers and tunnels. At that point in the war, we hadn't started the tunnel rat tactic yet. We had our only killed in action that day from sniper fire just after the perimeter was set up. It was several miles to the clearing at the edge of the trees. We had wounded and one dead to evac so we started moving back to the LZ. We counted five or six VC bloody bodies. They carried their others away.

We started back to the clearing where we could medevac our several wounded and KIA. We moved in the same formation that we came in the plantation with. It gave us the most all around security.

In an infantry war, it is important to always employ tactical formations where all your men can fire with slim chances of a friendly fire accident. On the way to the opening, we followed the same route we came in on. This is always dangerous; it raises the odds of an ambush. In this case however, we were caught out late and had wounded men to evac. We got to the clear area about thirty minutes before dark. The medic had already called for a Dust off when we knew we were about there. It was good luck we didn't have to fight on the way. That would have caused the wounded to spend the night in the bush. It would have been sheer hell for them. When the chopper closed, I went to the end of the opening and popped a red smoke. With both arms upraised I brought him in front of the medics and they quickly loaded our men. I shook hands with the first sergeant and he said; "Good luck Whitey and yelled out God bless you C Company". Just after the bird ran out over the trees, several gunship's came in and flew a daisy chain around us until dark. In addition we would have the gunship's and Puff the Magic Dragon on call all night. We were in luck, the clear area had quite a few bomb and shell craters in it. They were in a configuration that allowed us to use them to be down as there was no longer time to properly dig in. We put in all four platoon's and quickly got the trip flares and Claymore mines out. All platoons were on fifty percent alert all night. That meant one half of the men were awake until midnight and the rest until first light when we would stand to /maximum alert/. The Crater's were muddy and water was in the bottom. We tried to eat a meal of combat-rations but many of the troops were just too beat. I along with three of my men, were in a large crater. We had the platoon Claymore's sat up on several clacker's and dispersed in front of the five crater's we used.

The night was dark; if there was a moon it was behind the clouds. We had all got muddy and wet in the holes. It was crowded but most managed to pull their ponchos and liners at least partially over them. There were many very tired and stressed troops there that night. I had checked my men for wounds and ammunition. Most still had fifteen or sixteen magazines so that was good. None were hit but many were low on water. If we could get potable water in the can's brought in the morning that would be great. If we didn't get water in, then we would fill up at the first creek after we moved out. This would cause us to have to use Halazone tablets to kill any pathogens. I also made sure all my men took their malaria pills and salt. The next ranking sergeant would be awake until 2400 and then me the rest of the night. Few if any slept that night or hundreds more like it. I knew I had killed that day, but knew all that was ahead was more of it and didn't think a great deal about it. Just after midnight, the VC mortared us but missed as they traversed away just before they got to us.

When morning came we did the first light stand to. The Company Commander moved us back into the trees and we sat up a perimeter. This was a good tactical deployment because if we had remained in the open the snipers under cover in the woods would have had easy shooting. Many non military readers may not know what a gunship or Puff the Magic Dragon was. In 1966 we were still using what was described as the "D model" gunship. It had rocket pods on each side and I don't remember the size but they were deadly. Later on they were also equipped with a fifty caliber machine gun or a mini gun, the d model was a modified HU1b Huey. As 1967 came around the super bad Cobra Gunship came with it. The cobra is still in use in the Middle East, today. Puff the Magic Dragon was actually a C130 gunship with several mini guns of high caliber on each side. They also carried infrared sighting and seeing one in action at night was great. They could plant thousands of bullets in almost every inch of ground around an American unit. At night the sight of one in action was beyond belief, especially the first time. We moved into the plantation before mid morning. Evidently the enemy had been hurt bad because for the next two days they either stayed underground or pulled out of the area. When we reached the river on the west side the operation was terminated without further action.

We went back to the Cu Chi perimeter. By that time, mess halls had been set up and even field showers. It meant a great deal to the troops to get clean and have a good meal. We also had beer, rationed carefully at two cans per day, per troop. The troops had two days of rest even though we had to secure the bunker line. North of the Mekong River Delta was an area known as the' Plain of Reeds'. This area was near a river valley and Cambodia and our next operation. We sat up a company patrol base so the mortars went. This was when late spring started to wear away and the Monsoon approached. I was still acting platoon leader; I don't remember who replaced our first sergeant. We conducted several long sweeps in the valley but contact was not heavy. There was lots of sniper fire and booby traps. Our company had several men hit but no KIA. An LOH spotted a VC in the open leaving Cambodia and sadly he had his wife and little boy with him. He was heading right toward us and carrying a M-1 rifle. I would think the M-1 was from a dead South Vietnamese soldier (ARVIN) or a deserter. One of the rifle platoons soon had him surrounded. The CO called on him to surrender using our Vietnamese interpreter. He raised the M-1 as if to fire and was shot down. His wife and child were on the ground and not hit. The body and the woman and child were brought to the perimeter. He must have been part French as he had red hair. The Captain had already called a Dust off for the wife and child. As the CO walked by me he said; "White, get him under the ground".

Sometimes I wondered if I had an additional duty of Vector NCO. The Vet's reading this will smile. All joking aside, I was moving on down the emotional road by then and did not feel one way or another. Taking two of my men, we quickly got him underground. The wife and child looking on were no doubt horrified. She may have been a native of Cambodia as she was bigger than most Vietnamese. The little boy could not have been more than six or seven years old. They both looked horribly tired and dirty. In all the time ever since, when I think of the "Plain of Reeds," I see the shock and horror in that little boy's face. We had a Medevac coming in to take them to a Vietnamese Army Medical facility where they were cleaned up, fed, and checked over for medical problems. After that they would be sent to a secure New Life Hamlet out of the free fire zone. When the chopper touched down, I took the woman by the arm and carrying the child put them on the chopper. I managed to slip a small package of combat ration cookies in the little boy's hand. Someone else had given her a can of C ration peaches. It all was a bad emotional scene such as happened in hundreds of instances throughout South Vietnam every day. By that time, I was already getting to be very hard and unemotional. I have always remembered that little boy. I wonder if he still has horrible dreams about the big mean looking, uncaring strangers. I hope he is still alive and has put it all behind him. For a child to see his father killed by these horrific looking men and then quickly put underground in front of him, must have affected and deeply wounded him for life.

The Monsoon came soon after the Plain of Reeds operation. We spent a little more time in the Cu Chi perimeter. Southeast Asia has one of the greatest yearly rainfall amounts in the world. The rivers and creeks could go in a few minutes from a small stream to a raging torrent. The rain started slowly from a heavy shower in the afternoon to raining almost all day and night. We were seldom dry and I got to where I didn't really care. We continued to operate close to the border and rubber plantations, with a little more down time in between. In the middle of it all, it seemed like the VC were harder to bring to battle. I thought they may have moved over the border to Cambodia as their tunnels and bunkers would be flooded. I soon found out that was nonsense and they had carefully constructed their fortification system where they could stay dry. The main problem in the Monsoon, in addition to the enemy was to not get any of the troops drowned. Before the rain got too bad we ran a battalion sized operation west of Tay Ninh, at a place known as the old French Fort. The Battalion had seven to eight hundred enlisted at that time. Nam was a war where most US units had only a little more than half their TO&E. This operation in June got hot really fast even though we were soaking. We were heading for an area known as the old French Fort. In the air over the Nam, you almost always saw action going on around you in all directions. There were just so many airstrikes going on that you knew the entire province around you was very hot. On our French Fort mission we got in okay, but no old Fort was in sight. We were on a company sweep in our normal skirmishers formation. I had a platoon leader than and was back to platoon sergeant with the weapons platoon being operated as a fourth rifle platoon. We were moving across rice paddies that were wet as the Monsoon was just starting to get bad. Then we would enter areas with a few trees and high undergrowth. We had a reporter with us that took two pistol belts to go around. We put that fat ass on a chopper in the first hour. In a dark shady wooded area we walked right into a hidden VC hooch area. A heavy shoot out just blew up all around us in ever mounting combat. There appeared to be fifty or seventy five VC and we had a very tough exchange of fire and they ran for it. They were apparently as surprised as we were. They left seven or eight bodies and some wounded. Normally they tried to carry them off but we surprised them this time. One of our men bolted and ran over me. Then our Vietnamese interpreter ran over me also. I was wondering if anybody got the number of that truck. I only saw that happen one more time in that entire war.

It was a bad shoot out and we had eight or nine wounded and two badly. I got hit on my left arm above the elbow. A piece of phosphorus shrapnel still burning went into my arm an inch or so. It was burning and smoking and hurt like hell. I was laying on my right side and the medic was trying to extract it. Quickly he took a handful of dirt and put it into the wound. That stopped the burning as it cut off oxygen to the phosphorus. He took out a scalpel and washed out the wound with water and quickly dug out the shrapnel. The medic poured a disinfectant in my wound and bandaged it to keep it clean. He said to me; "Write you up for the purple heart, Sarge?" I was on my feet then and said;"no I am okay". I wasn't about to take a Purple Heart when I was still able to do the thing. Such actions are very poor leadership. We stopped when the VC broke contact. The Company Commander regrouped the company and we quickly formed a perimeter. We had wounded and needed at least two dust offs and fast. One of our wounded had his right leg blown off below his knee. It was a real horror; the medics were fighting to stop his bleeding. The first tourniquet failed and they rolled up his jungle fatigue shirt and forcefully jammed it in the stump. That slowed the bleeding and allowed a second tourniquet to work. He was in deep shock and white as a sheet and screaming. He was screaming for his mother, it was a bloody ghastly scene. We put him on the 1st Medevac with three others. The second chopper got the rest of the wounded.

We moved out soon back on our patrol route. Early in the afternoon we joined the other three Companies of the battalion. We were in a wide wet rice paddy with a small line of trees on the west side. Our company took position on the south side. We quickly dug in what I always referred to as a fighting position. Each man dug a one-foot deep trench as long and as wide as his body. The dirt out of the hole was piled in a mound on what would be the front side toward the enemy. Thus every man had cover, with his body under the level of the surface and a hump to fire from behind. The hole was perpendicular to the enemy. In this case it was even better because we were behind the paddy dike. Then we hustled to get our trip flare's and Claymore mine's out. The Claymore was extremely deadly, it fired a large number of heavy steel pellets out to fifty meters in a forty five degree sweep and not higher than a man's chest. In a night ambush or night action use of the Claymore was not as likely to give your position away as rifle or machine gun fire. The company that dug in on the west side was hidden by the small belt of trees. By late afternoon the entire battalion was dug in with linked up fields of fire. I was checking all our positions when all hell broke loose on the west side. I was kneeling in a position that allowed me to see in front of the west facing company. I saw a sight that I always remembered. I assume the VC only saw a small force of Americans dig in because of the trees. It was surprising to see thirteen black dressed VC armed with AK-47's and RPG's yelling as they rushed our position. Our company on that side killed them all in seconds. One of them was a woman armed like the rest.

After the short action everything became quiet and it started to rain as it got dark. We of course set up our normal fifty per cent night setup. My arm had started to bother a lot. The company medic who had treated me that morning checked up on me and gave me some Darvon. Since I had a platoon leader now, I would be awake until 2400 and then wake him up and he was awake until stand-to. I don't think anyone of us slept that night. Just before midnight the VC hit us with a large and prolonged mortar attack. I lay there and counted 64 rounds. Our company had one killed but no wounded. The VC and NVA seemed to only have mortar rounds with PD /point detonating fuses/.When a mortar round hit the ground the explosion and shrapnel goes up and out like a flower. Anyone lying nearby would be okay unless hit directly by the round. Men standing up would of course be hit. We had PD fuses also, but in addition had VT fuses. The variable time fuse would explode up in the air and thus rain steel down on anyone in the killing radius. If the target was in the open the VT fuse was by far the deadliest. We apparently were in close to a large enemy force. Just at daylight there was a tremendous arc light /B52 Air Strike/ pretty close to us. The ground shook and we could see the shock wave in the undergrowth and tree line.

Not long after the action near the old French Fort, which I never saw, we moved back north to the so-called" Iron Triangle "area. We passed the Nui Ba Dinh, "Black Virgin Mountain", near Tay Ninh on the way. The mountain just came up almost straight out of the Plain. The sides were steep, rocky, and wooded with high undergrowth. There were several hard core battalions of VC on the sides of the mountain. The top was controlled by a US Special Forces unit with mercenaries protecting a US communications unit. The VC never succeeded in taking the US position. The terrain in both 111 Corp and 1v Corp areas was flat and more rice paddy than anything else. The 1V Corp area was the Mekong Delta where the US Ninth Infantry division and large South Vietnamese forces tried to clear out a large Viet Cong enclave. In the French Indochina War from 1946 until 1954 the French had stayed out of the Delta(1). The toughest area of the Delta was the U Minh Forest at the southern tip of South Vietnam. American forces and our allies operated all over South Vietnam and the enemy had no safe haven in South Vietnam from us. The US Navy Riverine force entered the Delta waterways with the Navy seals working closely with the US Ninth Division.

The Iron Triangle area was flat and covered by Rubber Plantation mixed up with rice paddy. As was the norm, the VC had huge tunnel and bunker areas in the rubber. One of the little known facts about Nam was that US artillery shells and bombs, in many cases, went off in the treetops. In addition, the enemy had a big advantage in that they were underground and had grown up in the local terrain. The VC also blended right in with the Vietnamese people. In counter guerilla war, even in one that had a lot of conventional fighting; the blend in with the local population gave our enemies advantages, that our air support and indirect fires did not cancel out. The defending forces /US and our Allies/ had to defend all communication points, major population sites and roads, bridges and airfields. In our necessity to control the population and defend all built-up locations; the VC and NVA gained the initiative in most of the countryside over our forces. These facts along with their sanctuaries in Cambodia and Laos made our job very difficult. The Ben Cat area in the Iron Triangle was a good case in point. We went in while it was raining in July 1966. It was an entire battalion operation. We moved through the rubber in our standard skirmishers battle formation and down the length of the rubber tree growth. We had to be careful not to cross the rows so the enemy could not fire down the length and flanks of our formation. We had almost immediate enemy contact as soon as we entered the Rubber. We moved slowly trying to take out the tunnels and bunkers as we moved. It was a bloody shoot out at point blank range.

This operation in the "Triangle" as always, demonstrated the great courage and ability of the young American soldiers. Be they draftee or regular (RA) they took on the best the Communists had to offer head-on. In my memories, I still see them with their sleeves rolled up and a towel around their necks. They were all young and strong and no matter what their opinions of lifers or the Green Machine they were always faithful and loyal to the death. In the rubber at Ben Cat there was lots of death. Being watchful for ambush, we continued to move forward. The fighting was violent and at close quarters as always. In our company we had several badly wounded especially when we closed a drainage ditch in a slight opening late in the afternoon. Battalion wanted to stop and dig in at this ditch as we were caught out late. The slight opening gave us a little latitude to use our artillery. Our company had the usual artillery liaison group so the weapons platoon was a fourth rifle platoon. We had all four platoon's on line as our rear was covered by another company and we were linked up with other troops on left and right. At the ditch area, after we halted the enemies fire increased, since we stopped they could regroup. While we dug in, the artillery was increased to a continuous barrage all along our front. The artillery was 105MM and they were shooting HE with PD /point detonating/ fuse. In the company to my right, a young Sp4 was hit bad in the chest and looked near death. A Medavac was brought in for him and several more for other wounded. There was just enough clearing behind us for the birds to be brought in. On the bird for the troop hit so bad to my right, I was surprised to see the Battalion Doctor. When the chopper lifted out we put down a tremendous covering fire. I saw the Doctor with both hands holding a compress on the young man's chest trying to prevent a lung collapse, as it was a sucking chest wound.

The battle went on as darkness neared. The woods as always was dark and menacing and even today when near sundown I get that old feeling sometimes. I was moving down our line checking the troops' condition, water and ammo. We were down to 12 or 15 magazines per man but no one was hit. Our artillery was in fire for effect mode about 75 meters to our front. We were all down in our fighting positions with the exception of me. I was crouched as I checked the men. Suddenly, I was hit by a piece of our artillery shrapnel. It is not unusual for our artillery to have an occasional short round due to mass production. I was knocked towards the rear three or four feet. Luckily it was almost spent and hit my pistol belt. The breath was knocked out of me and I was lying on my back. The troops were yelling for a medic, they were yelling " Sergeant White is hit". Our medic's were always great in every way combat demanded. The medic quickly jerked my jungle fatigue shirt open. Then he laughed and said; "Sheeeet!" Shortly after he said; "write you for the purple heart Sergeant White?" By that time, I had my breath back and was ready to go. I told him, "NO, I would not take it for that". It took several weeks for the bruise to go away.

Just at dark we put out our Claymores. We had to be careful with them as they had a back blast from the C4 plastic explosive. Another factor to be considered with Claymore's was using them where we could see them, so the enemy could not turn them around on us. On the enemy side was printed, "This side to enemy." I always kept the clacker's disconnected so we could be safe as we set them up. I once saw a Claymore detonated by a radio handset, having a voltage leak. When the Claymore's went out that night, we put trip flares in front of them. The fighting had been so heavy, we stayed as low as possible during the setup. The position was soaking wet due to the rain and the ditch. We only recovered several enemy bodies during the day. The VC and NVA made super efforts to carry off their dead so as to confuse us as to our attrition of their forces. In the case of bunkers and tunnels, they often had ropes or commo wire tied around their bodies where if killed or wounded their comrades could drag them back in a tunnel to cover. It had been a long exasperating fight from tree to tree and from bunker to bunker. That night we lay exhausted and soaking in the usual fifty percent security setup. Just another long deadly night in the soaking forest watching the shadow's move from the artillery illumination flares. I guess in my 531 days in the infantry in Nam, hundreds or even thousands of bombs and shells had gone off near me. Today my hearing sucks and my VA hearing aids screech like those flares, as they floated back and forth under the parachutes.

The next day came slowly in the rain. The troop's rose to one knee at stand-to. Their aching wet bodies screaming at them. There had been no contact that night. Our artillery had continued until after midnight. The Iron Triangle was a free fire zone. After midnight there was a lot of harassment and interdiction fire from our heavy artillery that was 175MM from various American bases around 111 Corp. Harassment and interdiction fire became a bad phrase among the American student left. They of course wanted any excuse to say our own troops committed war crimes. H%I fire was only fired at likely enemy targets far away in free fire zones. Road or trail junctions in areas known to be enemy concentration areas were good targets. There were enemy troops killed in that war by artillery or B52s that were so far away the enemy never knew it was coming. That morning our artillery took a break, probably to bring up more ammunition. Thousand's of round's had been fired spanning a period of many hours. We were about to move forward when several air strikes were brought in to cover us during the artillery check fire. They were South Vietnamese Pilot's flying Korean War Sky Raiders. The Sky Raider was a prop driven fighter bomber that could stay on target longer than our jets. They dropped 500 pound bombs. One Pilot had too many bomadebom 29 beers and put a 500 pounder less than one hundred yards behind my platoon. We rose up in the air slowly and rolled over on our backs and hit the ground hard, then our helmets came down on our faces.

That morning after the air strikes we moved forward again and the enemy just disappeared. Perhaps they had enough or were running out of ammunition. When we came to the first area where we could get a chopper in, the resupply birds appeared. We brought in several with smoke grenades, who brought a complete ammo resupply; C Rations and Beer. We also got the Mail along with dry socks. In the Monsoon, socks were just an unneeded item. Then the rain started again. All of our operations were usually named but as 46 years have gone by I hardly remember their names. I think the Iron Triangle was named Wahiawa, after the town across Kam Highway from the main gate of Scofield Barracks on Oahu. There were a lot of Hawaiian troops in the 25th Infantry Division. There occurred on this operation the first use of tunnel rats; the first time I had heard of it. Smaller troops who volunteered became tunnel rats. This called for a small good troop with a rope tied around his waist and a pistol and flashlight to crawl into the tunnel. The Idea was to kill any enemy inside and find any munitions or any type of enemy supplies. This remained one of the most dangerous and daring tactics that our troops did. Troop's who were thought to be claustraphobic were of course never used. Later in the war, an entire enemy hospital and headquarters were found using tunnel rats. The American people will never know or fully appreciate the brave and heroic deeds by so many young American's in this war. Close to two million American troops went through the hell of Nam. I understand only 450,000 are alive today.

— Chapter Four —

Duty Whispers

So nigh is grandeur to our dust
So near is God to Man
When Duty whispers low, Thou must
The youth replies, I can.
—Voluntaries, Ralph W. Emerson

In late july or the start of august 1966 we returned to the Cu Chi base camp to get replacements and resupply. This also meant security on the bunker line, where a troop could get killed as easy as any place else in the graveyard called Nam. However it also meant decent hot food, showers, and clean uniforms. I even imagined that the Monsoon slowed up. Even with the replacements known as FNGs, our company was less than ninety souls. There was a squad Leader from third platoon who returned from the hospital at Bien Hoa.

He was a staff sergeant E-6 and had been wounded several months previously. He was shot through his thigh above the knee without hitting the bone. Policy in the Nam, only allowed for wounded too go home, if a bone was shot into or otherwise broken. There is one fact about infantry combat that absolutely cannot be denied. It does not matter how brave you are or how expert you may be in tactics or how wise about the war, if you are in an area that has thousands of pieces of lead flying around long enough, you will be hit. We very quickly moved out of Cu Chi and back to the deep bush. This time moving to the DUC HOA sugar mill area. The August days were passing and the Monsoon was slowing, I believe a bit early that year. Our company was initially alone in the area. We had taken the mortars, so the weapons platoon was set up in the patrol base perimeter. Intelligence had a VC hard core battalion operating near DUC HOA. We had patrolled out several miles from the patrol base in several directions without contact. The rice paddies were full of water. The Company CO had taken me out with the command group as well as my platoon leader. We had no artillery liaison party on that opertation, as sometimes happened. I guess he felt better to have two of us to handle fire support. After several days of fruitless patrolling; the CO decided to stay in the patrol base and double the ambushe's in the area. The leader of a night ambush should never leave the patrol base until just after dark. If you go out to early you may be seen. At that time DUC HOA was not in a free fire zone. The previously wounded staff sergeant was going out with his squad. I was in the act of sending one of our forward observers with his squad when, he said; "hurry up, guys, it is time to move out." It was still fifteen or twenty minutes before full dark. I said; "still not dark, sergeant." He replied, "I know it sergeant white, but I have a long way to go."

It turned out to be a dark still night and the rain stopped. The humidity seemed oppressive and it was to be a night filled with more than the usual danger. Even today my senses seem to be more on edge as darkness comes flooding all around me. It was not even midnight when we heard the M-16's and AK-47's start in. Why the M-16s were in action before the Claymores, I don't know. Perhaps the VietCong hit them before they were totally set up. The weapons platoon radio in the fire direction center lit up immediately, with our observer calling for fire. He made a quick adjustment and gave us fire for effect with ten rounds. We shot the mission with HE and as quickly we heard the patrol leader say: "we are being overrun." His platoon leader yelled into the mike, "blow the claymores and pull out". The Company CO reacted quickly, leading the rest of the third platoon to the rescue, while the other two platoon's held the patrol base. Just before he moved out he yelled; "white, you're going with us". We moved swiftly through the darkness as fast as possible. The area was open rice paddies full of water and that slowed us up. That is a very dangerous thing to do, as a large enemy force might be trying to lure the rescue force into an ambush. We knew that, but our buddies were out there in a combat to the death, and we had to try and save them. It was a situation happening frequently in that hellish place.

When we got close enough to the battle site the CO was on the radio to tell our guy's, "to just hold out, we were coming". I was moving very fast with the others, but my heart sank when I heard nothing from our ambush. The CO brought us on line as we entered the kill zone. We found our observer still alive, but seriously wounded, all the rest were dead. Their bodies were floating in the paddy; it was a NAM scene, a horrific scene. The water and the paddy dikes were blood soaked, with body parts floating around. The scene was something a troop saw a lot in Nam, it was usually the enemy who were killed. The young staff sergeant who had told me a few hours before, "got to go sergeant it's a long way," was hit in the face and it was a terrible wound. The scene was a horror for those not used to such sights; it was an old story for me. I felt a deep fury, perhaps at life itself. In the area of our ten round barrage, there were three wounded Viet Cong and many blood spots. Some days later a South Vietnamese patrol found twenty or so bodies crammed in a well near DUC HOA. We secured the area with a tight perimeter. The CO had the three VC brought into the center of our formation. We had a Vietnamese interpreter with us. When the VC were questioned they said, "they were walking home from the market at DUC HOA and were caught in the crossfire". That was a bold statement, as they all had their webbing and ammunition pouches on. The VC as usual had carried off all their weapons and as many of their casualties as possible. The Company CO turned to me and said, "take a squad and take these VC to the patrol base" and added, "MAKE SURE they get there Alive". I was terribly angry but got all three there alive; one could not walk and the other two had to carry him. I controlled my rage and proceeded carefully to our perimeter. The CO took the other two squads and swept the area at daylight. I was surprised there wasn't more action. The lack of more killing meant the VC were hurt.

In all counter insurgency war's or for that matter in all war, a steep moral slope may be found. I had read both of Bernard Fall's books about Vietnam(1) and understood the causes of the Indochina War. I also was prepared for the responsibilities of leadership. I knew it was imperative to never allow one's battle fury to cause a soldier to commit a war crime. In Vietnam, in all my 531 day's I never saw one dead child. I never allowed any troops under my authority, to violate the Geneva Convention or the rules of acceptable human behavior. I never heard of any violations of those principles by any American troop's, except at My Lai. I was in the hospital at Fort Riley when that happened. My Lai was a shame and disgrace to our armed forces and our Country. I was an aggressive American soldier, involved in a lot of killing and violence. All of my men knew that I demanded they do their duty, and that meant killing or capturing enemy combatants. I never kept score and cannot say how many I killed; however they were all armed and meant to kill me or mine. Vietnam was always a vicious close quarter's combat fought to the last extremity.

We finished the Duc Hoa mission without any more contact. It was not long after Duc Hoa that I saw a VC document that had been taken from a prisoner. Considering the discussion about the quality of the M-16 that has taken place through the years, the document is worth quoting here. The document informed all VC leadership to never engage an American unit near a road or an open area. The document went on to say, "be careful of any action with an American unit armed with the BLACK DEATH". One may take that at face value, I myself had great confidence in the M-16. I served in three different infantry company's in Vietnam and don't remember a single stoppage or misfire. We had ourselves and all our men load each M-16 magazine with two rounds less than the maximum load. We also had the weapon's opened and brushed clean each evening if the situation permitted. As August 1966 went by we had one more large sweep of battalion size near the border, west of Tay Ninh. We only made sporadic contact, I guess the enemy needed to regroup and get reinforcement's after the heavy contacts in 111Corp. We were breaking in a new company commander, to replace our captain we came in country with. He was a reserve officer, who was unsure of himself at first. No sweattie da GI, I saw lots of FNG's unsure of themselves in that Gethsemane of pain and sorrow. On that operation after midnight, I was checking our platoon security and found a troop asleep. He was lying on a small bunker about two or three feet high. I threw him off of it and he hit the ground pretty hard. I heard the new captain yell; "Sgt white, don't you hit that man". Well hell, I didn't have any intention of hitting him. If I had, you can be sure the troops depending on him for their safety would have backed me. The troop himself was a good man; he was just exhausted like all the rest of us.

When we returned to Cu Chi it was the last of August 1966. I had just come into the company area when I got the word to report to the Battalion Sergeant Major at the TOC. The Toc was the "Tactical Operations Center" and was underground with one level of banyan logs and another of sand bags on top. When I came in, he said;" have a seat white and a cold beer". He was drinking Pabst Blue Ribbon known among the fast set as a PBR. He said; "white, you're the last of the platoon sergeant's the battalion came in country with." If memory serves me well; we had eighteen platoon sergeant's which was either full strength are almost, when we got to Cu Chi. It was hard to believe, seventeen had gone, some killed, some badly wounded, some promoted and transferred. I had made platoon sergeant, just before we left Oahu, on December 5th, 1965 at the age of twenty seven, which was young for a regular army platoon sergeant. That made it for sure I would not get promoted, short of a Medal of Honor in NAM. The Sergeant Major went on, "I am going to transfer you to the 4.2 inch mortar platoon in HQ Company." He doubtlessly thought that would be a little safer for me. It sure did not work out that way. AS if to seal the deal, the VC chose that moment for a mortar attack into our battalion area. I took another big pull from my PBR and wondered if that was an omen.

I did not want to be in HQ Company and the 4.2 platoon. When I took over as platoon sergeant, I sensed immediately the hostility of the chief of the fire direction center. He was a sergeant first class like myself and didn't want to have a platoon sergeant of equal rank over him. The chief was very good at his job and errors were not made in that FDC. I didn't like being in 4.2 because I preferred to stay in a rifle company. There was also a wall between myself and the reserve lieutenant who was platoon leader and not long in Country. That's not to say I was a person that was easy to like. However I worked out a niche for myself. The platoon was short of forward observers so I sent myself out to be an observer for ambushes, several times a week. On one occasion, I adjusted in artillery and 4.2 concentrations for a battalion perimeter over near Cambodia. I adjusted from a light observation helicopter flying at 1200 feet. Fire adjustment was actually easier from the air, as you fired on the gun target line and made your corrections. The pilot, flew us off the map and I instantly knew we had crossed the border, and told him and we headed east. There were always standing orders, never to pursue into Cambodia and Laos. The maps were so bad prior to 1968, that many times we accidently crossed for short distances. The border restriction was never lifted until Nixon's Cambodia excursion in 1970.

I functioned well in night ambushes even though the danger level was high. In Nam, the danger level was high everywhere. In the first week of September the Monsoon had really slowed down and our Battalion moved to the Trang Bang area, northwest of Cu Chi on highway 1.Our Battalion was the 1st Battalion 27th Infantry Wolfhounds of the 25th Infantry Division. Actually being a night ambush observer for the 4.2 Platoon was a position below my rank. Nevertheless it gave me a way to stay in the most action. I wasn't looking for the MOH, but just felt better inside if I was doing what I did best. There were three incidents that happened on the Trang Bang operation that are unforgettable. One of the first nationwide elections in South Vietnam was taking place that month. On the day before the election every District Chief in South Vietnam was supposed to make sure that all the home folks got the word. The word was stay off roads and trails the night before the election. The night before the big day, we had every road and trail junction ambushed. We had been assured that the only thing moving after dark would be VC. Trang Bang was not a Free Fire Zone yet, it was also a hot area. That night after midnight, I was laying there listening to my RTO's radio set. We were on the battalion net and had no contact that night. Somewhere around 0200, I heard an ambush fire and it was heavy. The firing quickly stopped and I heard a very bad conversation over the radio. A cart with a young Vietnamese and his wife had rolled into a kill zone on a small dirt road. The ambush unit had followed instructions and killed them both. When it was a sure thing they were dead and NOT VC, the lieutenant commanding cried over the radio. I guess he had been in the war too long. The VC had put out fliers all over the country promising to stop the election. This bad scene was simply the fault of the Vietnamese District Chief.

The lieutenant was really broken up about it, but tears belonged in that far way place known as "The World", sorry about that. In Nam, I made efforts to be sure that my men or myself did not kill the wrong folks. Beyond that, after I had been there awhile, I tolerated no weakness in the platoons that I was platoon sergeant of or acting platoon leader. The army was short of small unit leaders in Nam, due to casualties and the Cold War. I was acting platoon leader more than I was a platoon sergeant. Several days went by and I had just humped into the perimeter with an ambush that I had been with the night before, when I noticed two figures quite a distance away. The Trang Bang perimeter was in a huge open rice paddy that may have been a thousand years old. This gave us great visibility and fields of fire. The enemy however could see us easily. The two figures must have been over half a mile away and still walking slowly toward us. I forgot them as I sat down by a bunker after getting my gear off. In a few minutes, low and behold,they were at the wire. The Company CO right in front of where I was sitting, "yelled out to a platoon leader to send someone out to run the two Vietnamese off." The captain also remarked; if we draw fire they might get hurt. They were both very old and crippled with age. A young troop without helmet or weapon walked out to them and said, "di di!" meaning get away. The old man, whipped out a hand grenade and dropped it at the feet of the GI. The troop was killed and they tried to run away from us. There was a wild scramble for weapons, and they were both quickly shot to pieces. I didn't bother to pick up my weapon; there were GI's between them and myself anyway. Did they have Cancer? Were they Grand Parents of the young couple killed a few nights before? Did they just want to die because they hurt so bad that they didn't want to live any longer? Hell maybe they hated us, Nam was a swamp of contradictions and hatred.

Just a night or so after the old folk's death, I was on a night ambush toward the south with a platoon commanded by a brand new Lieutenant. We were set up on the east side of a large paddy area where two trails ran together. I knew that at dawn the Battalion was sending a two company sweep, south of the perimeter on the west side of the clearing in front of us. At first light they moved just as we did stand-to. Six figures in black pajamas with no weapons started running away from them and headed across the paddy, running east toward us. We stayed down and they ran right to us. We captured them knowing they were VC and had them tied up with a rope the Lt carried. The Lieutenant was feeling his oats then but not for long. The Lt received a radio message to move quickly to the west, across the open and block for the two Companies. We moved fast, running on the paddy dikes. The two companies had several gunships supporting them. I heard the guns get the word: enemy running in front of us. One of the gunships said, "I see them running." I looked up and saw one of the guns was diving on us. I yelled, "DOWN" and everyone hit the ground.

I was waving my helmet hoping the pilot would see that it was an American helmet being held by a dirty tired GI. The Lieutenant was yelling over his handset; "You're on us! You're on us!" At the last second, the gunship seemed to slightly pull up but the pilot had already squeezed off his two rocket pods. That was sure death staring us in the face, I dropped, at the last second still yelling down. The rockets, thirty two I believe, just barely went over us and hit just behind us with the trajectory carrying the steel away from us. We jumped up and ran on pulling our six prisoners along with us. When we got to the other side, we quickly set up in front of our advancing troops. That was a bad move because we were masking the fire of our own troops. To do that, could easily cause a friendly fire accident. A heavy artillery salvo of 155MM /killing radius 100 meters/ was being moved forward in front of our line. The salvo just cleared us with the trajectory taking the sure death away from us. The impact was not even 50 meters away. The two companies stopped when they got to us. The Vietnamese intelligence guy our people had, quickly questioned our prisoners. He said," they no VC". I don't know how the hell he knew that quickly, but we had to let them go. There is one thing for sure, after that nice morning the erstwhile prisoners had, they were never going to be VC. The 155 Salvo was so close I was thinking; "man, can't sweat the Nam."

That's right, a GI can't sweat the Nam as death by many different means was all around. The VC had not been easy to find in the Trang Bang area. There were a small number of enemy troops killed and our battalion had several wounded. They were dug in those tunnel systems so deep, there is no telling how many just laid low and let us walk over them. "Stars and Stripes" magazine made a big deal out of the election, saying what a great success it was. They also played up heavily on the nation building theme. In the deep bush, we just dealt with the grim reaper every day and let the politician's talk the nation building, winning hearts and minds bullshit. When 1966 moved into the fall months, the enemy in our area had lost so many troops they were just laying low until they could be reinforced. We still had some heavy actions from time to time but the pace slowed. I was still the 4.2 platoon sergeant and was still going on the occasional night ambush as an FO to call for and adjust supporting fires. It was getting to early October and since the enemy was harder to find the battalion starting running a lot of "Eagle Flights". The theory was, a rifle platoon airlifted by usually five choppers (HU1B Hueys) with a gunship escort, would fly around an area that we thought was hot. If the enemy was caught in movement, the Eagle Flight would land in the nearest clearing and try to bring them to battle. When the VC was engaged, reinforcements were brought in to try to surround them. The Eagle Flight's had some success mainly as they could quickly cover more terrain than troops on the ground. In October we had one Eagle Flight meet with an unexpected bloodletting. It was a platoon from A company with a new Lieutenant. The choppers were low on fuel, so the troops were landed to make a sweep while the bird's went to refuel. They wound up in a very bad VC ambush and lost heavily.

The platoon was caught by surprise in a small clearing. Like most rifle platoons in Nam it was under strength, with somewhere around thirty troops. The platoon leader was hit in the head in the first burst of fire. More than half the platoon was wounded or killed quickly. The VC were in a wood line with hardened bunkers and machine guns along with the usual AK-47's. The platoon sergeant called for help and the Battalion sent the rest of A company immediately to the LZ. Both gunship's and other air support were sent quickly. The platoon sergeant charged the enemy bunker line alone and knocked out several bunkers, killing a number of VC before he was shot down. I believe he was recommended for the MOH. I don't know if it was ever awarded to his family. Late in the day behind a wall of fire, A company linked up with the few still alive. The 8 or 10 unwounded were brought to the battalion area in a truck from the LZ. I was counting ammunition in the 4.2 area when they came in. Their faces seemed frozen and white with shock. Some had to be helped from the back of the truck. The Nam had struck again as usual, extreme violence and killing could happen at any moment. I checked my seldom looked at calendar which had, just under seventy five days to go. There had been many times I had said to myself, "I may not make it." I lived them one day or night at a time. I had developed a psychological game that I played with myself, and it worked. It was about this time when I wondered when it was the last time I had laughed.

We knew that a real heavy duty operation was coming up in the Michelin Rubber Plantation. We were informed that our battalion the 1st Battalion 27th infantry would be OPCON (Operational Control) to the 1st Infantry Division (Red One). In the edge of the Plantation was a small village named Dau Tieng. I have never forgotten Dau Tieng or the date, which was November 3rd, 1966. There are several days of a year like march 12th and november 3rd that I always stop to remember. Hell, most of the time in that section of hell on earth, I wasn't even sure what day of the week it was. When we got the operations plan, the 4.2 platoon leader, the FDC chief and I were informed that our basic load of 4.2 ammunition, would be increased by 25%. We were going to leave the Cu Chi LZ in a Hook (CH47 Chinook) with the entire platoon and all four mortars. We would land at night, but in a secured perimeter at the Dau Tieng airstrip. I will never forget that airstrip since it ran uphill. When the C130's came into land, they landed " up hill" to slow down. They unloaded quickly and ran back downhill, to take off. Every time, either landing or taking off, when they went over the rubber, all hell broke loose. After our meeting was over, an officer from Battalion operations, casually remarked, "white, after the 4.2 platoon is dug in, we will need you at the TOC." My platoon leader nodded his head, to show he understood. That meant I would be doing some ambushing in the Michelin.

— CHAPTER FIVE —

DEATH'S CROWDED HOUR

Too busy with the crowded hour
To fear, to live or die.
Quatrains Nature, Ralph Waldo Emerson

On November 2nd, 1966 at about seventeen hundred, we moved our platoon, FDC section, all 4 tubes and our basic load of 4.2 mortar shells plus 25% to the 25th Divisions' LZ. The equipment and ammo was stacked at the side of the LZ waiting for us to load the Hook. We were in a loose line in the trees to the side waiting for the word. There were several rifle platoon's lined up in order, down a dim trail behind us. Then the battalion executive officer came over and ordered all Catholics out of line to the right side of the trail, and the rest to stay where they were. The battalion catholic chaplain came to the head of the trail and moved down the catholic line, giving each man Absolution. In the hot stillness, with sweat running out from under our helmets and down our faces, I heard a black troop behind me whisper to himself, "Man, I wish I had something like that". In the 1/27th Infantry, the catholic chaplain was always around, even going on operations with us. I was a very backsliden baptist and seldom if ever saw a protestant chaplain except when we had a memorial service. That was in my time with the 25th Infantry Division, later on in the 4th Infantry Division in the highlands, I never saw a chaplain period. I only prayed one time in Nam and I will get to that. The long Black Train was about to make a big move. In the next few days, there was enough violence and killing to strain the bonds and sanity of Humanity.

Just before dusk a hook (CH47) landed by our equipment and we loaded everything. To the best of my memory we had approximately 30 men in the 4.2 platoon. The Michelin Rubber Plantation and Dau Tieng had an evil name among the American units that operated in III Corps. At full dark the bird lifted up and moved out. The intelligence report had several hard core VC battalions reinforced by a company or so of NVA in the rubber and building up a large cache of ammunition and supplies. It was dark in the bird, which of course was flying with its lights out. Every soldier was alone with his thoughts; everyone was silent as the sound of the engines was too loud to talk over. In Nam there was really very little small talk anyway. When the chopper hovered over the LZ the crew chief opened the back door and turned on the red interior lights. We jumped out and it was a 3 or 4-foot drop into high grass.

When the Chinook lifted away, a degree of quiet returned and there was an officer from battalion to put us into position. The platoon had its work laid out for it that night. We were of course in the middle of a secured perimeter. Which means, as secure as anything was in Nam. Working through the night, all the 4.2 mortars were set up and laid in on the mounting azimuth with aiming posts out. The FDC Chief quickly had the FDC ready to go. The ammo was positioned and ready to fire. Then we dug in and sandbagged the guns. Our forward observers were with their assigned rifle company's when we left Cu Chi. The 4.2 Platoon was a very well trained and skilled unit that could put heavy fire on the enemy quickly. The FDC section chief, a sergeant first class E-7 like me, was the troop that made it all work. It was too bad the heavy fighting that occurred on November 3rd was just out of range for the 4.2 platoon. The 1st bn, 8th Artillery had a 105mm battery in the perimeter just to our right. They fortunately had most of the Michelin in range. There was only an hour or so for anyone to sleep when we finished and we did 50% but it really didn't matter. I doubt if anyone slept more than maybe a short nap. Stand to was at first light on November 3rd, 1966, as this was standard operating procedure. We all had a c-ration breakfast and some water that never really made anyone feel satisfied. The 1st Division had a battalion at the airstrip to secure it. We were under operational control to the Red One brigade operating in the area of the Michelin where Dau Tieng was. Just after first light, I still remember a momma san in black pajamas and white sampan hat that was walking down by the airstrip, trying to sell French sourdough bread. I went to the Battalion Toc as per orders somewhere about 0730. I was told to have a seat outside and cool it and they would brief me when it was time, whatever that meant.

All night long with their landing lights on C130 Hercules aircraft would come in to land. In order to land they had to circle low over the Rubber and land, up hill running fast right behind the gun positions. The first firing At Dau Tieng on "Operation ATTLEBORO" occurred when the VC in the rubber opened up with everything they had at those C130's. The firing continued into the daylight until an airstrike was called in on the approach over the Rubber. The strike was a large one with skyraider's followed up by gunship's. At the top of the hill at the end of the strip the C130s would stop and make a powered turn around. The C130's were unloaded very quickly and then made a fast run down the hill to take off. This went on every fifteen or thirty minutes all night and into the morning. After the airstrike the VC firing really slowed down. I never saw any of the C-130's get hit, at least serious enough to tell it. Sitting there waiting for whatever mission, I saw a sight that is imprinted in my memory forever.

Sitting in the shade of the 1st Battalion 27th Infantry TOC, I waited for the word, whatever it might be. That morning I felt some dreadful feeling deep down inside me, as if knowing that evil was afoot, yet not wanting to frame it into a thought. This narrative of mine of a great horror 46 years old is seemingly still born, as I can't use names of the killed in action. I also have avoided the names of those still living as it is very hard to remember all of their names. Nevertheless, these brave men are remembered always in the hearts of their loved ones. Like most small unit infantry leaders in that dark and evil place, I was living in a world of deadly violence. There where many loud explosions and the reaction was controlled by continuous radio transmissions. There by the TOC, I could hear many transmissions from all four of our rifle company's. I could also hear our battalion transmissions to the Big Red One /1st Infantry Division Brigade/ we were under operational control to. Movement caught my eye and I saw C Company, moving in line up the airstrip behind the artillery and 4.2 Mortars. Oh so many that morning who were my oldest and most valued comrades. Red One had an LZ there at the Dau Tieng Airstrip for the choppers to pick up the troop's for insertion into the rubber. The brigade needed to keep the air strip clear for the C130 landings and takeoffs. Charlie Company moved at a steady pace towards me. All of our other company's were already sweeping different areas of the plantation. I had seen the operational map for that day and saw our company's patrol routes and the 196th infantry brigade also under control to Red One. The 196th was several miles away from our battalion sweep location. The officers of Charlie Company must have been in a last minute meeting somewhere nearby.

The first sergeant was leading the long single file they were using for the short hump to the LZ. When the top soldier passed me, he glanced at me and said; "I wish you were going with us today white", I replied, "be careful today top soldier". There was never much small talk in that grim and hellish place. I have wondered if we both shared some dark and secret dread.

After the company had gone by, I continued to wait and sweat started to run down my face even though I was in the shade. The next several hours dragged on and I was still sitting there waiting for a mission. Then in the low buzz of radio talk, a sound of desperate need shot through my consciousness. I heard the battalion operations officer's quick rejoinder; "say again four and give me a six on your position." I knew instantly the call was from a Charlie Company call sign. If four was calling then six, / the company co/ was either dead or hit bad. Then very quickly, the operations sergeant stuck his head out and said; "saddle up white". I knew it was bad, if operations could remember a former Charlie Company platoon sergeant, that meant Charlie needed more leaders and right now.

I was ready to go and I think that I was going to ride the battalion commander's chopper as he was going to C Company very quickly. At this late date I am not sure what happened but operations failed to match me up with the chopper. The radio chatter continued to be bad. The Charlie company commander's RTO /radio Telephone Operator/ was cut off in the buffalo grass with several wounded men. On the radio chatter it became apparent that the entire command group was either dead or badly wounded. That meant the Company CO, XO, 1st sergeant, and weapons platoon leader, a young Lt who had taken my place. This also meant they had walked into a super bad ambush. In a few minutes, The Lieutenant who was on the radio and was call sign four had gathered together the remnant of the company in a wood line. He had managed to form a weak perimeter. There was no doubt they were fighting for their lives. The Charlie Company artillery forward observer got the battery of 105's who were set up at the airstrip adjusted and firing for effect. This helped Charlie four stabilize the situation until the Battalion CO arrived to take command. I was still sitting there at the Toc listening to it all and there was no doubt, it was a savage close quarters fight to the death. When the battalion commander's chopper tried to land, it was hit bad and had to crash land. The CO was ok but the sergeant major was hit badly along with some of the aircrew. The Battalion CO soon sent a report to our Toc operations and Red One. He said Charlie was caught in the open by a large VC force in concrete bunkers, with a large number of machine Guns, RPG'S and AK-47s. Charlie had eighteen killed and thirty five wounded in the first burst of fire. After the report, the artillery had a short check fire while they reloaded their ammunition supply. While this was taking place; I counted six airstrike's going in, flying right over our position at the airstrip.

The Battalion Commander wasted no time to provide the leadership necessary to pull the troops together. He addressed the ammunition situation first. Charlie had already run out a lot of M-16 ammo and grenades. The CO using code, ordered a complete basic load immediately. I could listen to all the radio chatter between our Toc and the Battalion Commander and Red One operations. Red One had already started ammunition resupply on the way. The airstrike's came in with napalm and 500 pound bombs. The enemy no doubt was getting hurt also. Apparently, the VC tried to make an assault because I heard the CO, yelling over the air; "Hold together Men, we will stand them off". Not long after that, the artillery was firing like mad again and our guys were throwing in everything we had. Our men were no doubt heavily outnumbered, but they were putting up one hell of a fight. The VC, were forced to stay in their bunkers, as they now had heavy casualties. Soon nightfall came and the VC fire slowed up. They were probably running down their ammunition supply without any quick means of resupply.

When darkness came on November 3rd I was still sitting outside the Battalion TOC waiting for the word, if there was going to be any, concerning me. I let my thoughts run through the wild and graphic radio chatter that I had been listening to all day. Not long after the Battalion Commander was on the ground and had taken command, the Red One operation's officer contacted him with a request for a body count of the dead VC. Then it was obvious that RED ONE three and Red One Six were both in command choppers in the air over the battle site. The operations officer being three and the RED ONE Commanding General being six. Our Battalion Commander was only a Major but courage was something he had plenty of, both physical and moral. The operations officer's request for a body count was absolutely stupid. The Major answered; "Get the hell off the net, I am in charge down here". Charlie Company's survivors and the Major were fighting for their lives and division operations wanted a body count. After a pregnant silence, Red Six said; "Hang on down there, guy's. We are going hit them with everything we have." This was a NAM moment where the dead were dead and the living must go on fighting. The entire 196th infantry brigade was just two miles north of the battle site. Then, "Red Three to 196th Six, heavy contact, reinforcement necessary, move south now". The 196th light infantry brigade six rto," we will as soon as we can do something with this jeep". Then wow, this is RED SIX; "PUT SIX ON THE HORN NOW". What, a one star general has taken a jeep to the Michelin Rubber Plantation? Then, 196th Commanding officer, "this is Six". This is RED ONE SIX; "leave that damn jeep and move south NOW, brave men are dying two miles south of you, RED SIX OUT". I think I heard someone in the TOC cheer. An hour or so after dark, the Major called Charlie Company's RTO who was lying fifty or more yards in front of the perimeter. He was an sp4 and had several badly wounded men with him. The Major did away with formal radio procedure and said; "lie still and quiet son, and tell those with you to do the same. The VC will search the grass looking for young troop's, in a situation just like you guy's. If they fire a few shots, don't fire back unless they are right on top of you. They will be trying to get you to give your position away. I PROMISE, that in the morning we are going to get you guys out of there".

In the morning at first light, RED SIX and our Battalion Commander were as good as their word. Division sent a tank infantry team with battalion strength breaking through the heavy undergrowth and linking up with the Major and the Charlie remnant. Then the guy's in the

TOC certainly cheered. The Major rescued the sp4 RTO and the other wounded quickly. The other three company's of our battalion also closed in on charly company's perimeter. The VC were moving quickly and trying to fight their way out. When the enemy ran for it, the rubber was full of dead VC. The total enemy body count for Operation Attleboro was over 1200 and the Charlie Company battle was the major encounter. Charlie lost eighteen killed and over forty wounded. There were over thirty VC concrete bunkers counted.

About midday on the 4th I was called into the TOC and told I would be picked up by a chopper on the pad in 10 minutes. I would be flown to the TAY NINH combat base and to wait at the TAY NINH LZ and several slicks (HU1B Hueys) would be bringing the Charlie company bodies there. I was to make Identification for the casualty section 25th Infantry Division. By November 1966, I had survived eleven months of infantry combat in NAM and was not a warm good man. Nevertheless, the thought of identifying so many of those fine brave men struck at my soul. In NAM, I never allowed any kind of human weakness for myself or my men, but I was extremely saddened. I was surprised at myself, for I had become part of the war and could not remember my last episode of humanity. Nam was an infantry war fought to the last extremity. When the chopper's came in, for some strange reason they carried only the battle gear and weapons of the killed and wounded. I was almost glad, and I picked out the 1st Sgt's gear and weapon. He always had his combat watch on his right shoulder strap and his name in duct tape on his weapon. It was a horrific site of blood and what seemed like body parts on the gear. The count came to just about eighteen and afterwards the 25th section leader said, “well anyway thanks for your help”. Then the TAY NINH LZ party got a message for me to wait at the LZ for the Charlie remnant which was in bound by chopper. There were tents with cots in the combat base set aside for the Charlie troop's to rest and clean up. When they off loaded, they were tense, almost white faced from their ordeal. They were a group of very fine brave young men who had fought a great fight. I took them to the area that had been set aside for them. I had already tried to lay on a good meal for them but the best I could do was a huge pot of ice tea, a large chunk of cheese and lot's of boxes of crackers.

As the day wore on, I managed by gentle persuasion to get them to clean up and rest. I said nothing about weapon maintenance and that may have been a mistake. They needed something to take their minds off the last thirty hours or so. After awhile I talked to one of my former weapons platoon sergeants who had always been a very good troop. He said; "well, sergeant, we were moving in heavy bamboo and undergrowth in the rubber. It was just horribly hot and we were making a lot of noise as we moved. We came to an opening in the Rubber. There was a mound out in the middle and buffalo grass all around. The Company Commander, knowing how hot we were;" said, we will move the troop's out in the open and checkout that mound. We are looking for a VC weapons cache anyway." He went on, "the weapons platoon was as usual serving as a fourth rifle platoon deployed behind the command group." Top Soldier said; "Sir, why not send the point to check the mound and keep the company deployed and undercover?" The Company Commander replied, "negative, everything is quiet." The sergeant continued, "when about half the company was in the open with our platoon just at the edge of the woods, it happened. There was a tremendous burst of automatic weapons fire and Rpg's. The command group were all hit at once."

As the long afternoon wore on I just sat and let the sergeant lay it all out. He told me, that all hell seemed to fall on them and they quickly formed a line in the edge of the rubber. The ranking officer, who was still unwounded tried to set up a base of fire, to cover those still alive in the buffalo grass. They were trying to crawl back to what was left of the company. The Lieutenant was the call sign four, who alerted the TOC to the disaster taking place. When the Lieutenant was sure that all who could make it to the hastily set up perimeter had done so, he gave the order to dig in. He knew the VC would try to move on C Company's flank and rear. The enemy was like us in one respect, they always went for the wipeout if they could. It was a good thing the artillery observer had survived the first burst of fire by being a little back in the trees.

He quickly brought in a marking round from the battery of the 8th artillery at the airstrip. Then he gave the command, "Add five zero, fire HE for effect and KEEP shooting". The sergeant went silent every few minutes and I didn't push him. He said, "when the artillery let up, a large number of airstrikes came in right on the enemy bunker line. Then the artillery resumed again." After a pause, he said; "The 1stSergeant was killed trying to rescue the wounded in the grass". He went on; "The Company Commander was hit several times in the chest. The medics managed to drag the still living wounded into one place behind a low mound. Several Medevac's came in at one time." After another pause, "he said, he thought the Company CO died as they put him on a loaded Dust-off." He shuddered as he said, "When the Dust-off lifted up blood just flowed out of the bird." The enemy as usual was blazing away at the red crosses. The heavy indirect fire and air strikes kept our men alive until the Major managed to get in. The chopper was hit and crash landed. The sergeant major was hit and the Battalion Commander, helped him get to the perimeter. I was not surprised when he said;' that the first words the Major said were; '"we are going to kick the hell out of those bastard's". After that he fell silent and lay back on his cot. I didn't bother him anymore. The combat base was hit by a big mortar attack that night. None of us were hit and not many among the garrison where either.

In a few minutes after the mortar attack, PUFF the MAJIC Dragon, showed up and cut loose sheer hell in the area the mortars were fired from. The rest of the night was quiet and the next day we were flown to Cu Chi. I thought after all the casualties I would be sent back to C Company, but had just over forty days left in country and was left in the 4.2 Platoon. I heard some rumors that the 196th Light Infantry Brigade had a new commander, but don't know that for a fact. The 1st Infantry Division Commander, call sign Red Six had a reputation of being a very tough and capable general. At Cu Chi I ran into a sergeant I knew from A company. He told me that when they fought their way to C Company, that he had never seen so many dead enemy troops. I would have preferred to have gone back to the company, as I never seemed to fit in the mortar platoon. They were a great bunch of guys and very skilled at what they did.

The second week of December 1966 came and I was a platoon sergeant who was short. One could always see a lot of troops with short timer's calendars and I respect that. Our troops were American citizens and free men, they were certainly within their rights to do that. The men who fought the Vietnam War for our country were some of the finest troop's ever deployed. I however was a professional soldier and part of the green machine and short timer's calendars were just not for me. Any man was free to refer to me as a lifer if he chose, BUT not to my face. There were many who used the term in a demeaning way and I didn't put up with it. It was not too common in 1966 but in 1968 and 1969 it was, and such things damage unity. The rest of December the battalion ran several operations over near the border, west of TAY NINH in which contact was sporadic. The 4.2 platoon was left in the Cu Chi perimeter most of the time. The platoon shot several missions for patrol actions near the perimeter. I didn't go out on any observer assignments with any ambushes in that time period. The duties of the 4.2 platoon sergeant were to coordinate with the gun crews and the FDC, concerning ammunition resupply and all platoon equipment maintenance and be the platoon leader's assistant. Near the end of December we went with the battalion on another mission near Cambodia. There were several heavy contacts and the platoon did some shooting. I went with ambushes as an observer when the battalion had more ambushes planned than assigned forward observers. On this end of year operation, I was out on one ambush and no contact was made. My first assignment to NAM was nearing an end.

In January 1967 our platoon stayed at Cu Chi and my time was up in the first week for sure. Nevertheless, I was in the unit for two more weeks and that put me 20 days over. I said to the 1st Sergeant; "what's the problem?" He told me, that "personnel was waiting for another career E-7 to replace me". Two days later I had occasion to be at Division headquarters. The so called;" repo depot" was across the street. I stopped by and no one was in the office except a personnel sergeant. We started a conversation and I told him I thought I was at least three weeks over my one year tour. He asked for my serial # and I gave it to him. He said; "hell sergeant, your twenty two days over DEROS"/ date expected return from overseas/ the date I could expect to leave the battalion for a new assignment in the United States. Then he asked, "Where would you want to be assigned?" I said, "How about Fort Sill Oklahoma?" He replied, "Don't know, but let me see what I can do." I went back to the unit thinking," I bet that's the last I hear of that." The next day I was doing my normal thing at the gun position and the First Sergeant came by and said; "white, turn in your weapon and gear and pack your bag". I left the unit in an hour and was at the depot waiting the next day for a chopper to Saigon and home. That night, I had a cot in a small tent with another sergeant who was also leaving the next day. Just after midnight, our area was hit by several mortar rounds and we spent the rest of the night in a bunker.

I have heard and read, lots of stories about the trip home on the so called "freedom bird". I was glad to be going home alive and not seriously wounded. The troop's on board were all very happy and singing. I was thinking about family and my wonderful wife. We had been married just over four years and had a boy and girl. I was also surprised at my next assignment. I was going to the ROTC instruction group at Texas A&M University at College Station, Texas. The flight was an air force troop carrier and for some reason it flew us over the entire length of the United States and landed at Fort Dix, New Jersey. When we crossed the Rocky Mountains, everyone was singing, "The Battle Hymn of the Republic". I wound up in a winter uniform and riding a bus from Philadelphia, PA on Interstate 70 through Pittsburg, Columbus Ohio, Indianapolis and stopping at the bus Station in St Louis. There was a thirty minute layover so I had a beer in the bar. I heard someone in the crowd talking loud about "baby killers" and was astounded when it became apparent they were talking about me. I was there a total of 531 days by March 12, 1969 and NEVER saw a dead baby. In any event I was about to hurt some SOB when two guys who were Korean war veteran's drug me out of the bar. They told me, "better get on the bus as the bartender had called the police." This was my first experience with the nation I thought I was defending and there would be much more through all the years.

It was after midnight when we got to the bus station at Oklahoma City in late January 1967 on a very cold night. My sweet wife picked me up in our old ford. We had a nice place rented in Ardmore, Oklahoma, which was the home town of both of us. Our parents were still alive then and also lived in Ardmore. My father was a veteran of both world wars and anxious to see me. At the end of the month we rented a home in Bryan, Texas about two miles from the university. I didn't know it then, but I would be back in NAM a short time after TET 68 and the long Black Train would roll again and much worse than before. It was the first few days of February 1967 and my family and I were so very happy in our new home. I turned thirty years old on February 23rd 1967 and my wife threw a surprise party for me. I believe it was around February 25th when I reported in to the University. The Sergeant Major was very competent, and a really nice guy. He told me that I would be there for years and never see NAM again. When he said that, I almost laughed in his face. The Army was in bad need of experienced infantry sergeants, there had been so many killed and wounded. This led to the establishment of the NCO advanced course at Fort Benning Georgia. The school's mission, was to train outstanding young soldiers to be sergeant's right out of advanced infantry training. They were outstanding young troop's with only four or five months service. When I reported to the detachment commander, he was a Colonel and a WW11 vet. He had been at Texas A&M for a lot of years. He asked; "sergeant what do you like to do?" I replied, "Fish and hunt, Colonel." He leaned back in his chair and said, "I know you have just returned from hell. Come in for duty on Monday through Thursday, and the rest of the week hunt and fish and by the way, don't screw the help."

— CHAPTER SIX —

DIVERSE PATH'S

Diverse paths lead diverse folk the right way to Rome.
—Chaucer

When I began my stint at Texas A&M in the ROTC detachment, I found my job to be extremely boring. In fact there were only three enlisted men, myself and another sergeant, as well as the sergeant major, whose name I cannot recall. Both sergeant's were doing the job that a SP4th class would be doing in a normal unit. On any given day, I might be storing weapons in the arms room or driving a pickup truck hauling training aids. The university had in the last five years started accepting civilian students. Before then, the CORP of Cadets had been the entire student body. If memory serves me well in 1967 there were approximately 1600 Cadet's and over Ten Thousand Civilian student's. Texas A&M was one of the top military schools in the country that sent commissioned officers to the armed forces. Most went to the army and the university had produced some of America's finest officers for many years. The CORP was very heavy on tradition and military values. The civilian students were already taking up the so called independent thinking nonsense of the 1960's. Some of the civilian students wanted to mimic the actions of the war protestors across the country. The young men in the Corp were mostly some of the finest young people I have ever met. I only found one thing about the Cadets that I found fault with, and it concerned only a few. In NAM young men from all of America's racial groups were fighting bravely and well for their country and of course some gave their lives. In the CORP in 1967, I believe there was only one African American.

In the CORP, as in many other military schools and of course at the service academies, harassment of the underclassman was a very old tradition. It was always believed to be a necessary requirement, in building discipline. However we live in a world where all good things and all bad things can be carried too far. I was the newest and one of the lowest ranking troops in the ROTC detachment. However, where discipline and leadership were concerned I had a world of real combat experience. The CORP had for a number of years, many Hispanic American cadet's who had always been totally accepted and who made fine Officers. I believe the young man in question was either the first or one of the first African American cadet's in the CORP. In the eyes of the Captains, Majors, and higher which made up the core of instructors, no one cared about an enlisted opinion.

It was my observation, that a very small number of upperclassman went too heavy on the harassment of this young cadet. I was sent back to the war before I got a chance to see if the cadet graduated and was commissioned. In Vietnam and during my other years in the Army, I served with some very fine officers of all racial groups. I am sure that the current Corp of cadet's at Texas A&M are a fine body of young men who are free of anything that could be considered racist. I said in the beginning that my Narrative would be factual as I saw factual. I shall write it as I lived it all the way through my narrative. In the normal course of life, I had good times and bad times at Texas A&M. The **chancellor of the university at that time was retired army** General Earl Rudder. He either led the ranger group at Pont Du Hoc on June sixth 1944 or was in it. I have heard him tell the story of the ranger's climbing the cliff under heavy fire. They had heavy casualties, but once on top they quickly wiped out the German infantry detachment that held the position. The heavy guns that were the objective of the attack had been moved back from the cliff and hidden in an orchard. The ranger's both found and destroyed them. The chancellor was addressed to his face as General Rudder, and certainly deserved it. He liked to be around US Army troops. Each afternoon when the business day was done, the General emerged from the admin building. He would wear combat boots and a WW11 Army pack on his back filled with rocks, and step off in a forced march.

It was not long before an occurrence at the ROTC Detachment improved my morale. Orders came down from Department of the Army that all ROTC instruction concerning small unit infantry tactics, had to be taught by a combat experienced infantry soldier. Well Big Woo, guess who, was the only combat experienced infantryman in the detachment. The officer instructor's and a large group of civilian instructor's protested to General Rudder. The officer's problem with me, was I was just an inferior enlisted man. The civilian's were pissed because I only had sixty hours of college credits. Someone told me that General Rudder said; "well, gentleman, I have checked this sergeant out and he is a real combat veteran and will instruct small unit infantry tactics at the ROTC detachment." I did the job for a few months before an infantry officer, just back from NAM was sent to Texas A&M. Gosh, I don't think I did the program any harm. I was at the university from February 1967 until September 1968, and met a lot of nice people both in and out of the Army. Both Bryan and College station were quiet Texas towns, filled with the kind of folks we will always risk our lives for.

During the two months I gave instruction on small unit tactics, I had to follow previously made lesson plans. There was a small area on the University grounds that ROTC used as a maneuver area. I ran the cadet's through all three basic small unit attack methods. I actually enjoyed doing the practical work and the instruction. There were so many other things that Sergeant Bob Earle and I did that were very boring. I was planning on doing a lot of fishing in the Brazos River but there was a drought and the river was in holes. One of the great things about Texas A&M was the alumni. Just outside College Station, an alumni, whose name I forgot, had a beautiful ranch. The ranch was on the bank of the river, and the ROTC detachment had a number of keys to the gates. We were always welcome to hunt and fish there. When the river went in holes, Earle and I fished a small hole for catfish. It was hard to believe, Bob caught twenty-two channel catfish from about one to three lbs. I was sitting beside him using the same kind of bait and gear and caught only three. I also killed a lot of Doves in September 1967 on the ranch and some Ducks on the river in the winter. I had started running a mile a day and increased it up to several miles, as I knew that NAM was always waiting. Since I knew I would be going back, I just took things one day at a time. I never mentioned it to my wife, but I know she was anxious about it. My wife was a hostess at one of Bryan's best restaurants and the lady who owned it let me hunt squirrels and quail on her ranch. My father gave me a Brittany bird dog named "King". He was a "King" that Hope and the kids loved. One night when Hope was brushing her teeth in the master bath, I heard her scream. I ran in there,

King's doghouse was just outside that window and he was lonesome and was sitting on top of it looking through the window.

This does not sound much like the platoon sergeant from NAM but he will be coming back soon. In some ways Texas A&M was pretty close to perfect but the large number of civilian students the university needed for economic reasons proved to be agents of change. It was normal for ROTC detachment personnel to have lunch at the student union. One day I had lunch alone there. The uniform for us was class a green or in summer khakis, and I was wearing khakis on that day. When I finished and had paid my bill, I heard some Army insults directed at me from a table where three young men and their girlfriends were sitting. The ugly nonsense from students all over America had arrived at Texas A&M via the civilian students. I was walking toward the door and stopped and turned toward their table. The room was suddenly very quiet. I walked slowly over and stood over them with my hands on my hips. They all looked at the floor and said nothing. Suddenly three or four upperclassman in uniform cavalry Boots were at my side. One of them was one of the CORP leaders. He said, "sergeant white, you might get yourself in trouble here, let us handle this." I left and heard no more about it.

When TET began on January 31, 1968, I was of course still assigned to Texas A&M. Every evening I was in front of the television set watching the fighting. There will perhaps be people who read this book who do not know what TET was. TET was the biggest Vietnamese holiday and is the Lunar New Year for all Vietnamese. It was a time to be off work and with family. To join with all family member's rejoicing in the good things of life, if there are any. In TET, the South Vietnamese Army would normally have a great number of troops on leave and stand down on all operations, if possible. The CIA and US Army intelligence had bits of intelligence that something big was coming. General Westmorland had informed South Vietnamese President General Thieu and asked him to keep his divisions alerted. The South Vietnamese President refused to go with the alert due to political reasons. Some of the South Vietnamese unit's in the Saigon area were kept near normal strength.

North Vietnamese Commander, General VO Nguyen Giap had carefully planned a surprise offensive over most of South Vietnam. The North Vietnamese had misjudged the situation thinking the people would rally to them. The people stayed with the South Vietnamese Government and the Americans. The enemy managed to get a suicide squad into the American embassy and two mp's were killed. Embassy personnel, Marine guards, and an airborne platoon landed on the roof, killed them all. With hard core VC already hidden in Saigon, the enemy managed to hold a part of the city and Cholon, the Chinese area. The South Vietnamese and Americans who were fighting house to house and street to street, soon regained control of the entire city. Most of the American action was outside the city with the 25th Infantry Division holding key bridges and access routes. In Hue, the situation was similar except the most enemy forces were North Vietnamese. In several weeks of heavy fighting, the US Marine's and South Vietnamese retook the city. There had been heavy fighting all over South Vietnam, and the NVA sent the VC ahead of them. The VC were almost wiped out and the NVA suffered huge casualties. Militarily, it was a great victory for both the US and South Vietnamese troops. Unfortunately, the American news media with Walter Cronkite and friends leading the way, falsely proclaimed a stalemate.

This was when Westmorland asked for 200,000 plus, more troops. Westy wanted to follow the enemy into Cambodia and Laos and finish it. The Communist forces were shattered, and with the antiwar group howling, LBJ refused the reinforcements and soon announced that he would not run for reelection. He also suspended bombing the North and asked for negotiations. These were actions that caused many American troops to have doubts about their sacrifice. This was a tremendous blow to morale in many American units. In my thirteen plus months with the 25th Infantry Division, we were fighting to win. After the LBJ decision, when I went back the fighting was heavier, and many times it seemed as if we were fighting for our lives. When the Nixon Vietnamization started, our forces started a slow pull out. In 1968 and 1969, on many occasions artillery and air strikes were harder to get. I always thought they moved the air force and artillery to positions toward the East China Sea at the beginning of the withdrawal.

At Texas A&M, time seemed to stand still. In 1967, Texas A&M had a great football team, winning the Southwest Conference and the Cotton Bowl. I don't remember their finish in the college football top 10 rankings, but it was high. I was told in February that I would be a drill sergeant at the August ROTC summer camp at Fort Sill. In March, the fighting in Vietnam had slowed down and it was obvious the communists had been badly beaten. The siege of the marines at KHE SANH lasted seventy seven days, beginning on 21 January 1968 and lasting until 14 April 1968. There were also two additional communist step ups in the action, during May and August of 1968. In all these attacks, the VC had almost disappeared and the NVA had thousands of casualties. I was sitting there watching it all on television and knew the communists were decimated. In June, as we were making preparations for summer camp, I got the word. Back to Vietnam in October 1968 and I would take a thirty day leave to move my family back home to Ardmore, Oklahoma in September. We had purchased a home in late 1967 and really fixed it up great, as my wife is a very good decorator. That evening, when I came home with the news, she broke down and cried. I felt awful about it, as it was our first home and she was hurt terribly. That started a period of depression for me that I managed to keep pretty well concealed. I started to get my mind and thought processes oriented toward the right frame of mind it took to handle the Nam. I remember going fishing on one of the lakes on the University property. I was fishing in my inner tube with a purple plastic worm and hooked a huge largemouth bass. The fish was swimming around me in a circle, spinning me around. The fight lasted for about five minutes then the fish shook the hook. I was so depressed about it all, I really did not care. I had already survived so much. I knew the odds were against me coming through alive again. I never told my wife this of course, I just made sure our will was in order.

So off I went to Fort Sill at the end of July, 1968. I rented a house at Medicine Park and moved my family there for the next three weeks. We sold our home to our realtor and were closing it in the first week of September. ROTC Summer camp was both physically tough and demanding and very boring. I had to make our company area at 0430 am and it was usually after dark when I got back to my family. The University of Oklahoma's second string quarterback was an ROTC Cadet in my platoon. I don't know what he expected from ROTC, as he dropped out of every run. It was all like a more extreme Army basic training episode, with commissioned officers doing things that were a constant violation of the cadet's civil rights. One afternoon the Captain that I worked with and I took the platoon through the infiltration course. Guess who got to demonstrate the course? One of the cadets was worn out and actually cried. The Captain freaked and started kicking him. I quickly said, "Captain, for hell's sake, you'd better stop before you hurt him." He glared at me and kept on kicking him. I saw a jeep coming and quietly stepped behind a tree.

In the world in which we all live, occasionally we see something that is noteworthy. I was behind my big wide cottonwood tree, watching the jeep as it rolled down the hill to the infiltration course. The idiotic bully, was still cursing and kicking the cadet. I stayed out of officer's business unless they were about to get troops killed by mistake. In this case this SOB deserved everything he was going to get. I had already seen the one star on the front bumper of that jeep. The jeep stopped in front of my tree, and very close to it. The General got out, and started walking toward the Captain like a man on a mission. The Captain finally looked up and snapped to attention. The General, took him aside and over close to my tree. In all the twenty years and a month I was in the Army, I never heard an ass chewing to equal that one. The General closed with a remark about efficiency reports that made the Captain cringe. When the General got back in his jeep, he said under his breath, "I saw you over there, sergeant. I also saw you the other day in garrison,and that Combat Infantry Badge, too." When the General had gone, the crestfallen Captain told me to march the platoon to the garrison area. It was late evening when I got them in. I checked their gear and weapons when they were ready. Then I left them with a remark, "men, the most important thing you learned today was how not to behave."

Well so much for little boy games and ROTC bullshit. We were in Ardmore after the labor day weekend and moved in a house we had rented. Then I was, Figmo (F&*^ it got my orders) and they sounded like action. I was going to the Fourth Infantry Division in 11 Corp or as some would say, War Zone two. The Fourth ID was headquartered at PLEIKU; this was an area that included many areas of heavy fighting the entire war. I was starting to get that old feeling of danger as the evening wore on. My sweet wife did not understand; there is no way a man can tell the lady he loves or his children what NAM was like. I would not want them to truly know what it was especially as I was going back. I would not know what infantry battalion until I was in country. I don't think I have mentioned this before, Walter Cronkite's buddy Dan Rather was once asked what being in the infantry in NAM was like. Rather answered, in a very true statement, saying; "It was sheer Hell." I had been to the gate of hell before, and this time would almost pass through. Nevertheless, I tried to enjoy the month of September with the family I loved more than anything. It was Dove season in Oklahoma, and I hunted a lot with my old hunting buddy. I continued to work out every day and ran several miles. My father was still alive then and he liked to hunt also. I was watching the news and knew that General Abrams had taken over from Westmorland in August 1968. The time seemed to go so fast. My children only knew that daddy was leaving again. My son was five and my daughter was four, just before I left.

In early October, I had to leave my wife and family and head for Ft. Lewis, Washington and McCord Air Force Base. From there, I would be flown to the NAM. My wife drove me to Dallas Love Field, which was still in full operation then. We took the children with us and it was an unhappy trip. I was already on the aircraft looking out the window and I could see my wife and children looking out the terminal window. The flight was delayed forty five minutes by a big thunderstorm. They were still there at the window, not leaving the terminal until my aircraft left. Suddenly I felt a terrible premonition that I would never see them again. My wife is only five feet two inches tall and they all looked so small and lonely standing there, my throat tightens as I type this memory. In all the world and all of life, there is only emptiness, if life has no love in it. This moment was the only time NAM almost broke me. When my aircraft landed in Seattle, the Army had a shuttle waiting to take me and some others to the overseas transfer company. We stayed in the barracks there processing and getting shots. We were also issued our jungle fatigues and boots. The 1968 World Series was on television and the seventh game was played the day we left. Mickey Lolich pitched the seventh game for the Detroit Tigers. I don't remember whom they beat. Lolich, was super that day and mowed them down. Within ten minutes after the game ended, we were on a bus to the tarmac at McCord. I was the ranking man in the group and so I had the roster. When we began to load in the rain, two of the troop's broke down. I told them; "too damn late for that crap; get on the bird," and away we went. Three days later I was at the airstrip at camp Holloway, and I was picked up by one of the dirtiest stinking troops I ever saw, in a wreck of a ¾ ton truck. Hell, I came in October and Jerry Horton, "Shake and Bake Sergeants"(5) came in December, it may have been the same troop Jerry mentions in his book as being so filthy.

— Chapter Seven —

They Shall Fall

But those that seek my soul to destroy it
Shall go into the lower parts of the earth
They shall fall by the sword, and be a portion for foxes
Psalm 63 9,10

I was sent to the 1st Battalion, eight Infantry and assigned to company A. I had to go through a two week refresher at Camp Enari that was child's play. The only thing noteworthy in the refresher was two Vietnamese truck drivers who were trying to urinate into an empty truck radiator. In this narrative of hell, I am going to use the names of those who survived, as I have been with them in a reunion group since 1999. This was an assignment in the toughest terrain found in all of the Nam. All of the central highlands were steep up and down hill. The Hill's were covered by a triple canopy of hardwood forest, with underbrush in many places over your head. There were bamboo thicket's filled with "wait-a-minute bushes" the Asian version of the American briar.

At the start of my narrative, I gave warning of the bloodshed and extreme violence that I would deal with in explicit language. You would not want children to read many of the details ahead. The Monsoon was raining walls of water in October 1968, when I rode a chopper to firebase twenty five, which was hill 687 northwest of the Ben Het Special Forces camp. Ben Het was on route 512, about fifteen clicks west of Dak To by road. This was some of the most dangerous country in NAM. The chopper found a break in the rain and landed at the firebase twenty five LZ. When I left the bird with my weapon and gear a young troop w/o his shirt, helmet or weapon ran out to meet me. He said; "HI my nickname is spider." I said; "my nickname is platoon sergeant white; where is the comand post?" Spider is retired, living in Florida now and a great guy. The Company Commander was a young Captain who had not been in Nam long. He told me I was the first career soldier in the company in months. He was a good young officer who needed experience. The company was approximately eighty men in total. That as opposed to the 144 and six officers an American rifle company was supposed to be. Just barely over fifty percent and we would soon have less. This was symptomatic of American units throughout NAM. LBJ would not mobilize the reserves and the Cold War plus NAM was draining away our strength. The CO showed me the perimeter and platoon positions. The actual summit of the hill was a little knoll just northwest and at least forty feet higher than the perimeter. I asked, "Sir, who do you have on that knoll?" He said "NOBODY, sergeant, THE MEN TOLD ME;" THEY WERE TOO TIRED TO GO ANY FARTHER." Remember, at the start I told you I would tell the ABSOLUTE facts. The anti everything attitude of the college bunch in the world while beneath contempt, had taken its toll. I was the first professional soldier with the company in a long time. The Captain assigned me as platoon sergeant of the 4th platoon and told me I would also be the field 1st sergeant. When I met the 4th platoon leader my mood improved immediately. He was a young 1st lieutenant with the right attitude and trying hard to overcome adversity. He was 1st lieutenant Andy LePeilbet and was a tough stud. We had a squad on the knoll digging in immediately. Just one NVA machine gun on that knoll would have wiped out at least half the company in a New York second.

Because of the rain we saw no real action until the rain stopped. We left the hill and started humping those 60 to 80 pound rucksacks on December 3rd, 1968. The company had a half battery or more of 105MM howitzers dug in on the hill. They never fired a round through October and November. There was a bunker right on top with a mess hall in it. They made breakfast every morning and we ate combat rations the rest of the day. On my first morning on firebase twenty five, there was a line on top of the hill for breakfast. They could only have been seen for many miles. Nobody had weapons or helmets or rank showing. I asked the first man in line his rank, he was a staff sergeant, HELL seven out of the first ten were sergeants or officers. I shamed the officers and sergeants out of line until their men had eaten. Thank God, there was that five or six week delay in action to shape things up.

Route 512 had some degree of importance in the 11 Corp operational area. It was a road built many years before by the French. The road ran generally westward from highway fourteen at Kon Hiao, to Dak To, and 15 kilometers on westward to the Ben Het Special Forces camp. The road ran westward down a valley, upon leaving Ben Het, it continued on westward approximately ten or twelve kilometers to the tri border where Laos, Cambodia and South Vietnam came together. The 1st Battalion, 8th Infantry supported Ben Het, from firebase twenty five with A company and a 105 battery positioned on the north side of the valley thirteen kilometers from Laos. On the south side of the Valley was firebase twenty nine, on hill 824 with C Company 1st Battalion 8th Infantry and a 105 battery. Ben Het itself had a good sized landing zone along with three companies of CIDG's, that's trained civilian irregulars. In the central highlands that usually meant Montagnard troops. They were led by American Special Forces advisers. Ben Het also had a battery of 105 MM howitzers and a battery of 175 MM howitzers capable of firing into Cambodia or Laos. There were also two forty MM dusters, a great anti armor and personnel weapons system. There were three hills at Ben Het making it a very defensible position supported by our two rifle companies with two batteries of 105 MM howitzers. Both firebase twenty five and firebase twenty nine looked down on Ben Het. Firebase twenty nine and Ben Het were in range of NVA artillery just over the border, fire base twenty five was just out of range. Ben Het and twenty nine took enemy artillery fire every day. The enemy guns were dug in on the forward slopes of hills and could be withdrawn into the hill. The air force bombed and bombed and could not take them out. All three American positions, Ben Het, firebase's twenty five and twenty nine had deep bunkers with PCP tops and many layers of sand bags. There were trenches that ran from bunker to bunker. Route 512 had always been a major invasion route from Cambodia and Laos into the heart of the central highlands.

All three positions had board sidewalks made from broken up ammo boxes so we could walk easier in the monsoon. The bunkers were always damp and filled with rats. Ledges were dug inside the bunkers where the troops could lay out whatever they had to sleep on. NAM like other infantry war's was just not a place where sleeping was a big thing. Firebase twenty five had been in use for several years and had been fought for in the past. When improving our positions at twenty five we usually dug up NVA bones. The trenches allowed the defenders when under infantry attack, to leave the bunkers and fight from the trenches. I made it clear to the troops, that if we were attacked, the first thing that would go were the bunkers. The NVA would quickly take out the bunkers with

RPG's with heat warhead's. We had three bands of command detonated Claymore mines around us and just beyond the mines were razor wire emplacements and many trip flare's on the outside. All three positions could reinforce the final protective fires of each other. In addition, at the DAK TO airstrip 15 kilometers from Ben Het there was Puff the Magic Dragon and many gunship's. There were additional air assets in the PLEIKU Area and for that matter all over South Vietnam.

At firebase 25, since we were not under continuous enemy fire we saturated the area with short range patrols called "srp's". These were recon patrols that sat up three to five clicks from twenty five, near trail junctions or other obvious places the enemy might be seen. A click was usually a grid square on the map and was thought of as 1000 meters. If the enemy were seen, artillery would be brought in and the small patrol would head out of the area. The difference between a recon patrol and a combat patrol is that the recon patrol is not to make contact but just find the enemy. The size of our short range patrol was usually three to five men. The leader of most short range patrols was usually a sergeant E-5 otherwise known as a buck sergeant. The rain was so heavy it could be dangerous; a small creek could become a raging torrent in a few minutes. This had led both the US Forces and the NVA to curtail operations in the worst of it. Everyone not out on patrol worked each day to improve the bunkers and trenches. At night we always had the normal fifty percent set up. Since I was the fourth Platoon sergeant, I stayed alert until midnight and then woke up Lt LePeilbet. On hundreds of nights in NAM I have stayed up for hours leaning against a tree or the side of a hastily dug fighting position. There were so many nights when I just lay there trying to put my mind somewhere else. When it was my time to be alert, I had a poncho liner wrapped around me and my rifle across my lap. I also had the night seeing device called a starlight scope. The ones we had were wet and you could barely make out movement in a green haze.

Discipline is the core virtue that makes a group of men operate effectively. Leadership must combine discipline and personal example to reach any objective with the smallest loss. At Bunker Hill when the Brits left their boats to attempt an attack, General Lord Howe said, "Lad's I will not ask ye to go a step further than I will go myself." In the NAM it was one hell of a long way from normal people acting in normal ways. When I saw that the men in A company had been without experienced combat type leadership for a long period of time, I set out to correct the problem and also restore morale as quickly as possible. One of my first problems required the personal touch. I had the platoon filling sand bags. It came to my attention that a soldier from the platoon was laying on his ass in a bunker. I walked in and said, "young man get outside and help the others." I knew this was the first test of my authority. He replied, "Screw you, white boy." He was lying on his poncho liner on an upper ledge in the side of the bunker. I still remember the cloud of dirt and dust when he hit the bottom of the bunker on his face. I never was much of a patient man when I had given an order. When he ran outside I followed and made sure an attitude correction had been made. When we had to dig in I always dug my own hole as I always took part in all hard work. I never sent a troop to do something I myself would not do. When the time comes for action the leader must lead.

I had noticed the first day I was at firebase twenty five that there were several dogs around. If they had been trained Army scout dogs, that would have been fine. However they were just dogs some of the troops had picked around Camp Enari. I decided when we left twenty five, the dogs were not going. Lying in an ambush position or moving, a dog barking could give your position away. One night in the first week I was at the fire base, trip flares started going off beyond the razor wire. Before any orders to fire the fifty percent on security opened up. This would not have been the way we would want to handle a night alert if it had been real. We would use the claymores and just the ones closest to the probe. I knew it was a false alarm immediately as no one was shooting back. Both Lt LePeilbet and I called cease-fire and finally got the firing turned off. A lot of M-16 and M-60 ammo had been wasted. When it got still and quiet, a damn dog came walking into the perimeter. When we took a resupply slick the next day, the dogs left with it. Battle experienced troops would not open fire without orders when they were not receiving fire. Considering what I had seen so far I was just glad the security had been alert enough to notice the trip flare. One of the big things I wanted the company to understand was the bunker's were for incoming indirect fire. In case of an infantry attack on our position, leave the bunkers and fight from the trenches. The bunker's would have been hit immediately with RPG's. I along with many others had learned that at Cu Chi in 1966. The company officers were good people, they just were not experienced. When we talked about things, they understood and made changes that were needed.

I knew I needed to go out on a patrol or two, to show the men that leadership would share their hardships and dangers. The current short range patrol SOP was only putting troops at rank E-5 and below out of the fire base and exposed to greater danger. I knew that none of the officers except probably Lieutenant LePeilbet had any idea if the srp's were going to the locations assigned. We were asking a lot, to expect inexperienced lower ranking troops to go a long way from firebase twenty five and find the right location to boot. If a srp was in the wrong location, it could be hit by our own artillery or airstrikes or even worse. If they ran into the NVA and we could not find them quickly they may have been wiped out. There came information from intelligence sources that the NVA had been using an old trail, that was two kilometers east of 25 and dead north of Ben Het. This was what I had been waiting for. I proposed to Lieutenant LePeilbet that I take six men and check the trail out or better do an all night ambush on it. The Company Commander's permission would of course, be needed. The company had been tasked by battalion, to see if this trail had been used recently. Since it was the Monsoon, sandal tracks like the NVA or VC used should be plain to see, if they had been passing through the area. Lt LePeilbet liked the idea and wanted to go.

The Company Commander went for the six man patrol with me leading it. The CO, told Lt LePeilbet he needed to stay with the balance of his platoon. I liked working with LePeilbet; he was a smart, hard charger. I selected the men I wanted and took my RTO so I could communicate. Since it was a one day patrol, I ordered two combat ration meals and two canteens of water on each man. Everyone would carry their own basic load of ammo and grenades. I carried Salt, Halazone and Malaria tablets in my rucksack and several smoke grenades. I had already made a map recon on the map that I would carry in my side trousers pocket. While making preparations that afternoon, it crossed my mind, that this would be my first patrol in the central highlands. One of the men I picked was an M-79 gunner. The M-79 was a great little grenade launcher. The only thing I didn't like about it was it had a small killing radius. I did not take an M-60 machine gunner, as this was a recon patrol. Yes of course, we would take action if we found the enemy. If I found a small force, we would engage them and use the battery of 105s on firebase twenty five. If a large force found us, I would use all the supporting fire I could get, and make a maneuver to get clear and get to firebase twenty five. I would need to get to a position where the Company could get to us if possible. I meant to leave the wire before daylight in the morning and move as quietly as possible. The 4th Division had done away with weapons platoon's and I was now a rifle platoon sergeant, which is what I preferred. Before I left, I also marked on my map, the position the only SRP east of firebase twenty five should be at. I was going to go and return by different routes that were not too far apart. I had it in my mind to determine if the SRP was where it was supposed to be. That afternoon just before dark, I stopped by the artillery section and coordinated with the FDC. We agreed that if I needed fire, they would mark center of sector and I would adjust off that.

Just before first light, I made a final commo check with the command post and led the way out past the wire. I had all ready verified that day's password though it would not be used, as we had radio commo to make a safe reentry. Password's were used, if a patrol had to fight its way to the firebase and the troops were separated and came in individually. I had covered all possibilities with my men and they were as ready as possible. The huge triple canopy forest had the usual heavy undergrowth and was still and quiet. There were few animals left in NAM, the fighting had gone on so long. Once in awhile we would see a baboon or a tiger, but not often. The NVA controlled all the elephants to carry their artillery.

There were very few birds, nothing really in NAM but men and most of them were insane killers. Once clear of the wire, I halted, formed a perimeter and waited for first light. In that hellish place, even at noon it seemed like the light was dim. When light came I set up with myself as point, since we were only seven and we moved downhill as quietly as possible. Every man had his weapon under his right arm with his thumb on the safety as per my instructions.

I was using an azimuth just short of 90 degrees that I had picked on my map recon, to hit the trail east of twenty five. In that kind of country, a patrol leader would need to look down his compass azimuth as far as he can to pick out an object. Then walk to it, he might use a huge tree or hill. He must use whatever he can see on the azimuth he is following. When he reaches it, he has to pick another object and so on until the objective is reached. I expected it would be close to 1200 before we reached the trail. I led the way on my compass with the patrol in single file. I moved slowly and kept everyone alert the first forty five minutes were consumed going down twenty five as it was steep. There was a lot of bamboo and other high vegetation on the hillside. I could hear the NVA artillery as they dropped 105MM rounds on Ben Het and firebase twenty nine. Every hour, we took a ten minute break. Since there were only seven of us, I didn't use a staggered numbering system like I would have with the entire platoon. When we stopped, I just set up a loose circle with everyone watching to his front. I called in a sitrep to the company every break. A sitrep is a situation report, which so far was negative. I always kept a good look around and used the clock system if I needed to focus the patrol's attention on something. The direction headed for instance was 1200. I was looking for Ho Chi Minh sandal tracks otherwise known as Goodyear sandals; they were made out of old tires. I was also looking for elephant or water buffalo tracks as the NVA used both animals to pack their mountain artillery and heavy machine guns. We moved silently, using only whispers or hand signals to communicate. I took a noon break when it was time and we drank water and ate combat rations.

When we had left firebase twenty five, the terrain had leveled out but it was still hard walking in the undergrowth. Whenever we hit buffalo grass, I stopped every few minutes to listen. I was straining to hear the buffalo Grass swish, as that is a warning that someone or something is moving near you. In the daytime there was not much noise from the small lizards that lived in the trees. If they were making a lot of noise and suddenly stopped, be on Maximum alert. The noise they made caused the troops to call them "Fuckyou Lizards". I only saw two crows in the highlands in 1968 and 69; I guess they had left like the other animals. We moved silently, following my compass sightings. It was about 1330, when I saw we were moving into a low swale and then we came up to the trail. I moved off to the side in some heavy undergrowth and set up a small perimeter. I told everyone to stay down and not make noise. I told two of my men on the trailside to cover me as I checked the trail. In addition I had a Sgt E-5 for assistant patrol leader and told him to stay on the backside away from the trail. When I saw the swale and knew the trail was close, I set up a huge banyan tree as a rally point in case we made contact and needed to regroup.

Except for the occasional faraway sound of NVA artillery hitting Ben Het and twenty nine, the dark forest was silent and depressing. When I felt that feeling, I always knew to be on extra alert. The trail was about twenty steps away and when I reached it, I dropped to one knee and moved slowly left and then back right. Tracks of NVA or VC or CIDG from Ben Het if recently made would be easy to see in the mud. Tracks are much harder to find in the undergrowth. At first, I saw nothing as I searched back in front of the men. Then at the side of the trail, I found it; just two Ho Chi Minh sandal tracks. No doubt they were trying hard to hide their tracks. The mud imprint was still soft in the tracks, indicating they had passed this spot today or at most yesterday. They were headed for Ben Het, which was south of us. Only two track's, also indicated they were a small group, perhaps just two or three NVA scouts on a recon. They were walking where the tracks would be hard to find, and trying to clean their tracks with small cut tree limbs of which one was still there. I checked the area again and found nothing else such as elephant tracks off to the side of the trail. I took a good look in both directions on the trail and then picked up the tree limb the NVA had used and brushed out my tracks as best I could. When I was back to our small perimeter I called the Company CO and relayed what I had seen. My information actually confirmed the intelligence report. We had done what we came to do, it was time to go. In the previous thirteen months in NAM, I had learned many things about small unit infantry war, both counterinsurgency and conventional. Perhaps that's why I was still alive and still learning. Certainly I was not Special Forces or anything black ops or elite, but was an ordinary grunt that had learned a few things.

Taking and extra two minutes, I told the men what I had found in a whisper and then asked for questions, there were none. I said we move and led out still using myself as point with my RTO right behind me. The men were keeping a good five to ten yard interval between them and that pleased me. Regular American grunts, were as brave as any soldiers in the world but they seldom liked being in the Army. I always made sure the last man in file kept the man in front of him in sight. I was a fanatic about not losing a man in that green hell. I was following an azimuth that was the reverse of my going out azimuth, plus five degrees. I was planning to arrive at twenty five on its southern slope. That should take me to the SRP position in about five or six hundred yards. I was watching my position closely not wanting to miss the SRP. The return trip was conducted like we went out and was without incident. When I was getting close to the hill, I stopped and set up a small circle. Then I climbed up a tree to get high enough to check my back trail and it was clear. There was no SRP; I found them in a bamboo thicket at the south base of the hill. After making some explicit remarks I attached them to my patrol. Then I called the CO and told him in code that I was coming in from the south.

The trip back into the perimeter was routine, just a long hard climb. The SRP that did not go out was from our platoon. The supposed to be patrol leader was on the E-5 promotion list and I had him taken off. He was normally a pretty good man, he probably was still "one of the boy's". There were lots of bad attitudes in American infantry units in the latter half of the War. Combat units seldom had a fragging incident; most men knew that teamwork and discipline were the keys to staying alive. Most of the attempted murder incidents were in the big base camps. When I reported in to the 1st BN, 8th Infantry at Camp Enari, there was a black troop chained to the Sergeant Majors desk and charged with murder. In the rear echelon, in late 1968 and in 1969, the officers and sergeant's were in many cases unable to control the troops. I never had much trouble with the troop's in the bush; most of them were good people. The young man who I took off the promotion list, I put back on the next month. During the time of the NAM, we were almost paid zero. I was the highest ranking enlisted man in A Company and one of the highest paid in the entire Battalion. My total allowable in the War was never up to $500 per month. That's approximately sixteen dollar's per day on a 30-day month. That's a high estimate rounded up. When I think of the thousands of nineteen and twenty year old troop's killed in action or maimed for life, it makes me furious. The young man I caught hiding his patrol probably wasn't making five dollar's a day and he had a family. In his case, his men might have been telling him they did not want to go out there. I always maintained an acceptable standard of discipline. I always let troops know that I was a man ready to physically back up his orders, if necessary. So many young men were killed, who were unable to care for their families and in many cases were draftees. Back in the United State's, there were many sons of the wealthy running around talking revolution. There is something really wrong about that.

When I had all safely in the perimeter, we sat down with the platoon leader. LePeilbet and I went over every aspect of the patrol. While I talked, we cleaned up our weapons. They needed very little, not having been fired. I saw that the six men I took were secretly proud of going. The rest of the platoon were also gathered around and it was easy to see they wished they had been taken along. Certainly if we had been in a bad scrape and some of us had been killed, the feeling would have been much different. When the Monsoon ended, it would only be a month or so until TET 69. When TET started; I knew we would be in the bush patrolling right on the border.

Lieutenant LePeilbet and I had a long talk about tactics and the best way to set up an ambush. The most imperative tactical consideration is to always have your men in a formation where all can fire without hitting one of our own. Almost all combat's in the Nam were encounter battles, in very tough terrain. In a War like NAM, we were nearly always in a recon in force. However, we never had enough force or more than half the troop's we were supposed to have.

On firebase twenty nine, across the valley from us, the artillery fire on their position increased every day. We communicated with them on the Battalion net quite a bit. We also heard all their communications with battalion. November was passing by and the rain was starting to quit. When the artillery pressure on twenty nine had reached a certain point, it was obvious that a big ground attack was coming. I had noticed stress and fatigue in the voices I heard on the radio. Charlie Company had not had many killed, because they were well dug in but there were some wounded. It seemed like every day, I watched a dust off fly through the dust raised by artillery shells to pick up someone. I watched it with binoculars and thought, “Why?” when we could defend South Vietnam and support Ben Het from positions out of range of the NVA guns over the border. The Brigade or Battalion Commander's must have been thinking the same. By late November, thousands of shell's and bomb's had been used over the border, the NVA Guns were still firing. Charlie Company was ordered to withdraw to the clearing halfway down the hill. Ben Het would send a platoon, led by a Special Forces officer to secure the clearing. Then Charlie, would fall back down the hill, link up with the platoon, and move back to Ben Het. We would saddle up our company and be prepared to be picked up and carried to the clearing, if needed. Our men had sat there day after day, watching the carnage going on. In the pickup, the Company Commander laid on fourth platoon to lead. That meant Lieutenant LePeilbet, in the first chopper and myself in our last chopper. When the first chopper came in, we had a refusal. I told him, what in hell are you going to do, stay here alone? He was crying and said; “I am not going.”

Well I guess that's what sergeant's are for. I had my gear on and with my rifle slung around my neck, I picked up his gear and weapon. Then with the other hand, I grabbed him by the shirt and cursing him all the way, dragged him to the bird. We were all ready to go, when Charlie made contact with the Ben Het platoon without having to fire a shot. Our mission was cancelled and we sent our refusal out on the next resupply bird. I don't think he was ever punished in any way. We had him charged with cowardice, but I don't think battalion thought it was worth the time. When the chopper came in, I walked him to it and told him in front of the entire company, "you are a piece of shit". I said in the start of my narrative, I would not pull any punches. In 531 days, I only saw one other coward and he ran, that was in 1966, we found him later on wandering through the rubber with a crazed look on his face. Such things set a bad example in front of the troops, when a yellowbelly gets out of it and nothing happen's. The vast majority of the troops being good men, they would rather face hellish combat than have someone they respected, tell them they were a piece of shit. The leaders must always lead and set an example of calmness and confidence. One thing that had great bearing on the incident, when the hook's (CH47'S) came into twenty nine to get the guns, two were shot down. Soon thanksgiving came to the Nam. On twenty five, I had some old tables that were built out of broken ammo boxes, put on the backside of the hill. That would keep the eating troop's out of sight of the border area. Recent intelligence said the NVA were bringing their artillery across the border with the aid of elephants. That would bring them in range of twenty five. They probably thought they had won a victory, since Charlie Company had been pulled off twenty nine. There were also reports, that patrol's in the valley near Route 512, had heard tank engines. When I heard that my thought, which proved to be correct, was that the NVA were getting ready for TET. We had a great thanksgiving, with more than we could eat of turkey and all the fixing's and more beer then we could drink. I have never had an addictive personality and could take it or leave it. That a US army rifle company out on the edge of hell, could have a meal like that flown into them says something about our army. The next day, we had Martha Ray, a Hollywood actress and comedian plus her front man visit us. We also had the donut dollies, USO girl's visit us the day after, with all kinds of pastries and wanting to play silly games. After Bob Hope, who I spoke to at Cu Chi in 1966, I guess they all wanted to get in on the act. Those are things that should have been curtailed; the NVA could have opened up on us at any moment. In those last days at twenty five, it seems like something different happened every day. We had approximately fifteen chopper's in formation fly over us in daylight, in CH34's. These were older troop carrying chopper's. They flew into LAOS in daylight; it could and probably was a SOG black op's mission. SOG meant special operation's group which was special force's or ranger's. Done in daylight, with so many choppers, one or two choppers could carry the patrol. The rest could scatter around the landing zone, and make so much noise the NVA could not be sure where or what had landed. Our special forces were no doubt, some of the finest troops that ever served this country.

I had heard the name, Jerry Loucks around the company before I knew for sure just which troop he was. He was in the third platoon and was known to dislike the army and authority. I heard him one day saying, "that morning he had answered the call of nature and went out to a toilet that was built in the wire". He said ,"that he surprised an NVA while using it; the NVA had torn up some buffalo grass getting away from there". I thought at the time that this guy is just a clown. If I had known that soon, I would be the third platoon leader and he would be my point man, I would have been surprised. Jerry is gone now, and wherever he is I wish he could read my words. After Charlie Company had been withdrawn to DAK TO, the shelling of Ben Het resumed. This time the gun's were in South Vietnam, the NVA moved them every time they fired because our counter battery was quick and deadly. DAK TO was about fifteen kilometers east of Ben Het on route 512. In 1967, two very large battle's had been fought at DAK TO and at hill 875 about seven click's southwest of DAK TO. The tri border area was one of the most violent places of the War. Before long, A Company was going to find out just how violent.

We left twenty five on December 3rd, 1968; the artillery battery and all its ammo and equipment, were picked up by hook's. We moved down the mountain in single file, fourth platoon bringing up the rear; that meant I was the last man to leave twenty five. In single file, if the platoon has a lieutenant, he moves behind the point and the platoon sergeant brings up the rear. In a company single file, unless we were leading we would not have a point. When the platoon's moved in single file, the troop's were numbered and in a short halt, every other man would face right or left, according to his number. Third platoon led that day, however it has been a long time, if so than Jerry Loucks was point for the entire company. We moved as quietly as possible, however the hill was steep and we were carrying sixty to eighty pound rucksack's and the underbrush was bad. It was very hot and still as usual, with no wind. There was an occasional artillery round on Ben Het, and their guns were shooting back in counter battery. While I was a platoon sergeant, I was also the field first sergeant. That meant, I ordered rations and ammunition, medical supplies, whatever was needed, for the entire company. Therefore, I always knew how many troops we had at the start of every day. I also knew how many were killed or wounded, and who they were. I received this info at the end of the day or night, tactical situation permitting.

We made it to the bottom of the hill and turned east to pass Ben Het on its North side. The Special Force's Commander of Ben Het, knew about our movement. All such movements of our forces were carefully coordinated, so the good guys did not shoot the hell out of each other. In late evening, we stopped in some heavy undergrowth on the north side of route 512. We did not ambush the road that night, as BEN HET was going to get a supply convoy from DAK TO that evening. This decision, to lay low in the bush was taken, because the convoy would be heavily armed and have a tank escort from 1st Battalion, 69th armored Brigade. The convoy ran several times a week, and had been hit by sniper fire and occasional artillery and the escort was super alert. We were in a good perimeter with claymores and trip flares out. Every man had dug his fighting position. We were about 150 meters off the road so we would not spook the convoy security. It was a quiet night; we were going to move on toward DAK TO at first light. The next morning we moved out early, even in the flat ground by route 512, it was going to be a good eleven kilometers to DAK TO. The convoy, returning to DAK TO from BEN Het was told to pick us up wherever they found us. When the link up was made, the other three platoons rode to DAK TO. The Company Commander, left us with orders to ambush the road near the bridge, over a large creek that ran by DAK TO. The road stayed close to the creek after the bridge crossing. It ran all the way to the DAK TO combat base and airstrip. Lieutenant LePeilbet and I, found a great spot for our killer team hidden by a drainage ditch under cover and right by the road.

The chosen spot for the ambush was a good one, the NVA, no doubt would like to take out the bridge. However, with 'all the off road equipment we had the convoy undoubtedly would have just drove across the creek. We stopped back in the woods to organize the ambush. Lieutenant LePeilbet sat up a rally point by a big tree that was down. The fourth platoon, at that time had just over twenty troops counting all. We had the ambush organization planned, and each man knew what section he would be in. We used two squads in the killer team, and the other squad would provide flank and rear security. We only had three squads, as the platoon was so short of troops. We planned on eighteen Claymore's hidden at the side of the road with big trees or clods of dirt behind each claymore, to absorb the back blast. There would be four Claymore's in a half moon arc behind us to cover our flanks and rear. There was a ditch over a foot deep at the side of the road, where the killer team would be under cover. Lieutenant LePeilbet would control the springing of the ambush, by blowing his claymore. When he fired his, the team leaders in the killer team would blow theirs. If fifty grizzly bears were caught in the kill zone, if any were left, they would be heading south at a fast pace. I would be in charge of the rear and flank security and have the four clackers of the rear cover Claymore's. The Claymore mine, when set up had in plain English, THIS SIDE TO ENEMY on the killing side. When fired, the Claymore with over 2000 large pellet's mashed into a hefty piece of C-4, would kill everything in a forty five degree arc to the front and not over waste high out to fifty meters. The plastic explosive C-4, was one of the most deadly explosive's, in the inventory. When we emplaced them, we never hooked up the clacker to the ends of the wires until the entire ambush was ready.

We stayed back in the forest waiting on dark. In the last moments of light, we would quickly move up and set up. I never used trip flares, because I wanted the target's if possible, to all be in the kill zone. When the moment came the set up went smoothly. Lieutenant LePeilbet moved to the other side of the road, and quickly walked the length of the kill zone, to make sure it could not be detected. Then the wait began, we were on fifty percent alert. We were all were lying side by side and could be quietly awakened. Soon after dark, Lieutenant LePeilbet had to sitrep the company command post at DAK TO. When he mashed the push to talk button on his handset, his Claymore went off like an A-Bomb. This sometimes but rarely happened, the handset must have had an electronic bleed. This was many of our troop's first ambush and everyone was wide awake after that. It is doubtful that the NVA could locate us from one explosion, because of the Daniel Boone scenario. Daniel Boone, wrote the following after he became old, "if you are alone hunting deer and you fired one shot, all the Indian warriors for miles, might hear the shot, but none would be able to pinpoint the location. If you missed, don't fire again."

We spent the night with the troops on edge from the Claymore detonation. We could hear an occasional artillery round impact at Ben Het. Their guns were shooting off and on all night. I suspect the new people, were a little unsettled because of the ominous feel of everything. The NVA no doubt, still had the bulk of their forces west of Ben Het. Well Hell, NAM was a great place to be unsettled. When morning came, we stayed low and ate some Korean war C-rations, washed down with water loaded with Halazone, because it came from the creek. Lieutenant LePeilbet wanted to move out at 0730. When it was around 0700, I heard an aircraft west of us but coming our way. It was a C130, and as he roared over us flying low, we all looked up. I remember with clarity, the agent orange settling on my face. Well our sitrep referencing the NVA was no joy; in addition we had these two other happenings to think about. The NAM had to be one of the most dangerous places that ever came along. I had a daughter born since the war that has had nineteen precancerous places removed from her body. I have had a melanoma taken off my face. We moved at 0730 keeping to the heavy forest and undergrowth, along the north side of the creek. In a movement in NAM, it was important, if we ran into the enemy to get the first shot. Then the chances we would fire the last shot's were higher, which would mean that all or most of us were still alive.

The fourth platoon's point man was a small likeable guy with experience, whom everyone called the flea. I did not use nicknames and I called him Pierce, that's Randy Pierce now employed by the TVA in Tennessee. Pierce got hit on March 12th, 1969; he was the fourth platoon's point on that day of course. There will be a great deal more, on that piece of hell later on. In NAM, anytime you were near a river or creek, the foliage was more tropical than in the hills or rice paddy areas. If one uses a watercourse in NAM to clean up or drink, caution is the main point to remember. The NVA, did not have a resupply system like us and they subsisted off the terrain and locals. In the central highlands there were few locals except for widely separated Montagnard's called by us "The Yards." The highlands were mostly a free fire zone as the yards had been moved by our side over east around highway 14 or near there. The Vietnamese, both South and North hated the yard's and the feeling was mutual. The Special Forces had lots of mercenaries and CIDG who were yards. Well, the flea moved us along as quietly as possible and carefully. He made sure we were following parallel, to the road and creek. Lieutenant LePeilbet and myself, as was our habit followed along with our maps. The flea from time to time, halted the single file and checked our location, referencing the road. As was SOP, every time we were in buffalo grass, we had at least one stop to listen for the grass to close after someone or something else moved near us. We arrived at Dak To about 1400 coming through the bunker line at the west end of the air strip, by the creek. That was just below an evil place known as "rocket ridge."

When we entered the perimeter, we were only supposed to be there a week, the TOC wanted a ready reaction force and that was us. When I was told that, I quietly thought to myself, TOC knows about something that may break loose. DAK TO Combat Base was one of many very dangerous places in the tri border area. In 1967, a terrific battle had been fought on rocket ridge. The NVA, had pulled out all the stops trying to take DAK TO. As a consequence, rocket ridge was bare of trees and covered with shell and bomb craters. The 173rd Airborne and the Fourth Division and ARVN defended the surrounding area. The NVA, kept attacking and lost thousands of troops on the hills in the DAK TO area, with the climax coming at hill 875, SW of DAK TO. The 173rd Airborne inflicted a heavy defeat on the NVA at hill 875. These were the October and November 1967 battles. I knew from what I had seen since October 1968, that the NVA was going to make another stab into the tri border area. While we set ourselves up in the TOC area, the flea somehow, got a puppy. The flea knew better, but he was young and liked dogs. When the dog started foaming at the mouth the next morning it lost popularity with the fourth platoon. Lieutenant LePeilbet killed the dog; the upshot of it all was that the entire platoon had to take shots. The shots kept us at DAK TO over Christmas, 1968. On Christmas Eve there was a maximum alert. Radio signals, had been detected on rocket ridge. The artillery fired an illumination mission over rocket ridge, just at midnight and it was beautiful.

Because we were delayed at the TOC, we got sent out on two different actions among the cluster of villages near DAK TO. TOC got intelligence that an NVA platoon was staying at night in a village, two miles outside the perimeter off Route 512 between DAK TO and highway 14. We left at about midnight, that day moving quickly without rucksack's, with just two meals of combat rations, weapons and a basic load of ammo. Our mission was to encircle the village in back and making a half moon come back to 512 on each side. We were in position by 0230 and tried to set up. Thank the good Lord, I was still on my feet and had not laid down. I smelled an old familiar smell, and was not surprised to see a mamasan come out of a hooch and drop her pants right in front of us. The troops on the ground began to moan and curse. Mamasan screamed, and pulled up her pants and ran for her hooch. It was awful; we put one squad in the creek at a time. Yes, you guessed it: NO NVA. The second mission was somewhat similar in that we encircled the rear of a village blocking a trail. At dawn a South Vietnamese armored company was supposed to roar down the road and hit the Village. This was all based on intelligence from the South Vietnamese district chief. About 0400 in the morning, there were a group of figures coming out the back of the village down the trail toward us. Lieutenant LePeilbet called out li day, that's halt in Vietnamese. We would not have warned them to halt, if we had been in the free fire zone. The figures, opened up on us with everything they had. We shot most of them down, their survivors ran back into the village. The Company Commander was with us and also another platoon.

When the figures still alive got in the village, they started firing at us again. I got up, and moved down our line to check our men and see if any were hit. It was light enough for the shooters in the village to see me. Someone started shooting at me with an M-79 and the other's opened up on me also. They were firing high and on automatic, and I knew they had no experience. When I got to where Lieutenant LePeilbet was, the Company Commander, Captain Sepansky was with him. I said; "there is something very wrong here. They are shooting at us with American weapons." Both Sepansky and Lepeilbet yelled in unison; "CEASE FIRE!" We stopped firing, and they slowly stopped. There were five very dead soldier's lying on the trail in front of us. There was one badly wounded, groaning horribly. We lay still and quiet until it got light. Just as I thought, five very dead South Vietnamese regional forces were dead on the trail. We did not have a man hit, I thought to myself, DAMN this war and all the district chiefs. The Company Commander, had already reported to DAK TO, and a command chopper, landed right in front of us. A Major General got out and some idiot whom I assumed was the government district chief. The wounded man died even though our medic did all he could and a dust off came in also. There was an old mamasan, who came out of the village with her mouth running betel nut, cursing us in Vietnamese and pigeon. She thought we were the number ten troop's of all time. In a little while, the Major General came over to us and said, "Captian Sepansky, the district chief has FUCKED UP. This is no fault to any of you people." He also said, "Take your men back to DAK TO."

We moved out in single file, with fourth platoon in the rear. The troop morale was somewhere in the toilet. One minute they thought they were heroes and the next they felt lower than whale shit. When we got to the perimeter, it was near dark and the troops tired and down. While we cleaned our weapons there was no talking. Finally, Lieutenant LePeilbet said something about what a terrible happening. I had been in the War a long time and I was callous and cold. I said, "well at least our men stood their ground and performed well." That was the only time in our long association that I know Lieutenant LePeilbet, was a little pissed at his platoon sergeant. He should not have been, as far more blood was about to be shed, and the long black train would go over the top. In the start of this narrative, I gave warning, this is something children and the young should not read. I will as I said, present the facts and pull no punches. In the NAM, killing was as normal as getting a traffic ticket in New York City. The flea and Jerry Loucks came up to me and asked, what do you think is about to happen sergeant? I said; "HELL, is about to happen. We will go to the gate, but let it be one hour at a time." When they turned to walk away I added, "remember man can't sweat the NAM." They were both veterans, esecially Loucks. They understood about sweating the NAM. Shortly afterward we flew out to a hill west of highway 14. It was hill 1089 and it was January 1969 and sheer hell only a short time away.

We were on the hill by 1600 and digging heavy with security to cover us while we dug in. It was A Company alone, also with no artillery observer party, of course supporting fire could be had easily from a number of firebase's west of highway 14. On call, we had airstrikes as usual, gunship or jet or the ever reliable skyraider. If the shit was deep enough, you didn't have to call for Puff the Magic Dragon. Puff was on call, at the Battalion TOC. I felt like our company had really shaped up, as small as it was. We dipped, to just under seventy troop's after

DAK TO and I was told we would get a few FNG's. In the company's I was in during that hellish infantry war, we didn't have problems with drugs or alcohol. Some of the troop's smoked but understood no smoking at night. It would be hard for any of them to smoke under a poncho and get away with it. The troops knew that as long as they were clear headed and ready for duty, I would not search their rucksack's. It was well understood out there in the bush that if you were straight, you had a better chance to live. Evening was advanced, when we finished with the position and had the Claymores and trip flares out. When we had an artillery party, they would normally shoot in a concentration or so close to us to adjust off of, that's if they could get the mission fired. If not, they would plot concentrations close to our map location with their fire direction center. Being field first sergeant along with being a platoon sergeant, I really didn't have time for anything else. Just before dark I got a call for smoke, a slick was inbound. The bird brought us the mail and beer and two FNG'S. One was an E-2 and seemed like another scared FNG, with one hell of a weight problem. If we hadn't been so short troop's, I would have sent him back. The other was much more promising, he was a shake& bake and looked and sounded like he could handle the job with a little experience. His name was Jerry Horton, and he was from west by god Virginia. The Company Commander, assigned him to us, and we gave him the squad the flea was in. The current squad leader was short and about to leave us. If I remember correctly, his name was Lestock, and he was a real good troop.

We sent out three SRP's that evening but at my urging the Captain, kept them in close. Just at dark, the Company Commanders RTO, monitoring the Battalion net, picked up a message from a SRP from another company. They were running for their lives, they had run into a large NVA force and the NVA were pursuing them. There were only three Americans and it was really a sad situation. Lieutenant LePeilbet and I, calculated from the cross conversation' that they were not far from hill 875. The SRP leader was very stressed. Their Company Commander told the leader to try to get to route 512. He would send gunship's and a slick and send a platoon to land on 512 ASAP. It was dark then, and movement in that area was difficult after dark. They would have to head north to get to 512; hill 875 was seven click's south of a big south bend in 512. This was the very thing that had made me have doubts about SRP's, when I first joined the company. In a few minutes, all contact was lost with the SRP leader, and that spoke for itself. The next morning the Battalion Commander came into our position in his command chopper. He told the Company Commander and the assembled platoon leader's, that disturbing reports were coming in about large caches of NVA rice and ammunition that were hidden in VC Valley. VC Valley was the valley the DAK AYUNH River ran through. In this valley on the north side of highway nineteen was an American perimeter called Blackhawk. Blackhawk was garrisoned by an aviation battalion and a tank company. South of highway nineteen on both sides of the river was VC Valley. It was in this valley that the NVA was thought to have large caches of ammo and rice. Intelligence said there was a VC hard core battalion and an NVA rifle company securing the caches. This river ran just west of the Mang Yang pass of French Mobile Group 100 fame. The Battalion Commander just wanted to pass this on to us. He thought in three or four weeks we would go to the valley to capture the caches. He said he would send one or two companies on the mission and just wanted us to be informed. Meanwhile South Vietnamese intelligence said; "they thought the NVA, had begun to move west from the border area." It was the middle of January 1969. He told the Captain," that in two or three days we were moving to a flat area on highway fourteen." Our mission would be, to secure a perimeter, for a meeting with the 11corp South Vietnamese Commander and some people from MACV plus the fourth infantry division Commander. Meanwhile in the next twenty four hours, patrol the area between hill 1089 and highway fourteen, and look for NVA. They probably had elephant's and water buffalo carrying their heavy loads. After the Battalion Commander had gone, the Captain told me; "white, take a recon patrol tomorrow from here in a northeast direction" checking for NVA tracks. Check the area to our east and south. Leave at daylight and be back at dark." The route would make an uneven circle on our east side that should find the signs of any NVA moving past us on the east. The Captain, Lieutenant LePeilbet and I, were sitting in the command post looking at my map, marking in the parameters for such a patrol.

This time, I took six different troop's from my recon off firebase twenty five. I resisted the urge to take our new Sergeant Horton, as he needed to get familiar with his squad. I took two men from each 4th platoon squad. I also took my RTO, and that gave us eight men with two meals c-rations and two canteens of water each. Everyone would carry his basic load in M-16 ammunition and grenade's. I would carry smoke grenade's as well as my normal basic load. I planned to leave the bunker line before daylight and back in, as light faded into the west. We went over frequencies and call signs, in case I needed fire support, as we didn't have an artillery party at 1089. This time, I didn't take an M-79 or M-60, since it was a recon patrol. I meant to move slow and careful; there was a large expanse of buffalo grass and a stream to our east. I figured if the NVA were moving by us, that stream would be as good a route as any. LePeilbet prevailed upon me, to take the fat FNG to check him out. I did not want to, but we needed to find out if he could keep up with us.

There was a little light in the east, as I took them out through the second platoon bunker line past the claymores and with a guide through the trip flares. When I was one hundred meters down the side of the hill in heavy undergrowth, I stopped and formed a tight circle waiting for light. The fat guy who I learned the flea had named "sump gut," had a hard time getting through the undergrowth. In a maneuver in the state's I would have felt sorry for him but there was no place or time for that in NAM. The other men had been around the NAM at least through some of the Monsoon, for the benefit of the FNG, I went over a few things in a whisper. "There will be no talking, period. If something needs to be communicated, do so in a whisper. The hand signal to come on line will be my outstretched arms shoulder high. There will be no shooting unless the situation requires it. If I fire, if you have a target, kill the SOB. We will move with weapons in the combat firing position, right thumb on the safety." Then, just addressing him, "You must keep up. We will move slowly, but you have to pick up your feet." Then finally, "This is the real deal and every man is responsible for himself." Having finished that and it being light enough, we moved out. Since we were only eight, I would be the point. I put the FNG in the middle so I could glance and see him. I had my first azimuth set for northeast, at thirty five degrees. We moved slowly and as quiet as possible. Our new guy kept stumbling and falling in the bush. In my thoughts, I cursed the Army for sending him out here. My other troop's were undoubtedly thinking the same. In the green hell, if someone can't do their part, the danger for everyone else is increased.

When we reached the buffalo grass area, I veered more easterly, increasing my azimuth to seventy degrees. The day was as usual hot and humid as the devil's hell. If the wind was blowing I could not hear it. After about fifteen minutes in the grass, I halted to listen to the grass. It was hard to hear over the loud breathing of the FNG. I finally satisfied myself that nothing was moving near us. I whispered, "we will take five here." It was the first break I had taken since our circle, just outside the perimeter. As there were only eight of us, I had not had the men number up. I kept them in a loose circle as we waited. The FNG started hitting his canteen heavy, and I was about to jerk it out of his hand when one of the troop's did. I nodded my head to him. In a green hell like NAM a troop must drink when he needs it, but only a little at a time. A new guy could founder himself on water and cause one hell of a problem for the patrol. When I moved on, I stayed at seventy degrees to be sure I got to the stream early in the patrol. Soon, we began to break out of the buffalo grass and into some tropical vegetation and high bamboo. I halted the patrol and listened, all was quiet and we were close to the stream. The tropical vegetation told me the stream was only a few meters away. Knowing such areas were very dangerous, since the NVA always used them for water, I brought my men up on line.

Ever so quietly, I moved the patrol forward. When I could see the water, I halted. I put the men in a tight circle, back to back. Satisfied that I heard nothing; I told them in a whisper, "stay put" and then went forward on my hands and knees. Lying in a bush, I took a good look up and down the creek and everything looked okay. I crawled back to the men and got the FNG. I told the men; "stay still and quiet while I check the creek bottom for tracks". I told the FNG, who I knew was close to the end of his physical endurance to "lie down in the water and cool off, I will be right back." I checked both sides of the creek and found what I was looking for. I managed to make out elephant track's in the mud. There were also water buffalo track's, spoor and sandal tracks. When the NVA traveled in force, they, like us, could not hide their tracks. When I was satisfied I had found what there was to find, moving low and slow I went back to the FNG. We moved back to my circle and I contacted the Company Commander and gave him the facts. There was no request from any of the other troops to get in the water. They knew we were in a place that was dangerous as hell, with only eight of us. I said,"we move" and back in single file we moved quietly away from the creek and then to another break in the bamboo. I saw that our FNG was very scared, he saw how I handled the stream and the reality of it came home to him. I informed the troops in a whisper of what I had found, and added one fact. The NVA, were in force and moving southeast, not far from our patrol route. When I moved out again, it was approaching 1100 and I altered my course to 195 degrees southwesterly. The FNG was white as a sheet from fatigue and fear. Nothing I could do about that, a troop had to learn not to sweat the NAM.

After another thirty minutes movement without seeing anything, I stopped for a ten minute break. We were sitting there in heavy cover back to back. When I moved again it was 1155 and I altered course again to 350 degrees, just west of north so I could approach the hill from the south. The walking got easier then as the undergrowth under the triple canopy wasn't so thick. We had all eaten some combat rations at the last halt and I was pleased that the troops including the FNG were drinking sparingly. Things remained quiet even though I knew not too far southeast of us, was a large unit of NVA. I took another break at about 1430. The FNG was getting closer to the end of his endurance and I had slowed the pace of the patrol to try and help him. I moved at 1440 staying on my azimuth and gauging my distance as to when I would be within 500 meters of the perimeter. The triple canopy was so bad I could not make out any big land features. I had to move very slowly because the FNG had about had it. When I stopped again, it was 1600 and I left the men in a tight circle while I climbed the tree they were sitting under. I managed to get up high enough to look north and it felt good to see 1089 out there about a short click. I also checked all around and our back trail, all clear. At about 1630 I moved again staying on my azimuth. I knew it was about 900 yards or a little farther to the bunker line. The last 500 yards was uphill. The sun was below the tree line when I reached the base of the hill. I called the Company Commander and told him; "coming in slow from the south." Then the FNG broke down and I knew I had to get him up the hill. I threw him over my left shoulder, weapon gear and all and managed to get him into the perimeter where I dropped him.

When I dropped the fat kid inside the perimeter I told him; "ever fall out again and I will leave you." I told Lieutenant LePeilbet, that we needed to quietly get him a job at base camp. I did not like to do such as it affects the troop's morale. When they see someone who can't hack it get a safe job, they feel the injustice of it. When you have someone who can't do his share, it increases the danger level for everyone else. Lieutenant LePeilbet told me we were going down on highway 14 east of DAK TO, to set a perimeter up tomorrow for the meeting the Colonel spoke of. Then I finished with the patrol members, explaining why I had done what I did and we got our equipment squared away and settled down for the night's dangers. This gave me time to talk to Sergeant Horton, once the SRP'S were out and fifty percent set up. I went over all standard operating procedures and then talked about patrolling, ambushing, set up perimeter, etc. I also went over proper digging of an individual fighting position and just dealing with the troop's in general. He asked a few questions that were normal for a new troop to ask. We had a very good group of squad leader's and Horton impressed me also. The night was hot and as usual filled with the night sounds, tree frogs, lizards and occasionally, far away artillery and an airstrike or so. We saddled up just as the sun came up and the Captain and the platoon leader's set up the company for the slicks to pick us up. We set down on a flat, at the side of highway fourteen just north of a sizable stream and a Montagnard village named KON HAO. By 1500 we were dug in with both Claymore's and trip flare's out. The Captain told Lieutenant LePeilbet, that the area was already scouted by several teams, don't send out any SRP's. He also told the platoon leaders and me, he was leaving on the next slick. Captain Sepansky was an okay officer and was replaced by a Captain Hockett, who I went the rest of the way with.

In the late afternoon, two CH47 hooks came in bringing a field mess hall and several tents and several staff officers. The Battalion Commander came in with the Sergeant Major in the command chopper. Soon after that, the Sergeant Major levied me for a twenty man detail. I had no choice in the detail, but felt they should have brought some base camp commando's, for that work. My men were fighting men, and were not in NAM to make leadership comfortable. The Sergeant Major made a face, when I made that observation. That night of course, we did the usual set up. Lieutenant LePeilbet told me the third platoon leader had left with Sepansky and I was now the acting third platoon leader, as well as field first. Well what the hell, LePeilbet was a damn good officer to be with. He asked me what I thought about Horton for platoon sergeant. I said, well he is brand new but seems to be a good man and is the highest ranking. I moved my stuff to the third platoon area and checked everything, and their setup was okay. That gave me Loucks for a point man and that was okay too. To get even with the stateside army bull shit, that night I crawled under the mess tent sides and took a twenty five pound ham and some crackers. The evidence was gone by morning, and my men deserved it.

When I remember senior officer's, sleeping and living in air conditioned house trailers with TV, showers and furniture, it makes me furious. The combat infantry in both the Army and Marine Corp lived in the dirt, their lives in danger at any moment. We had begun space flight, but supposedly the technology did not exist for us to have body armor. If a troop or marine was at grade four or below, their pay was so low as to be almost nonexistent. The next morning all the suit's showed up and had their meeting and then flew out. We were still in the perimeter awaiting our next mission. That evening just after midnight, just after Jerry Loucks whispered, "midnight, sergeant" there was a burst of M-16 fire straight north of us. There was a trail that went through our perimeter and went north. I knew one of the LRP team's had made a contact on that trail. The next morning the LRP's called for a safe entry from the north. We quickly passed them right on in. They had a shooter with them by the name of Randy Chrietzberg who was on security just after midnight. Chrietzberg, was very tired and trying hard to stay awake. Suddenly, he saw two figures in the darkness stopped in front of the LRP team and heard Vietnamese spoken quietly. They must have sensed the team and were trying to decide if action was needed. While they were deciding, Chrietzberg slipped his M-16 to full auto and blew them away. That is what American grunts were sent to do, in the near future Chreitzberg and our company had further business to tend to together. If you were going to be in a bad scene, you wanted troops like Chreitzberg with you. The word came down, that we would spend another day in the current perimeter and then hump north. We would move back into the hills on the east side of Highway 14. LRP teams, are long range patrol units, composed of deadly young men from higher headquarters.

I decided to take advantage of the delay and got permission to take my eighteen man platoon on a short patrol to the night before action site. I had new men, who had never seen a dead body and it was time they crossed the emotional line. LePeilbet, who was undoubtedly as bored as I came along and brought Horton and several other new people. When we moved in on the site, I felt it before I saw it. I deployed my men to Skirmisher's so if necessary, everyone could fire. I told them before we moved out, there are no good guys out there. The bodies were stiff and bloody and as usual covered with flies. The LRP's, had taken their weapons and gear and undoubtedly searched them for anything of value. The FNG's, were young and unfamiliar with death. If they lived through NAM they would never be young again. I put out nine men in a quick perimeter and let the other nine look at the dead NVA. Then

I had them lean over and touch the bodies and roll them over. Several thought they could not do it. Loucks laughed, and I told them; "do it, you have to kill to survive and this is your first look at it." The other nine had been in NAM awhile and were almost as casual about it, as Loucks and I. When it was done, I formed them up in single file, Jerry Loucks on point and returned to the company. LePeilbet did much the same and followed us in.

We moved just after first light on the trail to the north, slowly bending to the northeast. Captain Hockett had the fourth platoon leading, which meant the flea on the point. I was third between first platoon, Capt Hockett and second platoon. My point, one of the best I saw in the War, Jerry Loucks was unhappy because we were not leading. Hell, Loucks was as much a part of the War as I was. Loucks wanted to kill every day, just the kind of troop I needed, and he and I just kind of blended into this green hell filled with violence. I always demanded that we stay within the bounds of the laws of humanity and the Geneva Convention. In the free fire zones of NAM, it was like hunting season every day. I was becoming extremely hard and violent, but at least I recognized it. Lieutenant LePeilbet, and the flea, Loucks and myself, were very much alike. Horton was new and still had not seen the NAM in its true light. There would come a time very soon, when he would become a shooter, accepting the reality forced on him. We were all in some kind of international traffic accident, beyond our control. The terrain became steeper as we moved on northeast, on a long hog backed finger. Suddenly I heard an M-16 open up on full auto I knew it had to be the flea. Captain Hockett "yelled down" and we quickly set up. Since the company was together I had numbered my men. Even numbers faced right and uneven left. I heard a crashing through the underbrush to our left and downhill. Flea had come face to face with several NVA. They ran, and he opened up on them. If any were hit we could not find any blood trails. I know that disappointed the flea; he was a young hard reckless guy.

Finally we emerged on a high ridge and got to our hill. It was hill 908 which meant, it was 908 meters above sea level. The hill top was exposed and open, with dark wild triple canopy all around. At least, we didn't have to clear fields of fire as it was open to the wood line all around, about one hundred meters away. Within an hour we were dug in and had our Claymore's and trip flare's deployed around our fighting positions. The company had about seventy five men at that time, all included. That made us about one half strength, as compared to the table of organization & equipment. That night we sent out SRP's all around. I suggested we keep them no more than five hundred meters from the perimeter, with Captain Hockett agreeing. Loucks was grumbling under his breath. He wanted to lead one of the SRP's, I said; "No, I need you with the balance of the platoon." The next morning after a night of no contact, we received word that my enlistment was up, a chopper was on the way to get me. I had to reenlist or I would be sent home immediately. I heard later that the men were gambling on rather I would come back or not. Jerry Loucks was the most sure that I would return. Well I had a wife and two children and it was a tough decision. However there was nothing that offered a career in Ardmore, Oklahoma. I reenlisted for another three years and had a wild ride back to the company in a high wind. I did get a new uniform and a shower and a steak dinner. When I got there in my new uniform, Loucks yelled; "Oh good, another FNG."

While I was at Camp Enari, I picked up on the latest information and it was interesting. The NVA had apparently moved quite an amount of artillery and heavy mortars across the border. Ben Het and all fourth division firebase's, in the area of the tri border were getting incoming artillery amounting to a few rounds daily. The NVA was obviously registering from their new firing positions. That told me that TET 69 was going to start soon, probably in mid February. When I got back to Hill 908 it was just past mid January of 1969. The next morning we moved out on a trail to the northeast humping up hill's on the ridge heading for hill 1075. This time, I was leading with third platoon and Loucks on the point. By late morning we were getting close to a clearing on the trail. We suddenly ran into a group of Montagnard's and they scattered and ran down hill. They never knew how close they came, as we almost blasted them. I just saw in time, they were not armed. Captain Hockett stopped me at the edge of the clearing. The ridge had been tough going and the Captain thought there was a better route to our left and up a short but steep grade. We got to the top and everyone was breathing hard. There was another trail, and I turned Jerry to his right and we moved on up the finger. Suddenly the trail got very narrow with a steep drop to the left. Loucks stopped and motioned me to come up. He was about twenty yards ahead. When I got there I saw the problem. There was an antipersonnel minefield across the trail and about ten yards in depth. Hockett's call sign was twenty one and I was eighty nine. We had changed to numbers earlier in the month and I told twenty one, "you need to come forward." The column being halted and the Captain managed to squeeze through. I had been looking the minefield over and by the time twenty one got there, I had decided it was old and we could just step through it. The fuses were pressure and in plain sight and the dirt had been washed away by the rain. The mines were far enough apart to step between them. It still would be a dangerous decision to take.

When Hockett got there we talked it over and decided to keep moving forward if possible. First Loucks and myself, stepped through the minefield very carefully, no sweat. Capt Hockett stayed at that spot and as each man came up, he told them how to carefully step through. That caused a big delay as all seventy two men had to negotiate the minefield. One of the last five stepped on one and it did not go off. I kept the pace slow until twenty one called me; "and told me ok, let's move out a little." I am now going to use names and call signs as many of these men and myself have been in touch since the war. I will still not write the names of those killed in action to spare any family members grief, who might read this book. As far as the decision to chance the minefield, it was just too old and exposed to be too cautious about it. We finally reached a clearing just below the peak. I told twenty one, "I have stopped at clearing to let the column close up." When the company was closed up in supporting distance, I went to Skirmisher's with my platoon consisting of eighteen men, including me. I was in front of the troops, and said; "ok guys, let's move up." When I stepped out in the open there was only silence, and I kept moving up until I was at the top. The company was tired and it had been a hard, steep and stressful hump.

The top of hill 1075 was long and narrow and had both trees and undergrowth. The company commander called me to stop until the trail platoon had closed up. When I stopped, I kept my men in Skirmisher's and we dropped to one knee. I heard Loucks curse and I looked at him. He pointed to the far end of the summit, where eight or ten NVA were running like hell. When we saw them ,they were out of range for the M-16's and were gone before my machine gunner, Greg Rollinger could get set up to fire his M-60. When the rest of the company closed, we formed a perimeter and started digging and setting up both Claymore's and flare's. If we stayed longer than one night, we were going to have to cut trees and undergrowth for better fields of fire. Whenever we sat up on any position, I always interlocked each man's field of fire with the man on his right and left. I always kept our M-60 in final protective fire across our front and interlocked it with the M-60 in the platoon to our right or left. Final protective fire, is a cone of bullets that does not rise above a man's waist for eight hundred meters. There were few areas in NAM open enough to see eight hundred meters. It was fired by a machine gun across the unit's front that it belongs to. Final protective fire is a defensive measure, in case the enemy gets through the Claymore setup and any barriers that might be across the front of the defensive position. On hill 1075, it was getting late and while we were still working like mad, several NVA snipers opened up on us from the woods. We had no casualties and shot hell out of the woods and the NVA ceased fire. We managed to finish just at dark. Since we had already had contact, Captain Hockett decided on only sending out a four man listening post from each platoon and no more than 100 yards to our front. We were obviously in close to at least a small size enemy force. After midnight, all hell broke loose back down the long ridge at hill 908. One of the other 1st Battalion, 8th infantry company's had taken our place there. They had a bunker taken out by an RPG and had four KIA's. The NVA made an infantry assault on their perimeter, but was beaten off.

The next morning we were preparing to improve our position and heavily patrol the general area. Since I was the company field first sergeant, I received word that a CH47/hook/ NAM jargon (Chinook) was bringing us in a water trailer and ammo resupply. The pilot and I were on the radio together as he made his approach. I had just popped a yellow smoke on a clear flat area just inside our position on the south end, where the ridge fell away sharply. It was the only area that would fit the hook, and still be inside our position. As he moved in on my smoke, I held up both arms to show him where to land. Suddenly several NVA, dashed out of the woods between two of our outpost, and blazed away. They hit the rear engine of the hook, just above my head. The pilot was fighting the controls and managed to fall away with his rear engine on fire. He made a crash landing at the base of the ridge about five hundred yards down hill. Fortunately, the Battalion Commander was just inbound in his command ship. We hurriedly put a group of five men on his command ship. The Colonel and Sergeant Major quickly jumped out so the bird could carry the Chinook crew and our five men. The Chinook was burning like wild but none of the crew were hurt. The HU1B picked them up and returned all to the hilltop safely. When the bird was inbound, we cut loose on the woods to our west side for cover.

We stayed at hill 1075 for three more days patrolling out two clicks in all directions. The NVA just faded away which meant they were just a small force. I guessed and probably correctly that they were laying low waiting on a large TET '69 Offensive to start in February. We soon received orders to beat it back down the ridge to KON HIAO, where the meeting had taken place and my men had ham and crackers at midnight. We got there just before dark and used our fighting positions we previously had and quickly followed sop to set up. The next morning Captain Hockett was told to await orders, so each platoon ran a short patrol of one squad just to cover our front. The way to get hit by an enemy surprise attack in NAM was to get lazy and not patrol. While we were waiting, I noticed boom boom girl's coming out to us from the village. I gave orders to my platoon to keep them out of the perimeter and told the other platoon sergeants that would be a good idea. Boom boom girl's was NAM jargon for ladies of the evening. Civilians in an American perimeter increase the odds of a grenade incident like Trang Bang in 1966. However young men will be just that and one of my troops tried to score with a boom boom Girl. I was making an ammo and combat ration check when I heard someone yell, "sergeant she got my money!" I casually looked over and saw a young troop with his pants around his ankles. I calmly replied, "Young man, it is not within the purview of my responsibilities to retrieve money for a troop dumb enough to give a young lady of the night money with his pants around his ankles." That was one of the few funny things I saw in that Green Hell.

Just after noon, we received orders to move north on the west side of highway 14 to a hill numbered 830. It was between four and five clicks and impossible in that terrain to hump on foot in one afternoon. However an American armored infantry battalion came up highway 14 and picked us up on their M-113 armored personnel carriers. We rode on top with their troop's making for a crowded but quick trip. It was about 1400 when we dismounted, moving first west and then turning back north. It was a tough rugged hump. Soon after moving out in single file, I got a wait-a-minute bush, Southeast Asia's briar, under my left eyelid. It was hell, but Hockett stopped the movement while the medics used five minutes to get it out. The rest of the day I only had the use of my right eye. Then sergeant David Muck, one of my squad leaders from Michigan, fell in a cold hole of water about three or four feet deep. Sergeant Muck was standing on his head in paradise. Loucks and I, looking at each other in amazement, grabbed Muck by his feet and pulled him out. I am not sure Muck was grateful. The platoon leader of the first platoon got lost. We were looking for a long finger that ran up hill to 830. I was third in file and with my eye and Muck going swimming had not been keeping a close watch with my map. Captain Hockett halted the column and called me up front. The lieutenant of the lead platoon was crying, he was lost, no time or place for that shit. Hockett said; "white, get us out of here fast," it's getting dark and we are in this damned canyon."

The NAM, was a place hard on men and there were always a few who just could not handle it. The Lieutenant was young and inexperienced and he just folded under the pressure in front of his platoon. There was a man who may have known more about war than anyone who ever lived. His name was Napoleon, and he said, "brave men are not brave all the time." I found a large rock and climbed up on it working with one eye was not good fun. I managed to locate the tops of two hills in the area that I could identify on my map. I took my compass and shot azimuths to the two hills. Then I took back azimuths and using the captain's pencil drew in the back azimuth lines on my map. My resection showed that where the lines crossed there we were in a creek bottom. Having settled that, I looked at hill 830 on the map, and saw it was up the second finger to our left in the direction we were moving. We were at the hilltop with an hour to spare before dark. Working like mad, we managed to get linked up with fields of fire interlocked and dig fighting positions. It was a little while after dark before we had Claymore's setup and trip flare's out. We had fifty percent worked out and ate some combat rations before we tried to unwind. It had been a tough day for the old guy. I was almost thirty two, which made me the old guy. During the night the Captain explained our mission. We had so little time to make the move that he just now had time to brief us. An NVA unit had been detected moving west toward Highway 14 from the area we had just left. The South Vietnamese had deployed an armored infantry battalion just east of highway 14. Our mission at hill 830 was to be a blocking force in case the NVA tried to maneuver around the South Vietnamese left flank. Hill 830 was two and a half clicks west of highway 14.

That night the ARVN / Army Republic of South Vietnam/ and the NVA got in a bad firefight. At dawn the ARVN brought up some tanks and they opened up with a heavy fire, on the ridge east of the road. The ARVN wasn't using any artillery but brought in several air strikes with Cobra gunship's. I guess they thought they had the NVA pinned down. Just after daylight, Captain Hockett came by and said, "white, take your platoon and patrol straight east to the road. I want you ready to go in one hour, leave your Claymores and flares in place as we may be here several days." He added, "If you get in a fight I will move to you with the rest of the company." First Platoon extended to cover my part of the perimeter. My sector was in some huge rocks and it was an easy spot to remember. I called my squad leaders to my position and set it up. I felt really good about my squad leaders; David Muck from Michigan, Frank Novotny from Minnesota, and, Henry Scarver from Georgia and my ace in the hole, Jerry Loucks at point. I had several platoons in NAM and felt good about them all. The A Company troop's in general, were all very good; we just did not have enough of them. I said; "okay guys this is it, we move in one hour. I want basic load, two meal's and two canteen's each. Both myself and Loucks will carry smoke and extra M-60 ammo." With experienced squad leaders that's all that had to be said.

Before I moved toward the road the fighting was still going on between the NVA and ARVN. I checked my Frequencies and call signs with our artillery fire control party. The artillery party was usually a Lieutenant, his RTO and a sergeant. I moved on time which meant a departure in broad daylight. I should have been alerted to the mission the night before. Then my departure could have been covered by the darkness. My platoon was eighteen good men counting myself, which I believe was quite normal for NAM at the time. By this time in the War, considering the demonstrations at home, I felt like it was the green machine against the world. The triple canopy was as usual grim and quiet with heavy underbrush mixed with bamboo. Loucks was moving, as I directed east with myself and RTO about ten yards behind him. RTO short for/radio telephone operator/. The bamboo and buffalo grass was so heavy on that hillside I kept the platoon in single file. My numbering system was even numbers face right and uneven face left at any halts. Slowly and quietly, we moved down the hill which surprisingly was not to steep. My men knew the drill; no talking, just whispering if necessary, orders to be passed down the file if needed. As we moved, I began to think the NVA fire was dying away and I heard tank engines on the road. It took twenty or thirty minutes to reach the base of 830. Then to my surprise the undergrowth thinned out into a park like effect.

When we entered the thin undergrowth area, I stopped and set up a quick perimeter and took ten. After making my SITREP /situation report/, I moved on again in the same formation. I had my squad's, first, second and third, front to back. If we hit something Muck and Novotny knew that they would form a base of fire, first squad left and second squad right and third squad led by Scarver would cover the rear and be ready to maneuver if I wanted to. I knew that the NVA fire dying away could mean they had pulled back or were trying to get around ARVN. I took that opinion on no longer hearing much AK-47 fire and hearing the ARVN tanks moving on the road. We moved on carefully, every man with his M-16 in the combat firing position and thumb on the safety. Rollinger had the M-60 on his shoulder. The M-60 weighed eleven pounds and was called by some gunners "the pig." When we began to close the road, the forest lightened up both in thickness and visibility. It was about 1100 and I stopped and formed a perimeter, as I did not want my men to be seen from the road. Leaving sergeant Muck in charge, I took my RTO and Loucks, slowly moving from tree to tree we closed with the road. I stayed in the trees and watched the ARVN moving around on the other side of the road. It was easy to see that the NVA had broken contact. I called twenty one, and told him what I was seeing and he said; "okay the firefight is probably over." Then he told me to make a slow return and bow out to my right. That meant incline North making sure the NVA had not got around the ARVN left flank and had not crossed the road. When I turned back in a northeasterly direction, the always aggressive Jerry Loucks was cursing under his breath.

I was still going in the same formation to make the bow out that the Captain had ordered. Bow out; that's a strange phrase to describe a loop to the north as I returned to hill 830. I felt okay about it as I never went out and back the same route. If I ever did anything in NAM that I am proud of, it is in NOT walking troops, whose lives had been entrusted to me into an enemy ambush. On the return to hill 830 was the time when a baboon jumped out of a tree to stand on the ground behind our trail squad. What I can't remember is who it was that unloaded a magazine of M-16 on him. It might have been a small but very tough young troop named Ken McCormack from California. Several things are for sure one, is the baboon never knew what hit him and two was Captain Hockett saddled up the rest of the company. Three was that, Jerry Loucks was pissed he missed out on the great baboon shoot. I quickly called twenty one and said, "no contact, tell you about it when

I get there." I could not blame anyone for shooting the baboon. We were all on the thin edge of tenseness, and in the slightly dim light of the forest's floor, the baboon could have looked like an NVA. My men were certainly in a hair trigger mode. In NAM, especially in a free fire zone: when in doubt SHOOT. The incident of course alerted any nearby NVA that they were not the only bad asses in the woods. We made the loop without further incident. We pulled up to the northeast side of 830 and at about 1700. I then called twenty one to notify him I was coming in from the northeast side. I alway's made sure I had taken steps to avoid any friendly fire incidents.

When we topped the hill, I started the platoon getting set up again for the night. The entire company waited with excitement, to see what occasioned the firing of an M-16 magazine so close by. It did make an interesting story indeed. Captain Hockett sent out three SRP's that night, one each from the other three platoons. Since we had been out all day, I did not have to send out one. The next day we had one SRP lost, I think at this distance in time it had four men in it. One may have been killed. They were lost on a ridge quite a distance from us. They must have turned up the wrong finger in the night. That's the very reason when I came to A Company, I felt negative about SRP's. We had radio contact, which was a good thing. We recovered three of them luckily, and I could be wrong about the one being killed. Captain Hockett took a chopper and he managed to get there in a hurry looking for them. He saw two dead NVA and found Steve Benyshek from Kansas. Hockett brought him in swinging on a rope. He was swinging fast, but as he went swinging by me, I grabbed the rope and went swinging with him. When we came swinging back, several of the troops grabbed us. Benyshek, now back safe and sound, eventually survived the war. Perhaps there were only three: one wounded, a good troop named Crocket, who was picked up by a sling from the Captain's chopper. They also saw the Sergeant who had commanded the SRP, I think his name may have been Storm, and they picked him up. So if three was the correct number, then all came back safely.

February, 1969 came as we spent another day that was quiet at hill

830.We stayed at the hill for another day patrolling the immediate area and also to the north yet found no trace of the NVA. Then we received orders to move south, keeping route fourteen on our left and looking for signs that the NVA crossed fourteen, on the ARVN's south or right flank. TET was coming in late February and the NVA might be concentrating their force's in the tri border area for a push into South Vietnam. The Company Commander had also been told we might get picked up on the road for another mission. I was starting to wonder where the fourth division's aviation battalion's had gone. We had not had a combat air assault in more than a few days. During the move south, we were moving in file with fourth platoon leading and third platoon following in the second slot in the file, just ahead of the company command group. The hills were rugged and occasionally we could hear armor on highway fourteen to our left, which was east. The column suddenly stopped and there was a commotion up ahead in fourth platoon. I stopped, and put my platoon into the numbered position. Then Captain Hockett, told me to put my men into a perimeter and to go up front, and check out what the situation was. When I went forward, Lieutenant LePeilbet was on the ground obviously in great pain, with Horton leaning over him and looking very concerned. Then, as I walked up, Horton took charge and put fourth platoon into a perimeter. I rolled LePeilbet over to see where he was holding his back. The company senior medic was talking loudly and things were a little chaotic. I told the medic to speak softly and we would deal with the situation. Lieutenant LePeilbet was sweating profusely and seemed to be having trouble breathing. It looked like a spider or a centipede might have bitten him. Then Captain Hockett showed up and we decided to fall back into a small clearing not far behind us. Hockett turned the company around and we moved out, fourth platoon in the middle carrying Lieutenant LePeilbet.

We called in a dust off before we had a good perimeter around the clearing. Lieutenant LePeilbet was on his way to the hospital at camp ENARI very quickly, and Sergeant Horton was learning fast, as acting platoon leader of our fourth platoon. Pappy Rawls, who was one of the fourth platoon's best troop's asked me, what I thought just before we moved again. I knew what he was really asking, and I said; "Sergeant Horton can handle the job, like all platoon leader's he will need you veteran's support." That Pappy was a tough dude and looked like the oldest guy in the company by far. He was from Arkansas and now looks like one of the youngest guy's among the survivors. I was worried about LePeilbet. I knew the company needed him and I got along well with him. The first platoon leader, who had the emotional problem, was no longer with us. I did not know he left by a chopper while I was on patrol at hill 830. The second platoon leader had his six months done and was moving to MACV in a few days. Captain Hockett told me that we were to have two new platoon leaders inbound in a week or so. They both turned out to be real good men and just in time for TET' 69.

We went south after we medevaced Lieutenant LePeilbet. We were moving cautiously, with second platoon leading followed by first platoon, then the command group followed by Horton and his fourth platoon. I was bringing up the rear with the third platoon. The triple canopy and bad undergrowth was tough, taking a physical toll on the troop's all carrying sixty pound and heavier rucksacks. Well hell, that was everyday in the NAM dry season. We followed the south finger of hill 830, which was 500 to 600 meter's long and steep on both sides. By 1530 we were in the saddle between hill 830 and hill 710. Captain Hockett, stopped there and we sat up a quick perimeter. I checked the ground carefully behind my platoon in the saddle. If the NVA had gone around ARVN's right flank, heading west, they would have probably used that saddle. I found nothing, except I noticed a lot of broken branches. Men moving through that terrain, carrying heavy loads will break some branches. I saw no definite tracks, however the ground in February in NAM is hard as rock. I sat down at the base of a tree all alone and tried to make sense as to what might be going on. I knew that TET was coming soon as it had not started in late January. I felt a sense of approaching danger. In NAM, (6) /Leo J. Daugherty and Gregory L. Mattson/ stated on page 365, that TET 69 started on February 22, 1969. In the tri border area, it started very near March 1, 1969 as the famous armored attack on BEN HET was on March 3, 1969. TET 69 may have started on slightly different dates, due to the miles from south to north. Ever since we left firebase twenty five on December 3, 1968, we had patrolled many a mile and made only slight contact. I thought the enemy was lying low, awaiting a big offensive. There was another omen, the daily light shelling of all American and South Vietnamese firebase's in the tri border area. The tri border area was just to the west of our present position. At the start of my narrative, I warned about the violence and bloodshed and the long black train. Things had been dangerous but sometimes boring since December 3rd, yet now I was hearing artillery fire in the distance almost all the time. The only time, I heard that in my prior 13 months in the twenty fifth division, it was all American outbound. Now I was hearing as much NVA as American. The enemy would register, to zero in from a spot. Then the NVA gunner's would move quick because they knew a heavy American counter battery would be coming or an airstrike.

I quickly returned to the perimeter just as Hockett ordered saddle up. At about 1600, we started climbing up hill 710. I had heard Loucks several times cursing under his breath along with, "where in hell are those little bastards?" Seen in retrospect, we didn't have long to wait. The woods were quiet and it was getting dark as we followed a finger to the hilltop. When we arrived at the top of hill 710 about 1645 we were about a click west of LONG KON HOJAO village and the road. That put us halfway to our position at the Montagnard village and our old HAM perimeter. We sat up for the night on hill 710 with the usual sop and each platoon had a four man SRP deployed five hundred meters to the front. Every time I set up a platoon in NAM, I checked to see that every man had dug his fighting position and understood the interlocking fields of fire. It was just as important that the machine guns be interlocked, having a field of fire, serving as a final protective fire across their platoon front. Hell, in NAM'S central highlands, you could never see the required 800 meters as called for by the definition of final protective fire. Of equal importance was the Claymore and trip flare set up. I made it an obsession, to check everything as it was a part of my duty.

That night passed and was way to quiet. We moved at around 0700 and headed south expecting to make our previous perimeter at the meeting site by 1600. Before noon, I heard the artillery to our west start up again. The Captain stopped the company at 1300 and formed a perimeter. We had one of those great Korean war combat ration meal's with Halazone loaded water. I noticed that twenty one had been on the radio longer than normal, with the Battalion Commander Colonel Buckner. When the commander got off, he called for the platoon leaders. Change of plans, and we were moving east for the highway, just over a click away. We would form a perimeter at the road and be picked up by trucks no later than 1630. We were going to VC Valley, and the convoy would be escorted by an armored company of M-48 tank's as well as gunship coverage, all the way. He also said, "white take your platoon and lead the way." We moved out rapidly, with Loucks on point and I went on a straight east 90 degree azimuth. The company was moving in the conventional single file. The hills and undergrowth were pretty tough. We made it by 1600 without seeing anything, but red ants and leaches in the low wet spots. We formed a perimeter, on the west side of route fourteen and waited. By 1630, we were loaded and headed south for the highway fourteen and the highway nineteen junction at PlEIKU. Highway nineteen was a black topped surface, compliments of the US Army Engineers. We stopped at camp ENARI at dark and cleaned up, with a good meal, clean uniforms, showers and no security responsibilities. We moved east at 0700 on highway nineteen in the same convoy setup. By 1600, we unloaded without incident at the Blackhorse combat base on the north side of highway nineteen, near the bridge over the DAK AYUNH River.

Black Horse was a heavily fortified perimeter with an aviation and an armored infantry battalion, as well as an armored unit from the 69th armored brigade. The valley went south on both sides of the river. It was of course, the famous "VC Valley." To the east was a continuation of the central highlands and the MANGYANG Pass, which highway nineteen ran through. The pass was the famous ambush location of "French Mobile Group 100" in 1954 that closely followed the French defeat that happened at DIEN BIEN PHU. We set up inside the firebase. We had a platoon leader's meeting with Captain Hockett after dark, in a bunker where we would have lights. He said we would move at 0500 before daylight, so as to cross the road and get into the triple canopy jungle while it was still dark. The intelligence report said to expect, a VC Battalion and an NVA company somewhere in the valley, guarding a huge weapons and rice cache. The commander added that the NVA had some elephants. I was thinking, "and we are going in with only eighty troop's." I said nothing, as it was our mission, however anytime I thought our orders were insane I would certainly speak up. I don't remember if we got our two replacement platoon leaders before or after VC Valley, but we were rejoined by Lieutenant LePeilbet at ENARI.

At the Blackhawk location, the river was flowing southwest for approximately twelve clicks or better said kilometers. On time, in the darkness we checked through the Black Hawk perimeter and silently crossed the road and stopped, waiting for light. The fourth platoon leading, when we moved out with the flea on point. I followed, with third platoon then the command group. Then first platoon and trailing was the second platoon. We had an artillery forward observer group with us as was normal. They were moving with the command group. The night before, Lieutenant LePeilbet asked me how Horton had done, and I replied, "great." We were moving in single file and I was using my numbering security system. That morning, I had one hell of a stomach ache, and the medic gave me some antacid tablets. He said, "sergeant, you've been doing this shit too long." I thought, "well hell, a man can't sweat the Nam." I sensed, as we moved that this valley was an evil place, and used by the Communist Viet Minh in the French war from 1946 to 1954.In /The street without joy/(1) the author Bernard Fall page 15, states that the first Indochina war ran from 1946 to 1954. Like so many of our movements, the pace was slow due to the sixty pound plus Rucksack's in the brutal terrain. Everything was quiet with no birds or any animal life to be seen. For the first few hours, Lieutenant LePeilbet stayed back from the river and we only glimpsed it occasionally. There were several areas with buffalo grass above our heads, and each time we stopped to listen for the grass to close nearby. I had the best point man in the War, but it was easy to tell he was getting agitated by the lack of action. The valley was pretty flat and that helped us do five clicks the first day. We stopped on a low ridge on the westerly side of the river or you could say the right bank. We set up the standard perimeter with all fields of fire interlocked with Claymore's and trip flare's. Each platoon had a SRP out about five hundred meters, which also served as a listening post.

I was watching my men closely, for even the toughest of veterans can get slack and careless if you go awhile without at least a firefight. The second day was a repeat of the first, except that we went a little further. On the third day we stopped on a small hill at about 1600. We were close to where the river turned more to the south, and we were still on the right bank. On the fourth day, we stopped on a low hill about a click east of a small Montagnard village shown on the map as "DE TOUNG". Each day had been a repeat of the previous. Of course we did our standard perimeter on the hill. The next morning we tried a tricky move that sometimes worked. We made a lot of noise as we ate our morning rations and threw the cans loosely around on the ground. Normally, we buried everything, like our enemies. We were trying to make it appear that we had never been there. I was leading that day, and we made a lot of noise as we moved out. When we were about twenty minutes out in rough country, I turned and we quietly moved back to the hill. Sometimes we would find the VC at the hill scrounging for food and digging our sumps. This time, as we moved up the hill we caught one lone Montagnard or "Yard" as the Special Forces called them. The poor man was scared to death. We gave him several meals of rations and sent him on his way.

When the yard went out of sight plus fifteen minutes we moved out. Captain Hockett was following his patrol route from operations at the battalion TOC. I was leading behind Loucks, and I took us straight east to the river. The river was very swift and rocky and about 150 yards wide and from knee to waist. It was deep and difficult with a heavy load on your back along with your other equipment. Captain Hockett surprised me when he opted to stop and take a bath. I am probably cleaner than most seventy five year old's but doing that in NAM was very dangerous.

He sent the first platoon upstream on security and second platoon down. When third and fourth and the command group finished, we would take security while first and second bathed. When I arrived at the river, I had turned slightly northerly because I saw a sharp bend. Crossing at a bend helps to hide you from a long view up, or down river. The bend also helped hide us from anyone, a long distance down or upriver as we bathed. We waded in uniform and boots and washed our bodies as well as our uniform's with the few pieces of soap we had in the company. It was not necessary to tell the troops to hurry. In thirty minutes we were ready to go again to the east bank of the river. Since I was leading, I had to lead the river crossing, something that was in my experience. I set up my platoon on the west bank in skirmishers. Captain Hockett, put the rest of the company in a perimeter right behind my platoon. Leaving Sergeant Muck in charge of the platoon, Loucks and myself tied close together in a long rope about 5 yards apart, started moving across. Sergeant Muck let the rope out from the center of my platoon as we moved. It was a tough wade and both of us fell down at least once. It was very lonely out there, totally exposed. When we reached the other side we swept it out to 100 yards and up and down. Being sure there was no ambush, I signaled the Captain to move the company across.

It was now the afternoon of the fifth day and we turned south. The east side of the river was lower, flat and swampy with high buffalo grass. It wasn't long, before we were totally soaked in sweat and feeling the mud in the swampy terrain. Every thirty minutes or so, I stopped the company and we gave the grass a listen with the company using the numbers system for security. At about 1600, we found a little higher dry ridge and stopped for the night. Both Loucks and myself felt an ominous feel in the air. While we were setting up for the night in our normal NDP /night defensive position/, in the fading light of the sun, I saw a flash of light twice to our east. I thought, "they are watching us with binoculars." Captain Hockett and I had a talk about it and scanned the east horizon with our binocular's but saw nothing. In the NAM, death came suddenly and in many ways. We just had to increase our vigilance and be mindful of the chances, as the NAM was one hour at a time anyway. The company was really pooped when we finished with the Claymore's and flare's, Hockett said, "The guys are tired. Let's forget the SRP's for the night." I said; "Captain, we should at least put a three man listening post out in front of each platoon, maybe a hundred yards." The Captain replied, "No, we have enough security for right now." Attitudes like that have killed a lot of troops. In that cataclysm of blood, violence and killing, it was impossible to be too careful. When the NAM lets you slide for several weeks without a contact, you better look out. It was mid February 1969 and TET was bearing down on us.

The morning of the sixth day in VC valley we were moving at 0730. I was in the slot, behind the company command group with fourth platoon behind me. The patrol route took us south for about four clicks to a double hill with a saddle in between hilltop's. It was hill 742, in the flat river bottom, even though it was so muddy and filled with buffalo grass, we could move faster. However, it was total swamp until we approached the hill. There was one creek that flowed to the river from the east that had a wide watercourse about a foot deep and muddy as hell. It was a great place for an NVA ambush, and we had seen the flashes to the east the previous sundown. Since I was just behind the command group, I suggested to the Company Commander that we slow down and move with two platoons as skirmisher's side by side. We could then deploy the rest of the company following in single file. Captain Hockett was younger than me and a sharp guy. Maybe I was getting on his nerves, as he said a little sharply, "NO sergeant." It is better to be overly cautious and alive, than have a landscape littered with bodies. When we had hill 742 in sight at about 1600 the Captain took a break, and we went into a perimeter. While we were there, Lieutenant LePeilbet said to me very quietly; " I thought sure as hell, he would slow down and sweep ahead for an ambush at that watercourse." LePeilbet and I always were thinking similar to one another as we swept through that green hell. We had now gone six weeks without a large contact, by far the longest I had ever gone, and the odds were building fast against us. I knew, it would not be long before sheer hell and much death was going to break loose.

We moved on to hill 742 and worked up a good NDP setup. The company possessed all together eighty eight Claymores. It would cost the enemy a big butcher's bill to come through that. Any enemy assault force would also have to face our M-16's and machine guns. Each time we stopped, the artillery observer party, plotted in two concentrations on each side of us. In 1966, more times than not I succeeded in adjusting the mortar concentrations on each side of us with White Phosporus. Some might say, "why give away your position to the enemy?" Hell, they know where you are anyway. We had taken a resupply bird on the morning of day four to reload combat rations and were going to have to again in the morning. The morning of the seventh day we received a resupply bird early and fresh water in jerry cans. The patrol route, called for us to move east to a wide swampy creek bottom. My platoon was in position on the west hill facing the river, two clicks away through a swamp. The Captain came by before we were ready to go and said, "White, leave your claymores out. I am going to leave you here in ambush. I want you to hold this position until noon, then follow me to hill 744 to the east four clicks." That was smart, and it showed the Captain had still been thinking about those flashes in the east two sunsets ago. I liked the sound of that except four clicks was a long hump in one afternoon. He went on to say;"we took that resupply bird and will be loud and high on the hill when we leave. If they are out there they may try to come in here, after we leave to police up any food we left." He smiled and added, "maybe they will see you anyway, and think you're an easy mark. Whatever, either way, if I hear you firing we will be back double quick." I sure as hell was never an easy mark and would be waiting; of course I knew he was kidding about the easy remark. He might have felt we were a little tense, after the water crossing in the swamp and wanted to let me know we were okay. That proved in a few days to be not the case.

I kept my men behind the hilltop and gave them the lowdown. Loucks had the first pleasant look on his face in days. The only thing about the

Captain's plan that was not good was we were only eighteen men ordered to hold a double hill that should have taken a large company to hold. Since we had all the Claymores on the west side I concentrated my men there. No Sweat GI, I kept my men low in the grass on the back side of the hill with no movement, nor sound. I was lying in a patch of high grass on the hilltop with good visibility. If I saw them coming, I would encircle the hilltop with the seventeen men I had. That way we could fire in any direction. They would probably come from the north through the swamp ground, that I had my machine gun covering. The day wore on, with the sun super hot and Loucks cursing under his breath. I moved at noon as ordered, moving in a low wet swamp for a click and a half. I used the standard single file with Loucks out in front no more than ten yards. Then we moved up on higher ground that was dry, but open as hell. I was out three clicks and it was late, when I came in sight of hill 744. I knew the company would be there and they were. We were set up by nightfall

The eighth day in VC Valley came bright and hot at hill 744. Nevertheless, the small pimple of a hill exposed us against the skyline of the surrounding flat low terrain. The plain, in most places was wet and soft mud. One positive feature was that there weren't any big hills or cliffs covered with super bad undergrowth, or "wait a minute bushes." Despite the wet mud it did not take as long to hump somewhere in this soaked, desolate valley. When on the plain, the buffalo grass over your head kept you hidden. As the Bible say's; "the rain falls on the just and the unjust," so the enemy was hidden as well. The patrol route called for a hump east to a swampy low stream. We did the combat rations and cold water, picked up our equipment and moved out with the fourth platoon leading. I was the rear guard as we made it to the stream and swamp in one and a half hours. We were moving cautiously and stopping every few minutes to listen. The NVA could easily lie in wait in that terrain. If they were around, they would certainly know where we were because of our resupply birds and terrain exposure. When we got to the watercourse, it was at about the halfway point between its start and intersection with a larger stream to the north. As I was bringing up the rear, the Captain sent me to my right south, to check the bottom paying special attention to the small creek banks. The Commander, waited for me with the rest of the company in a perimeter where we had hit the stream. I was getting that feeling of being watched and told Loucks to be slow and careful. We found nothing and turned back north still moving very slowly. When we reached the company they were lined up and ready to move. The flea and Lieutenant LePeilbet lead out and in one minute found the mother lode.

Dug into the right bank of the stream, with a large bush in front, was a recently dug cave. One of the eye catcher's, was that there were no other bushes around like the big one supposedly hiding the cave. We stopped and formed a perimeter. The flea and Lieutenant LePeilbet very cautiously approached the cave opening. Looking out for mines and booby trap's, was imperative at the cave's mouth and inside. It was very important all over the whole damn area. In just a moment the flea and Lieutenant Lepielbet came out with a hundred pound sack of rice. There turned out to be over 100 sacks of rice, some of them marked with US AID. There were over two hundred boxes of 7.62 ammunition, and a big bunch of RPG warhead's both anti tank and anti personnel. The Captain called for a hook and notified the TOC of our find. This was mission successful,however security was necessary while we loaded it out. The Captain, put fourth platoon on security, while the rest of us did the work. There was quite a bit of toil and sweat. The hook came in soon, and I set him down in the buffalo grass and mud right by the streambed and cave. There were two gunship's flying a circle around us. The Battalion Commander came in to pat Hockett on the back and say, "when you're through here go to hill 744 for the night." The district chief came in with his tiger suit bunch and went to a small Montagnard village nearby to question the locals. I can hear them now saying, "ME NO VC."

We made it to hill 744 in an hour and were well setup by dark. The horizon problem in the flat area remained. Any enemy, in the buffalo grass anywhere on the plain around us would have us sky lined. We could not see the enemy unless they attacked us. The area, everywhere on the east bank of the river was a sniper's paradise. After midnight, as was my habit being the field first sergeant, and my prerogative, I checked the entire company security. The fourth platoon was sound asleep. Of course, they were exhausted, but in combat that is no excuse. Yes, they were some of the best. Horton was a very good platoon sergeant, but still no excuse. Their own lives were at stake as well as the entire company. If the enemy had probed our position, and found a way through the Claymore's, flare's, and the fourth platoon, the company could have been decimated in a few seconds. The AK-47 like the M-16 with the advantage, is sheer death. I knew where Horton was sleeping from the setup the evening before. I leaned over him and softly called his name and he awakened instantly. Cursing and so angry I was almost over the edge; I chewed his ass and got the entire platoon up. I am sure LePeilbet woke up, as well but said nothing. Sergeant Horton made the necessary corrections and cursing under my breath I walked away back to third platoon. The fourth platoon leader, platoon sergeant and troop's were as good as could be found in any battalion, Special Forces, rangers or any unit. This was a bad mistake, mostly caused by extreme exhaustion. However, the security of the other three platoons was alert. Being human one time too many in the NAM, was sure death. It did not matter that we had gone weeks, without a bad fight. That just ensured that death was lurking out there in the undergrowth, trees, and in the darkness. I said nothing to Captain Hockett about it, and as far as I was concerned the necessary correction had been made.

The ninth day, in VC Valley came bright and hot. The patrol route called for a move west to hill 742, our double hill. It was a three click hump, with a tired company, that had been seen sky lined on 744, for many hundreds of yards around. Captain Hockett had second platoon take the lead and I don't remember if our two new lieutenant's had joined us yet or not. I think they joined at camp ENARI several days later, and just before the long black train gained speed. We managed to get to hill 742 without incident; we were still exposed to the entire damn area. That night, I made a count for resupply for the next morning, before we moved. When I called Battalion rear; they said, "birds not available in code. What in hell happened to the best led, best equipped, best supplied, best paid, Army in history? I called again, and in code, told battalion we would only have one days rations left in the morning. The answer was the same, but battalion did say, twenty one would be informed. Captain Hockett came by third platoon and said, "The air cavalry was in a bad scene up north, in the AShau Valley and had lost a lot of choppers." WHAT the hell? We could be in a bad scene any moment! I could only assume this situation had existed for the last month as we had been trucked everywhere. The scene in the AShau finally terminated at the end of May with 101 Airborne's savage shootout at Hill 937, known as Hamburger Hill.

The tenth day in VC Valley started like the other nine, with us totally exposed on hill 742. We moved at about 0800, with the third platoon leading in single file, numbered, and Jerry Loucks 10 yards in front. The patrol route took us west to the river and I aimed for a sharp bend. I knew we had to make the ever dangerous river crossing. It had now been almost thirteen day's since we got clean uniforms at camp Enari. That meant that the majority of the company's legs were bare from the knees down, with many bites, scratches and bleeding. There were also many troops with bare arms and sleeves rotted out from sweat. The troop's, were about to get very hungry, but only the Company Commander and field First sergeant knew it. I had moved with usual caution, especially as we had been so exposed on the small hill's. We stopped at least twice between hill 742 and the river, to listen to the grass. I did the usual, at the river, keeping the platoon down in skirmishers hidden in the grass. If Loucks or me came under fire while in the river, they could cover us as we tried to get back. In case the NVA, were on that other bank or on the high hill on the other side, Loucks and I were dead anyway. When I went back in 68, I never thought I would get home again. The Company Commander was lying there with my platoon and said, "Good Luck." WOW. I checked what I could see up and down river, the other bank and hill with my binoculars, but saw nothing. This bend was extra sharp if we could call that comforting. Hell, in the NAM death could be anywhere or anytime.

The water was cold, swift and waste deep as we entered it roped together. The ever experienced sergeant Muck paying out the rope as we waded. About halfway across, I saw something move on the hilltop. Loucks saw it also and asked me, "what do you think?" We were a little closer to the far bank and I said, "keep moving." When there was only ten yards or so to go, Loucks slipped on a rock but I caught him with the rope in the swift water and we made it to the far bank. I did not give the signal to cross until I had checked the far bank thoroughly, and went halfway up the hill on a finger that was 150 yards to our right, west. From the finger halfway up I didn't see anything on the hilltop. Both Loucks and I were staying very low in the grass. The Company Commander must have wanted to move quicker but to his credit, he waited on his most experienced NCO to give the signal. Reluctantly, I gave the signal and the crossing began. If we had lost some or all of the troops in that river, I would have never been able to forgive myself. In one of the other platoon's a troop had dysentery really bad, so the deeper water must have been a blessing to him. Hell, there were no birds to resupply us or send him to the hospital. Damn the Fourth Division, what if we had got in a bad firefight and had wounded. When the company was finally over the river we rested for ten minutes and then I got the word. The patrol route took us straight south over the hilltop. It was hill 700 and was very steep with only small clumps of vegetation on it. I said, "Hell, Captain, we can go 150 yards west down the bank and go up on an easy finger. The men will not be exhausted and if we get hit we can deploy for close combat."

In all my twenty years and one month in the US Army, I endeared myself to very few officers. I don't know what was bothering Captain Hockett, but he insisted on climbing the hill and made it an order. That was plain damn crazy, and I said so. His response was, "that's an order, sergeant," and he was loud with it. He probably thought that my everyday attitude challenged his authority. I always had problem's with some officers like that. I was the oldest man in the company at almost thirty two, and by far the most NAM experienced. My point man loyally said, "I will take it, sergeant." I said, "No, Loucks, you have crossed both the river crossings leading. I will take this one." Hell, I am no mountain climber and in all the years since, have not paid some super dude to drag my old ass up Mt Everest. I gathered up the rope and tied it around my waist. It proved to be just long enough to get to the top and the company come up on it, one at a time. I slung my M-16 over my back, and my ammo belt over one shoulder angled over my other side, like I always carried it. I left my rucksack at the bottom of the hill for me to later drag it up by the rope. I started climbing, and it was one hell of a job. The rest of the company came up on the rope, but I had to free climb it. I kept my mind off what might be on top and took it like I took the War, one moment at a time. I just kept working my way up until I reached the top. Once there, I tied the rope on a tree as close as I could get to the cliff. Then I checked my rifle and searched the hilltop. Lucky me, there were big places in the high grass mashed flat and elephant crap everywhere. Just beyond the elephant dung area, was a large area of small indentations where many NVA had lain. It was all fresh when I checked, the NVA had gone south. They must have left there that morning, as the elephant dung was still soft and smelled. So much for going straight over the hill's.

I finally gave the signal and the Chinese gang fuck began. First, I had to pull up my rucksack and then throw the rope down. The seventy eight man company, climbing on the rope one man at a time began climbing. We had to do it one at a time; if one man slipped, anyone below him was going down with him. Then each Rucksack had to be pulled up and it was almost dark before the exhausted company was on the hill. It was hard to believe that no one was hurt. We set up as best we could in the gathering gloom. After we finally were set up, Loucks who had been laughing to himself finally whispered to me his story. While I was climbing, the artillery observer, a first Lieutenant came up to the Commander and said, "Captain, this is the craziest stunt I have ever seen. You are going to ruin your company. We," (his Sergeant, himself and the RTO) "are going up the finger sergeant white told you about!" hill 700 was a straight up cliff, nothing like the gentle sloping Hill's of 742 and 744. In any event, I showed the Captain, where the NVA and their elephants had been, and how fresh the dung was and that they had gone south. When I started to walk away he said, "good job white." I don't know what got him that day as he was normally a very capable officer. We ran out of combat rations that night. The eleventh day began early, with fourth platoon leading and the patrol route, headed south down the right bank, the west side of the river.

We moved in our normal single file, third platoon following the command group again. There was a good possibility that the NVA was somewhere to our front. The troop's had not yet complained about running out of food. This was the only time in all my time in NAM that I knew of an American unit going hungry. I had informed my platoon and the other platoon sergeants and said;" I was sure the Battalion Commander knew about it and was working to alleviate the situation." On toward the middle of the day, we had gone through some tough country with a steep cliff on our right. The Company Commander stopped about a click down river from hill 700, and had a radio message from the battalion. A light observation helicopter (LOH) came over and threw out a case of Pepsi Cola. I was amazed, the Pepsi case hit a big rock and all the cans busted. Wow! Pepsi Cola, out of combat rations, I was wondering what would happen next. The Captain called the platoon leaders over and informed us, that we were going to be picked up at a road that was down river. It was another click and then west, one more click to a trail head. There was a tank company escorting the trucks for us, and would be at the trail head in two hours. We moved out, and the Captain told Lieutenant LePeilbet to pick up the pace a little bit. We were in hilly terrain that was not too steep but the undergrowth was tough. We were passing the point of the steep cliff to our right, when I found out what was going to happen next. Two Gunship's came flying up the river towards us and made a rocket run on a steep hill, about 500 yards down river from us. Then they turned and made a second gun run on the hill. The Captain stopped the company quickly and we formed a perimeter. He said he had received no information or radio contact concerning the Gunship's or any expected NVA contact to our front. That was very out of ordinary, for an airstrike to happen near an American unit and for the Commander to not know anything about it.

We moved on cautiously and the Captain finally got a message from battalion, it was an ARVN Cobra mission and beyond that, they had no information. Hell an allied air strike near an American unit and we don't know why. That was unprofessional and pissed me off. The fourth platoon, with flea leading veered away from the river and we humped for the trail head. I had a thought about the biblical verse: "If the bugle blows an uncertain note." The cache find had been the high point of VC Valley, everything else after that sucked. We found the convoy at about 1700 or 5:00pm and loaded. I guessed that something was up and the battalion was in a hurry to get us back to camp ENARI, the Fourth Division base camp at PLEIKU. The convoy had both a tank and a gunship escort. We were in our company rear area by dark, "the word was clean up, clean uniforms, showers, hot steak dinner and no bunker line that night." We actually slept on cots that night and were clean and well fed. It was the last time I ever saw camp ENARI and the Fourth Division base camp except for the hospital. When we got up at 0700, the word was "to get ready to move out." TET 69 had started and the NVA were moving in force and heavily supported by prepositioned artillery.

— Chapter Eight —

Sacrifice

When empires arise they are prepared to sacrifice their finest young men. When empires decline they are only prepared to sacrifice their NCOs.

—Menachem Begin, Leader of the Irgun

March 1969 came in NAM and brought TET'69 with it. There were many people alive in NAM when March 1969 came, who were not alive when it was over. I had already experienced a lot of close quarters combat in 1966 in the twenty fifth Division in 111Corp. There was always the required number of chopper's to lift the entire company and we had more troops then. We had all the gunship's, SKYRAIDER and Jet airstrikes and arc light, (B-52) airstrike's, needed. We also had, Puff the Magic Dragon as well as tremendous artillery and mortar support, as much as we could possibly need. In 1968 and 1969 the fourth division was scattered in small packets of fifty percent under strength units, all along the western boundary with Laos and Cambodia. This was General Abrams plan, to catch the NVA coming in and hold them until reinforcement's could reach us. The amount of artillery support and airstrike's available to us, was much less than my previous experience. In Washington, congress had refused to allow increases in the budget for Vietnam. We left camp ENARI at 0700 on the next day after VC Valley. We had clean uniforms that were not in tatters. Every man had three days of combat rations and their basic load of ammunition. We were equipped as usual, but the situation in the tri border area had changed. The company was seventy two men including our artillery observer party. We had gained two new Lieutenants, Andrews from New Jersey and Porter from Texas. Both of these young officer's would prove to be fine soldiers and Leader's.

We were in another truck convoy escorted by a tank company from the sixty ninth armor. The sixty ninth armor came to NAM with the twenty fifth Division in 1966. The sixty ninth armor was a battalion with the twenty fifth. Since then, the sixty ninth had been given the huge mission of patrolling all the black top roads in at least 11Corp and 111 Corp. I believe they were enlarged to a brigade then. We had several Cobra Gunship's around. The platoons were so small each truck could carry one. I had the usual 17 men but they were some of the best. We were the last truck in the convoy and supposed to pick up the bridge guard's as we came to them. We were going north of PLEIKU on highway fourteen through KONTUM CITY and on north to Route

511. We would take Route 511 west on the north side of the DAK BLA River, when the road changed to dirt it was a few miles to the POLEI KLENG Special Forces camp. There was an air strip at the camp with a few utility chopper's and gunship's. The camp was home to a Special Forces detachment, controlling a company or so of CIDG troops. The camp also had mortar's and an artillery battery for support. The air strip was constructed of steel matting. The trip was uneventful, except that my driver thought he was a country music star. I only had to pick up one pair of bridge guards and they were from Charlie Company. They were black and I thought they looked high when they got on the truck.

We were going west when I thought I heard something different in the back of the truck. There were two African Americans in third platoon, Sergeant Henry Scarver and specialist Paul Summerlin known as Airborne; these were both good men and fine soldiers. The NAM got them both with cancer thirty years later. The road finally wound around a long hill and crossed another river the DAK SIR where there where Montagnard children playing in the river. Then the road went up a small hill and through the gate of the heavily fortified Special Forces camp. The truck's stopped on the south side of the air strip, where there were several utility chopper's and gunship's setting. They made great aiming points for the NVA guns in the hills. We were downhill from the command post, and as I swung out of the front door of the truck, an officer was walking down to meet Captain Hockett. When I walked to the back of the truck, I saw the two black bridge guards still looking high, but shaken. Sergeant Muck and several others were fighting with all their might to keep Jerry Louck's M-16 away from him. Blood was running down the side of Loucks face. When someone fucks with my point man like that, I can get very mad very quickly. I pointed at the two blacks, both of whom still had their rifles, and said, "you two son of a bitches get down here." They both eagerly came down out of the truck. I said, "stand there and keep your God damn mouths shut." That cooled the situation, and I said, "Loucks, you have to give me your word that when Sergeant Muck gives you your weapon back, that you won't kill these two bastards." Loucks was so filled with rage he could barely nod his head. I turned to the two bridge guards and said, "okay, which one of you two cocksuckers butt stroked my point man." They both looked at the ground and said nothing. I told Sergeant Muck, "to unload the truck and take the troop's over to the rest of the company." I said, "Sergeant Scarver, stay here with me, I want to know all the details of this incident."

I had already cursed these two sorry examples of humanity to where I myself, could be facing judicial legal action. Sergeant Scarver, obviously not wanting to speak, started speaking haltingly. He said, "Sergeant White when these two chucks," (at that time, some African American troop's referred to themselves as "chucks"), "got in the truck, they started coming out with racial insults directed at the whites." I said, "Go on." "Well," he said, "an argument started and Loucks spoke up louder and more direct than the rest of the guys." Sergeant Scarver then told me; "that the larger of the two had butt stroked Loucks." The rest of the troops, including Scarver and Airborne had got between Loucks and the two low life's. Sergeant's Muck and Novotny, managed to jerk Loucks rifle out of his hands before he killed them both. Those two lucky bastards had come very close to being killed by a very deadly man. I took them across the strip to their Company Commander and told him the story. Anyone could see, they were high and I wanted them court martialed. He just looked down at the ground and did not speak. Another US army officer in 1969 scared of his own troop's

When I got back across the strip, Captain Hockett asked me what had happened and I told him. I also told the Captain;" that I would sign the accusation myself when we got back to where we could do such. Later on after I had cooled off, I suddenly recalled I had forgotten to get their names and serial numbers. In the maelstrom to come all that went by the way side. The Captain said, "we will be right here tonight, and I will have a meeting later on to give the next day's operational orders. We will not be needed on the bunker line tonight. The Special Forces will take care of it." We deployed our men down the side of the air strip and set ourselves up for as comfortable a night as possible. Then Sergeant Scarver and Airborne, who was Paul Summerlin, came to me and wanted to talk. They told me, "they, being only two chucks, were nervous of about going to the bush with all us white's." I called the platoon together and got down to facts. First we were the green machine and we were fighting this War together. Both Sergeant Scarver and airborne were part of our brothers in arms and we would always be glad they were part of our group. Instantly, Loucks and the rest clustered around Scarver and Airborne, shaking hands and hugging each other and the racial incident was over. Late in the day at POLEI KLENG a chopper came in with three FNG's on it. I thought, "WOW,I would not want the good old USA to give us too much help." I needed a full time RTO as the one I had went home, lucky rascal. One of the FNG's was a trained RTO, so I got him. He looked every bit of sixteen and ninety pounds soaking wet. I had no time to really tell him our call signs and radio procedure. I made it super clear, where I went there he went also, and if he heard eighty nine, my call sign, to hand me the handset.

It was after dark when the Captain called the platoon leaders together. Lieutenant's Andrews and Porter were sitting in on their first field operation meeting, and it probably was not what they expected. We had just barely time to shake hands. The Captain laid it on the line and it was a real serious operation. When the meeting started, we could hear the artillery start up in the hill's and in the far distance, see "Puff" working out. We were going to air mobile out at 0700 in the morning. We were only going to have ONE bird available. Due to the elevation and heavy usage on the transmission, the chopper could only carry five men. If that was not direct enough, guess which platoon was going first? The landing zone was hill 744, and there were lots of hill 744's in Nam. It was three clicks from Cambodia, and overlooking the trail that branched off the Ho Chi Minh Trail and entered South Vietnam via the PLEI TRAP Valley. The Captain mentioned this operation was named "Wayne Grey" and involved the entire Brigade. He went on to say; "it was TET 69 and the NVA was making an all out effort." I was going to take third platoon in first, five men at a time. It would take all day to move the company. I do not know about the rest of NAM, but the fourth division was in a bad fix for equipment and man power.

The turnaround time from POLEI KLENG to hill 744, was twenty minutes if all went well. In addition, the daisy cutter bomb the air force had hit 744 with, had not made a clearing for a landing zone. I was taking two chain saws, along with my four men. This was a dangerous mission in a hellacious place, where danger and death were commonplace. I got the troops together and went over it with them. I would be taking Loucks of course and Rollinger and Procter with the M-60 and my new RTO. I figured that I would set up Rollinger and Procter in the best firing position I could find. Loucks and I would cut tree's with the chainsaw's and my RTO would stay close by. I went over the M-16 with the little RTO and made sure his weapon was loaded. I also made sure he knew where the selector switch was, and how to use it. He asked, "When do I shoot?" I answered, "You will know." Someone said, "Sergeant White when that bird comes in without a single gunship, the NVA in the area will know from the sound of one bird, exactly where you are." I gave the only true answer in just one word: "Yes." We settled down to try to relax and rest. I put tomorrow out of my mind remembering Jesus said, "THE EVIL THEROF WAS ENOUGH FOR THE DAY." I guess the NVA knew our FNG's needed to get broken in, as they landed a mortar salvo just inside the perimeter. They probably aimed at the chopper's on the strip. The Polei Kleng artillery opened up but after a few minutes all settled down. Loucks whispered, "Sergeant White, midnight," as was our operating procedure. Loucks stayed alert from dark to midnight and me from midnight until stand to. The rest of the platoon was always on fifty per cent. Just after midnight, a CIDG troop on the bunker line cut loose with an entire M-16 magazine. I don't know at what or why he shot. Afterward all was quiet in the dark night, stars shining brightly. My new RTO lying by Loucks and myself, kept rolling over and over and mumbling something.

Daylight seemed to come quickly, during the night I had heard heavy gunfire far away to the north. Ben Het was hit by a large artillery barrage and a tank infantry attack. The NVA did not know that the sixty ninth armor had put an M-48 tank platoon at Ben Het. The sixty ninth tanker's knocked out two pt76 soviet tanks and two armored personnel carriers. One M-48 was slightly damaged and no Americans killed. The NVA carried away many bodies. That may have been the only American and NVA tank action of the war. It was March third and the NVA with their soviet tanks could not cut it. The chopper, came in for my daring band of hero's and this small group of the best led, best armed, best paid, best fed army in history left for hill744. I could feel the tension in the chopper; it was so bad that Loucks went to sleep. The RTO's eyes were as big as fifty cent pieces. The chopper came in on the hill and slowed down trying to get us as low as possible, as we had to jump. When the pilot closed he took a blade strike off a large tree. The prop began making a very bad sound. I leaned over the pilot's shoulder and asked, if he could get back to POLEI KLENG. He said, "I hope so." I replied, "we are jumping right now." It looked like thirty feet into high undergrowth. I looked back and nodded my head; Loucks went followed by Rollinger and Procter. My RTO was frozen with his eyes closed mumbling, and I threw him out. In Nam we had to jump many times, usually from ten to thirty feet, and let the undergrowth catch us.

When I landed it was on top of my RTO. When I got up, he was crying and Loucks was in his face enraged. I handed Loucks a chainsaw and said, "let's cut some trees." I stood by the RTO for a few seconds, and then said, "DRY IT UP! When you cry in this world, you cry alone." I went on saying, "now, son, you have got to toughen up, I want you to go home alive but a lot of it is totally up to you. Get a grip and don't cry again around me." Loucks and I cut trees like mad; a chain saw can be heard for miles. I had Rollinger set up at a place where he and Procter had visibility to do their best for our security. There was no doubt at the very least there were hundreds of NVA in the trail area below us. Why they did not come up and do us in, I will never know. I didn't say, but knew that the turnaround time right now was going to be more than twenty minutes as another chopper had to be obtained. Well, it wasn't the fourth division's fault as the US lost approximately 2200 chopper's in NAM. The years had ground down one of the finest groups of fighting men ever assembled. Troop morale had also been adversely affected, by the disorder in the streets of America. The democratic politicians who sent us to war had cut the budget for NAM. The budget was the main reason for troops occasionally being hungry and having manpower and equipment shortages. But we were there and whatever, we had to do our best. Loucks and I kept cutting trees and I knew if Rollinger fired, then we would fall back on the M-60 and shoot it out. I had told Hockett, if we got hit to look for us somewhere between hill744 and POLEI KLENG.

If the NVA had come up hill744, five men would not last long and probably not be able to leave the hill either. Nevertheless, we kept our nose to the grindstone and in an hour I heard another bird coming. I popped red smoke, and there was room for the bird to land with five more men from my platoon. It was almost 1100 and we were ten, by 1800, we had most of the company and were digging in and setting up Claymore's and flare's. Why the NVA never came up, I don't know. I could occasionally see NVA, far away on the trail below. I also thought that after dark we would draw indirect fire and maybe an infantry attack. Perhaps those at battalion operations thought so to, because just before midnight "Puff the Magic Dragon" showed up and flew a circle around the hill. That was enough to strike fear in the hearts of those in the brown with the AK-47's in the woods below. The night was quiet and I heard Loucks cursing under his breath. Here we are in TET'69 sitting right in the middle of thousands of NVA, at the entry point of South Vietnam off the Ho Chi Minh trail and not a shot was fired. I hardly ever smiled in NAM, but was slightly amused when I thought about Loucks, because I knew he would not have long to wait. TET '68 was the only thing worse than sixty nine as far as big NVA offensives go, except for their attacking ARVN after the withdrawal of our troops. Blood and violence in an atmosphere loaded with anger and bitterness would soon be prevalent all around us.

Morning came at hill744 after a noisy night of artillery in the distance to the east. We were sitting in place while the Captain waited for the Battalion Commander to fly in. Meanwhile we got a chopper inbound on our smoke. We were down to one day's rations and the slick gave us a reload of two days. In addition to rations, there was another FNG replacement for us. He had a note for me from the A

Company rear detachment at camp ENARI. The note read, "Sergeant White, this man is one of McNamara's 100,000." Well fine I thought, just what in hell is McNamara's 100,000? Since Lieutenant's Porter and Andrews had been in the State's since me, I asked them. Neither one was sure, but Andrews thought it might be a Defense Department program to help young men from the core of the big cities. The FNG was black and looked very uncomfortable. I said, "young man, obviously there is something special about you, what is it?" After a moment he answered; "Sergeant, the Governor told me if I got back alive, I would be pardoned." After another moment, I asked, "Governor of what state? He said;" Illinois." I said;" what were you in for?" He stammered and said, "She was in a house." I thought about a moment and asked, "did you kill your wife?" He said,"yes, and the man with her. I got life." I almost felt sorry for him; he was so down and inept. The NAM, did not allow for human feelings when you're looking downhill at the Ho Chi Minh Trail. I said, "what weapon did you use to kill them?" He said, "I shot them." I said, not meaning to humiliate him, "see these men in green uniforms around us? They are our friends. Now make damn sure you don't shoot any of them and don't shoot anybody unless your squad leader tells you to." He went to first platoon as they had one less than the other three platoon's. Remember, in the start of my narrative, I said, I would give you the absolute facts.

I don't remember if he was still alive when NAM finally caught up with me. I hope this guy made it and built a new and positive life for himself in Chicago. The troops with their nickname mania instantly named him "Joliet Jake". This is an example of the American power structure's opinion of its own soldiers in 1969. Millions of young men from the upper income bunch, stayed home. Years later in pinstripe suits they assured people that they were right wing patriots. The Battalion Commander did not stay long and said, "good job, men!" when he got in the bird. We knew he meant well, but in that far away piece of hell it meant nothing. The Captain sent for the platoon leader's and had a quick meeting. The Battalion TOC had an opinion, that today an NVA regiment, two battalion's was moving south hidden in a stream at the base of 744. On the map the stream was referred to as YA LON whatever that means in Vietnamese. Captain Hockett said, "In one hour, I am taking third platoon and fourth platoon and going on a recon in force to the creek bottom." He went on, "first and second platoon's will remain in place and occupy the entire position until our return." I knew it would not make any difference to point out we were splitting our force in the face of the enemy. After all, it was General Abrams operational plan.

As we walked away to our platoons, Captain Hockett added; "Colonel Buckner also said, they are using elephants to carry their mountain guns and heavy 50 caliber machine guns." Hill 744 was a hill far too big for a seventy some odd man company to defend. There was a second summit that jutted out to the west with a finger that sloped down to the creek. I don't remember who was senior, Andrews or Porter. The artillery observer's party was going with us. Two very under strength platoon's with a total of thirty some plus troop's, were being left to defend a hill that actually would need to be defended by a battalion. I said earlier, I don't remember when Andrews and Porter got to us, but Wayne Grey may have been their first operation. They both wanted to talk to Lieutenant LePeilbet before we left but time was short. This was the MACV plan, for the Fourth Division to watch the western border of 11nd Corp, with it's under strength unit's well scattered out. That was just exactly what Captain Hockett was doing, following orders. We would seek to engage an NVA regiment, with a very small under strength company spread out over a click or so. We would be using reconnaissance in force as we moved in on the creek. Most movements to contact in NAM were "recon in force." This tactic is kosher, when you are not sure of the enemy's position. The size of force was sadly lacking, while it had no meaning to NAM, that's exactly the tactics Custer used at the battle of Little Big Horn, ninety three years before. We saddled up quickly taking all our Claymore's and equipment. Captain Hockett told fourth platoon to lead out and I would take the rear with the command group in between. We moved initially south then inclining back west downhill on a long finger. When night fell we were on a low hill overlooking the creek. We were about two clicks from the other platoon's. We stopped early enough to set up in a small tight perimeter with Claymore's and flare's out. Every man was in a fighting position just deep enough to get the trunk of his body underground. All fires were interlocked and all machinegun's on FPL, interlocked if possible. We sent a three man listening post, fifty yards out in front of each platoon. If either listening post heard anything, they were to get back to us quickly. The undergrowth was heavy around us and the hill had a triple canopy overhead. The artillery forward observer had concentrations plotted all around us. In situations like this I never worried about what might happen. I just prepared to deal with whatever,one hour at a time. It was a dark and somber nightfall. The tree lizards started up their song as the highland night chill began to be felt. In the highlands it was hot as hell in the daytime. At night however, it could get pretty cool and put that with a wet sweat soaked raggedy uniform, and it could be chilly. Most troops were wrapped in their poncho liners. I normally carried two poncho liners. I had not even dozed when Loucks whispered, "midnight, Sarge." somewhere around 0200, I heard the elephant's start trumpeting in the valley below. An FNG whispered, "what's that?" I whispered back;"peacocks, relax." At stand to, at first light, we pulled the listening post's in.

I noticed how tired and stressed they looked. There were certainly some of the troop's who had been around long enough to know, those were elephants right below us. When we were going downhill the afternoon before, the company commander was a short distance in front of me. When we got to a good looking hill higher up, I suggested we stop there for the night. Captain Hockett wanted to keep moving as dark was still over an hour away. If we had stopped when I wanted to, we would have had a better chance at surprising the NVA if they were right below us. The low hill we stopped on was so near the creek bottom, if the enemy was where I heard the elephants they would hear us when we moved. That's just subjective thinking on my part but we would need all the advantages we could get, if we got into that bunch. Captain Hockett said, "let's hurry and get ready, I want to get to the creek ASAP." He had already told me to take the lead today. Just before we moved, I managed to get a whispered conversation with Loucks. He told me yes, he had heard the elephant's and expected that the enemy was right in front of us. I agreed, and told him that if he came under fire, I would immediately set up a base of fire. Try to get to us as quickly as he could. I also told him if he got hit, I would get to him ASAP. I had already asked the Captain if he had heard the elephants, he was grim faced when he said, "yes."

When we lined out to move I walked past Lieutenant LePeilbet, he was also grim faced and just shook his head. When we were ready, I looked at the Captain and he nodded his head. I whispered to Loucks, "let's do it and be very careful." We started downhill slowly and carefully, and I had Rollinger with the M-60 right behind me. I had already told Muck and Novotny when all hell broke loose, form the two squad base of fire and Scarver would link up with the troops behind. We had not gone fifty yards when we were among big mounds of elephant dung and tracks where the undergrowth had been knocked down. It would have been normal for the NVA to stake the elephant's out a small distance from their NDP. Every ten or twenty step's, Loucks looked back at me and I signaled straight on. I knew there had to be a trail on one side or the other of the creek. The undergrowth was just too heavy to be quiet, and I remember feeling of my M-16 safety on the selector switch. One of the most dangerous things about recon in force is the movement to contact. The attacker is at a disadvantage as the enemy may get the first shot. If the NVA was still in their night defensive position we were going to be in one hell of a fight anytime now. Suddenly Captain Hockett called for a stop and a perimeter right quick. We did and I used the trees and rucksacks to give my men cover. The Captain was getting a message from the Battalion TOC. The situation had changed and we were ordered to pull back and link up with the other two platoon's. I heard Loucks curse under his breath and I had to fight back a smile. Captain Hockett turned the company around, with LePeilbet leading and third platoon following we moved uphill.

We moved at a normal pace back up the hill. I kept as much of a look as possible behind us. To me there was no doubt, they lay there thinking, just a little bit closer and we will pin them down flank them and wipe them out. After all, it's just a small group, dirty and tired in raggedy uniforms. I looked up through the column seeing so many who were totally unaware of what they had so narrowly escaped. We headed southeast on the ridge until it turned north. What we had humped yesterday in seven hours we could make easy, well before dark. It was late afternoon when we made the summit and all Leader's were glad to see each other. I walked by Lieutenant LePeilbet again and he gave me a tired smile and shook his head. Loucks was disappointed but also glad to be alive, I read it in his look. Loucks had seen heavy action on firebase twenty nine over Ben Het more than a year before. The Company Commander was getting another message from the TOC and I had to reorder rations on the log channel. This would be a good time to make two points. The US media, and liberal left and animal lovers at home, made much of the fact that our gunship's killed all the elephant's and wild buffalo they could see from the air. When you read this narrative of mine, you can see why. The use of the word "gook" was used to inflame the academic bunch against us also. This word was more an emotional ploy, to make it easier for the troop's to kill. Young Americans have never been raised up to kill and many have a hard time dealing with it. All armies, in all Wars have used words like this to make the mental barrier easier to overcome. For Instance, In WW11 we fought the "kraut's, eyetie's and the nip's." It was an attempt to gloss over the humanity of the enemy. I know from experience that few, if any, thought of the enemy as inferior.

This time the battalion wanted a probe to the northwest on the long finger I spoke of, to check the creek for the enemy at that point. The morning came quickly and I knew it was March 7th, 1969. In this operation the whole company was going, our force was small but at least they could not fight us in detail. The Company Commander told fourth platoon to lead, and me to bring up the rear. I wondered if he had become totally aware of the serious situation we were in. It was very obvious that the NVA had large forces in the area. Perhaps the Captain wanted to use his most experienced platoon leader's at the most dangerous spots, until our new officers were broken in. He need not have worried they would know the ropes very quickly. The northwest ridge was more open than the other side of the hill. The flea and LePeilbet moved slowly and carefully. Each platoon was numbered, and at each quick halt everyman faced his direction. The flea, young, experienced and reckless was showing more stress than before. The MACV operational requirement on the fourth division was certainly a strain for those who knew the odds. This time, we halted further from the creek and dug in. When we were in the ground, we had eighty eight Claymore's around us. We had done it all, fields of fire interlocked and the whole works. We used the fifty yard deployment for the listening post's again. The next morning, March 8th, 1969 we were recalled again.

We started moving back to the hilltop landing zone as soon as possible. We took a different route moving at first east on the hillside to another finger. This was to avoid an ambush but the hillside was tough going. Suddenly, we came on a mound and a Christian cross on our right flank in a little clearing. First platoon was leading and I was following. They stopped and several troops started walking toward the cross. I quickly said, "get back in formation." This seemed so strange and unusual, but there was probably an unexploded large bomb underneath a pressure release fuse, below the cross. In NAM, one of my most stringent requirements on troop's was "if it's not yours, leave it alone!" I said, "let's move," and passed the word to the rear to stay the hell away from the cross. The NAM killed in many different ways. We made the hill top position by noon. This time we were flying east to a clearing two clicks east of a creek called Dak Hodrai. Well I knew it, my platoon was going first. This time the chopper's would carry six and we were getting two. The distance was shorter than from POLEI KLENG to hill 744. We also had a loach gunship circling. I yelled in my RTO's ear, "let's go," and we hit the ground running and made a quick short sweep on line around the clearing. We had no contact, and I formed a quick perimeter around the clearing and waited for the chopper's. We had the company unloaded in the clearing by noon and ready to move. We started west to the creek and the terrain was flatter than usual. We were in a valley, near the junction of the DAK HODRAI and DAK

ROTIL creeks. Loucks was leading, and very soon we both began to see small trails going west also. There were also sandal tracks and lots of broken branches.

The undergrowth under the triple canopy was typical, thick and with bamboo clumps. This was a very dangerous area and I was getting that old feeling. After several hours into the afternoon we began seeing more tropical vegetation and I knew the creek was close. We closed the creek with about an hour to spare before dark. We set up a perimeter on the creek's east side. My platoon was facing the creek. While we were digging, I glanced back the way we had come and two NVA grunts just came walking up and stopped in front of the second platoon. They must have mistaken us for NVA, as we were very dirty and our helmets were off as we worked. Troop's on that side froze as they sensed something was wrong. I made a move for my weapon, yelling their NVA kill the bastard's. I could not shoot as our troop's were between me and the NVA. They started running like hell as the second platoon shot the trees and undergrowth down around them. I think they may have both been hit as there was a blood trail. It was just one of those things that happen in a war. We could hear artillery firing nearby and it was not ours. We started getting sniper fire from across the creek and returned it, which not having a target should not have been done. No doubt the NVA was here and knew we were also. Sergeant Scarver came over to me saying, "Sergeant White, I can't get so and so to dig." He had not been with us a long time.

An attitude adjustment was required and quickly as the situation was serious. I moved to Scarver's squad and took care of things. It is not necessary to mention the young man's name, and he turned out to be a good troop anyway. When darkness came it was easy to see that if our mission was to find the enemy, we sure as hell had done that. The NVA guns kept searching around the area, around here and there. This told me that their infantry might not have an artillery forward observer with them. I suspected they did not have an NVA observer close to us who could adjust fire. Because of the creek and knowing the enemy was close, we did not send out any listening post. We were on the normal fifty per cent after dark anyway. We had the creek in front of third Platoon, Claymore's close in and trip flare's on the west bank. I sent Muck and Novotny and their squad's across the creek to set the trip flare's. Loucks and I crossed also and gave them cover while they quickly did the job. Sergeant Scarver and his squad were watching our flanks. The company's flanks, both east and west were covered by eighty eight Claymore mines command detonated. We would be one hell of a tough job for any NVA unit. The artillery observer at my suggestion, tried to shoot in several concentrations to give us the opportunity to have artillery on a very quick response. The forward observer's battery fire direction center refused the mission, saying they were firing everything they had for a company that had been ambushed. It was TET 69 indeed and someone left the door to hell open.

The night was dark with no wind or moon; there was lots of NVA artillery fire around the area. It was very obvious that every time they shot they moved the battery position. They no doubt feared our counter battery and "Puff the Magic Dragon" who was doing his thing to our south west. We were approximately twelve clicks in from Cambodia, that's about seven miles give or take. We were in position with all our fires interlocked and platoons on fifty per cent alert. I doubt if anyone other than perhaps Loucks or me even dozed. I was leaning back against a tree right beside my fighting hole. I was wrapped up in a poncho liner with my M-16 laying across my lap. My helmet and ammunition belts stacked beside me. My M-60 gunner, Rollinger was positioned to my right, with an assigned final protective fire to his left across the face of the platoon. The night was deep and dark, maybe that's why I thought about that verse by Robert Frost, "the woods were lonely dark and deep," etc. To my left was my RTO with the radio between myself and him. During that dangerous dark night, my RTO kept mumbling. I was thinking about shaking him but when I leaned over I heard it, "yea though I walk through the valley of death," etc. I felt an emotional response that I had long ago put aside in the hellish situations I had lived through. Now that I knew why he mumbled all the time I felt a new respect for him. At midnight Loucks leaned over me and whispered, "midnight, sereant." I whispered back, "no shit" he tried hard to control a snicker. At first light it was March 9th 1969, this was a day when the long black train picked up speed.

When March 9th, 1969 came, it was hot as hell and our sweat soaked rags were weighing on the troops nerves, along with a woods crawling with the NVA. We had two meals of rations but being aware that it might be awhile to get rations and ammo with all the fighting going on, I called for a reload. Counting the artillery observer party, we had seventy two men. The word was it may take awhile on rations and ammunition, birds overcommitted and uniforms in very short supply. I have stated several times in this writing that it would be the truth and it is, as God is my witness. Captain Hockett was aware of the troop's bare legs and arms and the scratches, bug bites, leaches, and he was the same way. Since all was quiet around us, the Captain suggested we put five men in the creek at a time, for one minute to try and help some of the discomfort. That was a good thought but it was very controversial. When the second five were in the creek, the enemy called the play. The NVA opened up on us with a machine gun firing down the middle of the creek from the south. The Captain ordered, "white, take your men across the creek, feel out their position and if possible get that gun." Then he ordered LePeilbet, "take your men down this side of the creek and you and white support each other. The first and second platoons maintain the perimeter staying ready to support either platoon as needed." Just before I crossed, I heard the artillery observer being told to standby overcommitted. I put down Muck's squad and Navotny's also to cover my crossing. Then moving quickly, I took Scarver's squad and Loucks and waded across. When I had crossed with no return machine gun fire, I set up a base of fire and brought Muck and Navotny across. The third platoon was really maneuvering, all seventeen of them. On the other side, I set up Muck and Navotny's squads in skirmisher's facing south. I had fourth platoon on my left across the creek, which gave me flank cover on that side by some very good people. Then I put Scarver on my right in single file from the right end of Navotny's squad.

To advance on a heavy communist machine gun with seventeen

men, is a wild and crazy proposition, but MACV and General Abram's had called the play. I and Loucks were in the middle between Muck and Navotny and I brought Rollinger there by Loucks with his M-60 with Procter his assistant gunner on his right. Before I moved, I said, "this is a tough call but we must get that gun, follow me and if you hear a metallic click to our front hit the ground quick." Communist heavy machine guns had a handle on the side similar to our fifty that the gunner could pull, to be sure he had a round chambered. We moved out keeping our line with Loucks in line and me slightly to the front. I was moving south down the west side of the DAK HODRAI creek. I knew there must be a trail to our south or the NVA could not have got that heavy machine gun into this area. I can only imagine what my men were feeling, as far myself I felt cold, almost detached. I glanced at my RTO, he had his eyes open and they were big, but he was doing okay. When we moved on, the brush lightened up and I saw the trail. At that point we came under heavy AK-47 fire, they must have moved their machinegun not wanting to chance losing it. We returned fire with everything we had, as we hit the dirt.

The NVA fire dropped away, and I supposed that they were pulling back when the encounter took place. One of my men had a minor wound in his arm. We moved forward and swept the contact site. There were several large pools of blood but no bodies. The NVA always carried off their killed in action, if they could. Then two loaches flew over, armed with mini guns. One of the pilots called eighty nine and asked if I had a mission. I told them I thought the NVA was running west on the trail where they passed me. I was looking for a clearing to dust off my wounded troop. It is hard to remember all the names, but I think his name was Don Cheek, a fine young troop. I found a clearing and having already called dust off it did not take long. I formed a perimeter around the clearing, and smoked in the chopper and our good troop was on his way to the rear. Before I moved on, the Brigade Commander landed in the clearing. He was a full Colonel and had the Brigade Sergeant Major with him. I maintained my perimeter with my now sixteen man platoon. Hell, that's not even two table of organization squads. The

Colonel acknowledged my salute with a quickie. Then the brass said, "why didn't you put a wall of steel in front of you and walk over them?" I said, "well sir, we have not heard anything from the artillery in days except they are overcommitted. However, I went on, "we had placed heavy fire on the enemy and they had pulled out and I sent those two loaches after them on the trail to the west." The Colonel frowned, and the sergeant major spoke up and said, "Sergeant, why haven't you had your men clean up and shave? They look like savages." Never in all my warring have I heard a statement as stupid as that. We did not even have potable water; potable water is water you can drink without boiling or treating it We were drinking creek water that had to be treated to kill the pathogen's. We never had even a small amount of soap and it came from combat ration's.

Then something surprising happened, my men were in the prone position in my perimeter and Jerry Loucks stood up. When he did then the entire platoon stood up. Standing there, as brave as lions, with their ragged uniforms falling off them and covered in dirt. I was surprised, but the Colonel and Sergeant Major were stunned. This was an eye opener for the brass, there was one man there who could for sure control these men and he was the platoon sergeant in front of them. I saluted, they got in the command ship without another word and left. I have always supported the army's power structure and the law, I always will. Senior officers and their Sergeant Major's have to understand that the troops doing the actual fighting, get tired of officers in chopper's always demanding close to the impossible. No one should be critical of the troop's efforts at great risk of their lives. I never saw a command ship in NAM that didn't have a large cooler of ice water and beer. The troops knew the brass lived in air conditioned house trailers with showers in the big safe base camps. I don't want to be to critical of this Colonel and his Sergeant Major, as seventy two hours later they flew into a hellish situation, to bring us ammunition. This was a heroic action by both of them sadly the Sergeant Major was killed. The troops I was with in NAM always supported their company officers and sergeant's, as we were out there all the way with them.

I moved from the clearing with my men in single file, going west at the side of the trail. Loucks was back on point with us staying off the trail, but in sight of it. While I was delayed at the clearing by the Brigade Commander, the loach Gunship's had been firing heavy, down the trail. I came up on the area very carefully, there were two dead NVA, shot all to hell by the mini guns, their blood and guts running through the dust. They died like so many, with their sightless eyes open. The grass was on fire around them and they were burned and smelled. I took their AK-47's, grenades and ammunition. I didn't see anything of intelligence value. While Loucks and I searched them, Sergeant Muck had the platoon in a perimeter around us. We quickly, moved on guiding on the trail. I gave twenty one, an overdue SITREP and about that time heard fourth platoon firing heavily to my east and rear. In case LePeilbet needed my support, I turned and headed toward him. We were moving east, when we came across a heavy blood trail and a land line commo wire. Loucks was like Custer on an Indian trail, when he saw that blood and wire. I of course turned the platoon south, to follow it. I had to pull Loucks off to the side of the wire by 5 yards, in the heavy brush. By not walking on the wire, I was guarding against ambush if possible. I gave twenty one another SITREP about the blood and wire, he said okay. Lieutenant LePeilbet's call sign was forty nine and I heard him tell twenty one, that they had killed two NVA. I slowed Loucks down, and we moved on south cautiously. Every step, we moved farther away from twenty one and the rest of the company.

I knew the enemy sometimes laid a commo wire to try to walk an American unit into an ambush. Keeping that in mind, I moved slowly with the wire just in sight. When I was another 500 yards or so south, twenty one gave me a recall saying there was need to regroup. I turned and headed back north in single file, Loucks leading. I could hear heavy artillery fire to the south. A big bluff type hill called Chu Ming was down that way, firebase swinger was on it. The firebase was southeast of POLEI JAR SIENG village, which was the name of the map sheet I carried. When we hit the east west trail, I turned east staying on its south side, and moved back to the contact site. It was then about 1330, and my men had been shooting and moving for almost seven hours in full battle gear. I left the contact site and headed for the company, staying one hundred yards farther from the creek than my route in the movement to contact. If you go back on the same route you went out, you are inviting ambush. The heavy wooded jungle type terrain was dark and silent as we passed carefully through it. I saw a chopper land at the company perimeter, as I was deciding I was close anyway. I could tell my men were pooped and needed a break, so when I saw I was about twenty or thirty meter's downstream from the company, I headed Loucks to the creek, and we walked the last few yards getting wet below the waste and walking very slow. It was about 1730 when I was passed into the perimeter. Lieutenant LePeilbet and his crew were already there and the company was saddled up. The chopper had already gone and the Captain wanted to move to a nearby hill.

When I came into the perimeter the Captain said, "white keep your men saddled up, We are moving." I said, "Captain my men are really beat up. We left here at 0730 and back at 1730. That's ten hours of constant humping, shooting and stress, and I need to get them some rest." I knew when I said it that the Captain was right, that position had been maintained too long. We moved quickly to a small hill position not far away to set up. Before we got much done, we heard the NVA guns fire to our southwest five or six 105MM rounds sailed over head and impacted close to our old position by the creek. Captain Hockett was certainly right on that one. I said, "wow, who was that dumb sergeant that wanted to take a break?" In any infantry war, but especially that one, shoot, move, and communicate was the only way to go. Before we were dug in, Hockett sent third and fourth platoon's to a hill just south of the one we were on. The other two platoon's and command group were going to set up where they were. The hill, to the south had two trails coming from the east and joining, before coming on over the crest of the hill. Hockett wanted an ambush there and it was the thing to do. When we got there I took the north side of the hill and LePeilbet the south side. The entire area was full of NVA and our artillery was hitting to the south, possibly near the NVA gun position that had just fired. We had several Gunship's over that area searching for those guns. LePeilbet sent the flea and two FNG's with two Claymores ahead to the point where the two trails joined. They set a Claymore on each trail and set up a temporary listening post to cover us while we dug in and did the NDP set up. The flea decided that they were hungry and sent the two FNG's back to our perimeter ambush site, to get their combat rations.

We already had our fighting holes dug and lieutenant LePeilbet and I were getting our machine guns set on final protective fire. We set up, interlocked fields of fire with the M-60's covering the front of both platoon's. Just as the FNG's reached us a Claymore went off at the flea's position. We hit the ground with weapons ready. Coming uphill from the east the flea was running in yelling;"don't shoot, it's me the flea!" I asked, as he jumped down among us "flea, did you kill a GOOK?" The flea with his southern accent replied, "they wuz either gook's or the two brownest Mexican's I ever saw." I almost smiled something I never did in those times. Loucks almost split his sides with laughter as we still stayed low. Lieutenant LePeilbet brought up a squad on line to sweep the area. With the flea leading, they moved down the trail to his position to check the situation. At the ambush position we covered, suddenly I heard laughter and LePeilbet called out, "coming in." When LePeilbet came in he was carrying two sets of Ho Chi Minh sandals and two rice knives. The flea, always brave and sometimes reckless, became startled as the two NVA suddenly appeared, and in the excitement he got the two Claymore clackers mixed up and blew the wrong Claymore. The two NVA were so scared, they jumped clean out of their sandals and dropped their rice knives and ran like hell. They just might be running yet forty three years later.

After the two NVA had left the area, we finished an NDP that also served as a good night ambush location, as the two trails joined and then fed right into us. We had our two platoon machine guns interlocked on an FPL that covered our platoon fronts and the trail also. We had all our equipment and forty three Claymore's, after the flea had detonated one. Our ambush site covering the trail made a great kill zone. Being in a perimeter, we had good flank and rear security. We still had plenty of Claymores, to provide additional flank and rear firepower. We had covered the flank's and rear with trip flares. LePeilbet called in the flea and the FNG's when we finished. We had decided on the hill to our left, where the rest of the company was as the rally point, if one was needed. Both positions were close enough together to support each other, and the artillery observer could have surrounded us with artillery concentrations, if he could get the missions. The two platoon's together had only thirty three men, which gave us a tight formation easily defended. Being so close to the rest of the company we did not select an alternate ambush location. It was 2355 when Loucks nudged me and said someone was coming on the trail. I passed the word by a whisper to both platoon's. Lieutenant LePeilbet was just about ten feet to my right. We as always had a few FNG's with us and I heard their safeties start to click off. I passed the word quickly, no firing unless I or the Lieutenant blew a Claymore. We had gone over all that while it was still daylight. We would only use the M-16's and M-60's at night if the enemy was getting through the Claymores. Few NVA would be able to come through that Claymore setup. I was listening to the footsteps, four in a series. I knew instantly it was not human. I passed the word, relax it was four legged.

The steps came up to the edge of the trip flare and Claymore set up and stopped. I guessed it was probably a tiger, as there were still a few in NAM. Then we could see its eyes, and it started working to our right relying on its sense of smell to get around us. That tiger certainly knew what it was about and worked around us in a half circle and came back to the trail on the downhill side and moved on off in the dark. When the tiger's steps faded away in the night, I could sense the relief in the troops around me. The nights in the NAM were always full of danger. What the hell, the days were too. I took over from Loucks when the tiger's footpads faded away and Lieutenant LePeilbet took over from the Flea. The squad leader's outranked the point men but they had their squads to control. Sometimes I used Loucks as an assistant platoon leader according to the situation. I sat there against a tree with my rifle in my lap and the starlight in my hand. The starlight was a night vision device that allowed a small bit of night vision, crude by today's standards. When we set up Claymores, we always wanted them to be as close to us as possible. We had to make sure the enemy could not crawl up and turn them around on us. That called for a tree to be behind the Claymore to absorb the back blast.

The rest of the night was totally uneventful. Possibly the afternoon Claymore incident had alerted the enemy to our location and they did not want to engage that night. The morning was hot as always and it was March 10th, 1969. We had passed through the fabled "Ides of March." Soon after daylight, Hockett came to our position with a squad from second platoon. The Captain, told me to set up a listening post down the creek bottom to our south, to watch the flank. I decided on a three man listening post, led by specialist George Sams who was known as Snook. I took them down the creek about 500 yards, and set them up with two Claymores in a hidden position with good visibility to the south. I had Loucks and two FNG's with me. We returned to our hill position and just got there when a Claymore went off. I quickly saddled up the platoon, and fourth platoon covered the hill. I moved out, going down the creek south in single file, Loucks out front. I gave twenty one a SITREP and he replied, "keep me informed." We moved quickly, and I was a little concerned because the terrain to our left was high. However, I had to get to my men. I detected movement on the high ground and I put the men down in some brush to give it a quick look. Specialist Ken McCormack, a very experienced troop was the rear guard. McCormack's back was to the creek. Then an NVA soldier with his AK-47 walked out in the open on the other bank. I passed the word to McCormack to kill him. McCormack simply could not move to turn and shoot, as the NVA would have seen his movement. The NVA grunt would have fired a magazine that would have passed through the entire platoon. We were just unlucky in that incident and the NVA vanished in the brush.

I could see no NVA on my left flank on the high ground, so I moved on quickly to get to snook. Snook had killed two NVA, one definitely an officer on the east/west trail with the Claymore. He had seen a number of other NVA with them, and the others had made themselves scarce.

Snook had a slight wound on one arm from a grenade. I moved forward to the two dead NVA at the side of the trail. When we moved up we came on another NVA who was wounded. The NVA tried to crawl away in the underbrush. Both Loucks and I shot him and he was hit bad, but below the waist. Then I saw he was unarmed and told Loucks to hold his fire. I managed to get a chopper to land on our smoke on the trail. I had quickly formed a perimeter and we sent the NVA to the POW collection point, with his wounds treated and a drink of water. His buddies had deserted him and took his weapon. I gave twenty one a SITREP, and a few minutes later he told me to ambush the trail at my present location. He also told me C Company was moving east on the trail, to wait there and pick them up and lead them to our company. That battalion wanted to group two company's is indicative of the enemy contacts in the area. I took careful actions to set up a perfect ambush on that trail. I had 11 Claymores hidden at the side of the trail in the kill zone. The other 11 covered around the flanks and rear of our perimeter. We had fighting holes and I put the M-60 by the trail in the killer team. I dragged the two dead NVA to a depression and had two of the troops cover them with dirt.

When I put the two dead NVA where we could quickly cover them up, I just needed to do away with the smell in that tropical heat. I had no feeling in a moral sense about that. In a war like NAM, policy governs such things and it can endanger your men to an even greater degree, if you make unnecessary noise. I always tried to avoid noise and never linger in a place where we had just had a contact. There had been so much noise and movement, including the chopper. To Medevac that NVA at that moment was controversial on my part. To do it just after a contact was very dangerous to my men. Given the situation we needed all the prisoner's we could get for intelligence about the enemy. The fact that I had to ambush the trail as well as pick up C Company, kept me from moving too far. After a contact it was always best to quietly move. The afternoon began to slowly pass by, and just after 1600 I heard a heavy amount of AK-47 fire slowly answered by M-16s. The firing was to my west and I concluded that C Company had been ambushed not more than a mile from me. I gave the order to saddle up; we were going to C Company. The Battalion Commander flew over just then and called me on the company net. He wanted me to move to C Company and hit the NVA from the rear. I told him, "roger" I was already getting ready to go. He said the NVA were in some rocks on the north side of the trail. He was not sure how many NVA but wanted me to get moving. I had the platoon in single file with Loucks leading on the north side of the trail in the brush. I was not going to take any unnecessary chances of getting ambushed. If I got hit too, that would not help C Company or my seventeen man platoon. I had gone almost half a mile when the NVA broke off the action and moved away. They probably had scouts out who saw the command ship hover over my platoon and drew the correct assumption. The Colonel called off my mission and twenty one told me to stay where I was halted and set up another ambush.

I set up another kill zone on the trail at 1730 with 11 Claymores hidden on the north side of the trail and the other 11 in a half circle covering my flanks and rear. I had Rollinger with his M-60 with myself, Loucks and Sergeant Mucks squad in the killer team. Sergeant's Scarver and Navotny covered flanks and rear. Each man dug a small but deep enough fighting hole, and I interlocked all fields of fire. When I was satisfied, I looked up and down the trail to check the situation. I gave twenty one a SITREP and he told me C Company would not be coming down the trail, just kill some gooks. The Captain also told me the NVA who Loucks and I had shot died in the Medevac. Just before dark, in a whisper I went over what was probably a very dangerous situation with the platoon. With the area loaded with NVA, I designated our previous setup as an alternate ambush location. We were probably 800 or 900 yards from the rest of the company and all of it in heavy bush. At dark, I registered an artillery concentration across the trail from me about 200 yards south. I was surprised they shot it in. About 2100 I heard a noise to our rear. I quietly moved to the rear to Scarver's squad and waited. I asked in a whisper if any of our troops had gone out on a nature call. The answer was negative, and then two figures loomed up in the darkness about ten or fifteen feet away. I whispered to the troop beside me to blow his Claymore, they were right in front of it. He was new and froze, I put my hand on the clacker, flipped off the safety and squeezed.

When I fired the Claymore, the NVA in front vanished from the waist down. We could plainly see him in the blast and his clothes were blown away with his legs flapping in the light. The other NVA was hit bad and fell to his right against a tree. Sergeant Scarver calmly let him have a twenty round M-16 magazine in the trunk of his body that should have finished him. I quickly had a Claymore fired by each squad leaving us 18. I did that, knowing the possibility that the NVA were all around us, considering the afternoon's action. I called the artillery and asked for six rounds on the concentration. I gave the order to pick up the other Claymores, secure all ammunition, weapons and grenades. We were moving to the alternate ambush location but leaving our rucksacks behind. When artillery told me on the way, I gave the order to follow me and keep as low as possible. We moved to the alternate location covered by the artillery, and our sound at least momentarily was absorbed by its impact. I gave Red Leg a cease fire and thanks for a good mission. We got to the alternate site without contact and set up in the darkness as well as possible. I put the kill zone on the trail again. The moon came up and strangely the moonlight filtered through the trees. I whispered and passed the word, "do not fire if you hear shooting. If they come at us, we will use the Claymores first." We lay there quietly, each man with his own thoughts, letting the sweat of a tough day dry. In the distance, the sound of Puff the Magic Dragon working out came to us through the still night air. I could hear artillery fire in every direction.

I whispered a SITREP to twenty one and then we heard a shot. I thought the NVA was firing a random shot hoping we would return fire and show them our location. It must have been after 0200 on the 11th when I heard NVA artillery so close, I could hear the breechblocks close. In the clear cool night air sound carried farther than in daylight. When they fired we could barely make out the flash to our south. We were about five or six hundred yards from an NVA artillery battery. I called twenty one, his RTO answered, I asked for twenty one and the RTO said to tell him the message, and he would relay to twenty one. I gave him the enemy battery location as 500 yards south of my location. I heard nothing for fifteen minutes, I called twenty one again and was told he had my message. I drew my own conclusions, I had only seventeen counting me and the NVA battery no doubt was heavily defended. I considered attacking the NVA battery, but had to consider the fact, I had just been in contact. There were many enemy grunt's in the immediate area who would be searching for third platoon. If I moved in the dark, I would give my position away. I knew my men would be badly outnumbered and we needed the advantage of surprise. When daylight came, twenty one told me he was moving to my location to back me up, when I swept the night contact site. When the rest of the company was close to my position in a perimeter, I put my platoon in skirmishers, and we carefully swept the contact site. I moved as quietly as possible with Loucks at my side. When we reached our site the first NVA was only half a man, it was a bloody horrific sight. It was a NAM sight and the one Scarver shot had been hit all over. He had put the muzzle of his rifle under his chin and finished himself off. We picked up our rucksacks, after searching the two butchered NVA we moved back to the company. When we were linked up, twenty one put the company in single file, third platoon in the rear and we moved northeast to higher ground.

When the company got to the top of a small hill, the DAK HODRAI was west of us and DAK ROTIL was to our south. We formed a perimeter on this hilltop and the date was March 11th, 1969. Captain Hockett had a mission from battalion and all platoon leaders were called for a quick meeting. The day before, which was March 10th, there had been an arc light strike (B 52) three to four clicks to our southeast. There was thought to be a large NVA base in that area. That would put the NVA base area sixteen clicks from Cambodia. The base area location must have been the destination all the NVA units we had been fighting were moving to. The trail, running from east to west, to Cambodia and the Ho Chi Minh trail, was their prime avenue to penetrate Kontum Province. The trail followed the DAK ROTIL creek about two hundred yards south of it. Captain Hockett had orders to do a bomb damage assessment of the arc light area. The patrol route called for us to move east another two clicks to a hill north of the DAK ROTIL, and set up there. We would move southeast across the DAK ROTIL and into the area on March 12, 1969. It was almost 1200 when we got moving again with 1st platoon leading then second platoon and fourth and third in that order. We had gone about half a click, in really bad bamboo and underbrush and crossed a low place then uphill to a small clearing. We formed a perimeter at that clearing and a chopper came in to take Captain Hockett on a recon.

We were waiting in the perimeter for Hockett and watching the bird, which was a light observation reconnaissance helicopter. They were making their recon over the area where we thought the trail must be. They found the trail it was 500 yards to our south on the other side of the creek. Suddenly a forty millimeter anti aircraft gun opened up on the chopper and it was very loud, even at our location. The pilot did some fancy flying to avoid the enemy fire even though a heavy machine gun began firing also. There was no doubt, if our mission was to find the enemy we had sure as hell had done that. They were heavily armed with artillery, both anti personnel and anti aircraft weapon's, backed up by heavy machine gun's. There would have to be a large concentration of troop's to secure that kind of firepower. There were additional NVA forces of size, in the base area unless the arc light had creamed them. In NAM it was best to always operate on the worst case scenario. We had a seventy two man unit, with four machine gun's and 82 Claymores. The Claymore was normally a defensive weapon except when used in ambush. When the Captain came in and the chopper left us, the Company Commander looked a little grim. It was starting to push 1530 when we moved on east another click and more to the hilltop. The triple canopy overhead was thick and the underbrush was heavy. We moved slow and careful, while the recon had found the enemy, it also showed the NVA exactly where we were, when the chopper landed. We made the hilltop after 1630 and dug in with our normal NDP defensive setup. We had a short meeting to mark the next day's patrol route on our maps. We should enter the arc light drop zone about 1300.

We were almost finished with our night defensive preparations when a chopper called me wanting to bring in the mail and resupply. We didn't need any combat rations as in the last two day's we had been reloaded. Third and fourth platoon's needed some more ammunition. I didn't want the bird to come in and show our location, when we were nearly in contact with the enemy. However, I knew how important the mail was to the troop's morale and Captain Hockett agreed with me. I brought in the bird and we received our mail, two beers a piece and two FNG's. The bird also had us more ammunition. In all my time in NAM, regardless of whatever unit I was in, an attempt was made to get the troop's two beers a piece, when it was possible. In that heat the beer just sweated right through and no one was ever impaired. The Beer was also a morale factor, which along with the mail helped us relax. March 11th, 1969 was an evening that A Company, 1st Battalion 8th United States Infantry needed a morale pickup and a little diversion. I knew intuitively that tomorrow, March 12th was going to be a very dangerous day. It was like an evening before a huge storm hit. The mail was welcome with most troops and I got a great letter from my wonderful wife. However, of all times for it to happen, my point man received a "Dear John Letter." Loucks was carried away, struck very hard with anguish and anger. He looked at me and said; "if I get home I am going to kill that bitch." I replied, "Jerry," this may be the only time I ever called him by his first name, "get a grip. You're a very tough man and you know as well as I, that the world is full of lovely women." I continued, "you and I have been in this war a long time and we can read the signs. Sometime tomorrow we are going to be ass deep in heavily armed NVA, and in probably a large bunker complex. You are going to need all your skill and courage, to get through this one and help the company get through it also."

Oh hell, did I ever turn out to be just loaded with foresight. Loucks knew that what I said was absolutely correct. He worked hard on his emotions to get himself back in that hellish place, and away from his personal problems. When night fell, the lizards in the trees got much louder which suited me just fine. The floor of the wooded jungle was dark and gloomy. The troop's were very quiet, no whispering and even my RTO was very quiet. I can't remember my RTO's name but if he had known what was a few hours away, he would have been praying. It seemed like no time at all when Loucks whispered, "midnight, sergeant," and I took over. I felt strangely on edge and very alert to the jungle sounds and stillness around us. We had no listening post that night, opting instead for a very alert posture knowing that the lizards would suddenly go silent, if something was coming. Captain Hockett knew we had been in contact almost every day for the past week and he wanted the troop's to relax if that was possible. I was sitting there quietly against a tree, when the two FNG's that had come in earlier that day, wanted to ask me something about what was happening. I don't remember now what platoon they went to but it wasn't the third platoon. We had two sick troop's fly out with the slick that afternoon so the count was still at seventy two. They seemed like they were going to be good troops. Hell, they were combat veterans by the afternoon of the next day's deadly combat.

I sat against a tree from the first minutes of March 12TH, just after midnight until first light and stand to. After the FNG's had finished twenty questions and went to their holes, I put my mind to what probably was ahead in the next twelve to sixteen hours. AT hill 875 in October 1967, the NVA had employed a tactic they referred to as the "hill trap maneuver." The height of ambition for a mid level or senior NVA officer was to command a unit that overran an American unit. I found this out by reading Intelligence summaries, while I was still at Texas A&M. The 173rd Airborne, one of the finest brigades in the US Army, had the mission to take hill 875. Hill 875 was southwest of Dak To airfield and rocket ridge and southeast of Ben Het. A large NVA force had been spotted on top of 875, which was steep and covered by thick triple canopy trees and some bad underbrush. In the beginning, the 173rd had sent a battalion to take the hill. The hill trap was really not complicated, an NVA unit, would show themselves on top of the hill to suck the Americans in. There were large NVA forces concealed in the terrain near the base of the hill. The 173rd Battalion sent two company's up the hill, one company leading the other that followed in support. The other two company's remained in a perimeter near the hill in support, as well as to hold a landing zone. The NVA on top put up a stiff fight, which delayed the lead company. Then the NVA struck, sending one battalion up another side of the hill to try to cut off the lower 173rd company, from the company in the lead. This being done, the NVA then struck at the rear company from behind and almost overran it. The American company command group was wiped out in hand to hand fighting. The NVA, then threw everything they had against the survivors of the lower company. The paratroopers were fighting like tigers, surrounded by NVA. The upper company could not move back down to help or the NVA on top would take them in the rear. With heavy air support and artillery, the lower company remnant, fought their way through the NVA and linked up with the company, higher up on the hill. They formed a perimeter but had suffered heavy casualties. They were surrounded, but held out as the 173rd Battalion Commander instantly committed his reserves against the rear of the NVA. The "Sky Soldiers" were outnumbered, but won the battle and NVA left for Cambodia leaving large numbers of dead men on the hill.

The hill trap maneuver was very much on my mind at daylight on March 12th, 1969. Loucks and I, in a tense whispered conversation, went over maintaining linkup with Lieutenant LePeilbet's rear guard as the fourth was leading and third along with the command group following. Then came the first and second platoon's. Just before we moved, we had a LRP tracer team join us briefly. They had a real shooter with them, Randy Chrietzberg from earlier in my narrative. The LRP leader and I disagreed as to our exact location. In the ensuing conversation, both Captain Hockett and Lieutenant LePeilbet supported my map position as correct. We had far more serious things to worry about than that. The LRP team, moved out about twenty minutes before us and went to our left front, moving southeast.

The LRP leader was guiding on hill 783, which was a small hill on the horizon. That kept the LRP team moving ahead and to the left of our patrol route as they were following a more easterly route than us. During the day, I never heard them firing as the volume of noise around me prevented anything far away, from being heard. They ran into a large NVA force and were fighting for their lives. Only Chrietzberg and a wounded troop survived, and rejoined the company either at dark or the next day. I don't know much about their ordeal but am certain that only Chreitzberg's skill and courage led to their survival. Fourth platoon leading meant the experienced flea in front. They moved downhill slowly and carefully. We were going just east of south at about a 170 degree azimuth. There was a wide shallow flat with water about a foot deep, at the point where we crossed the DAK ROTIL with buffalo grass above our heads. The water course was actually a swamp, that was four or five hundred yards wide at our crossing point. Lieutenant LePeilbet was always a tactician, and halted the company for a listen just over halfway across. It was hot, still and very quiet and we stayed there longer than usual. Perhaps the flea or LePeilbet thought they heard or sensed something. I glanced back at my men all perfectly facing their assigned directions, due to my numbering system. I felt something ominous and thought, "I sure hope I don't lose any of these guys today." In a few more minutes we moved on, thankful for being able to get wet. It was at least an hour or more after we moved out of the NDP that we began to come out of the water. We started uphill, still on about a 170 azimuth and as soon as the entire company was in the trees, Captain Hockett called a halt and we quickly formed a perimeter. This halt was at the map coordinates in the after action report and not for the location of the ferocious combat to the death, that now was only a short time away. The Captain called in a SITREP to the TOC from the halt location and never had time the rest of the day, to give another position report on the battle site.

I am sure, I had never done it before yet for some strange reason at the halt, I glanced at my wife's last letter that was in my pants pocket. I felt no premonition, but rather a cold, detached feeling. The flea and Lieutenant LePeilbet started up the steep hill at about 0930. The hill was very steep even though the hill top was elevation 515. We must have been halfway up, climbing in single file when the flea, stopped the company. The hill was so steep the troop's were clinging to it with their huge rucksacks pulling them backwards. I could hear the troop's breathing hard, while most of the troops were in good shape they were exhausted from day after day of NAM. The word was passed down for me to come up front, which was hard to do as I had to work my way through the entire fourth platoon. When I reached the front, Lieutenant LePeilbet told me that the flea thought he saw something on top. We both looked with our field glasses and saw nothing. It is amazing how much detail you can see with field glasses, in heavy undergrowth and trees. About that time, twenty one called up and asked;"What is wrong?"LePeilbet replied,"just being careful."

Lieutenant LePeilbet told flea,"let's do it," and the climb resumed. When my platoon got up to me, Loucks said, "what?" I just shook my head and we moved on toward the door to hell. When we arrived at the hilltop, fourth platoon had moved to their right, heading south down a long hogback finger. I noticed a small clearing close to the hilltop just to our left. We followed fourth platoon with Loucks staying close to their rear guard. I passed the word back to McCormack to make sure the command group saw the right turn. The woods and undergrowth, with lots of bamboo as expected, was very quiet and still. I had examined my map carefully that morning and knew that the flea must be closing in on the arc light site. As we moved downhill the hogback got narrower, in retrospect (Thank God) we went through a bamboo thicket about 400 yards downhill, from the hilltop. The hogback was so narrow at the bamboo thicket we almost had to cut our way through it. We were just barely able to squeeze around it on the right. The term hogback ridge describes a ridge with a very narrow sharp top, just wide enough to walk on. Not far after that, Loucks pointed down to his right where lay a long sock filled with rice. Most NVA troops carried two rice socks tied around their necks. Looking back over the years, the time we left the bamboo thicket must have been around 1045 or maybe 1100. Suddenly, the fourth platoon slowed up and then moved on more slowly. We started to see large bomb craters on the sides of the hogback. Then I heard a grenade go off and heavy M-16 and AK-47 fire broke out. The shout came down the line, "sergeant white to the front." I yelled over my shoulder, Muck, form an oblong perimeter and link to fourth platoon rear." Loucks followed me, but I told him, "get back to Muck and tell him, if necessary use the rucksacks for cover." I moved quickly to the front, and LePeilbet was down and bloody as hell. I rolled him over and he yelled to me over the sounds of the ever mounting combat, "whitey, get back!" and then he passed out. I looked around, and saw that they had stumbled on to a big NVA bunker complex with bomb craters having just missed them on the left side.

Horton the fourth platoon sergeant was shooting and yelling to his men to keep firing. The fourth platoon machine gunner, Campbell was firing straight ahead at several NVA bunkers. I yelled in Horton's ear, "my platoon in a perimeter right behind you!" Horton nodded his head and kept firing. LePeilbet had been trying to tell me that we had to fall back on the rest of the company. I knew that, but first we needed a clean break so a running fight would not develop or preclude our being able to fire and maneuver, while falling back. I could already tell that there was a hell of a lot more NVA here than our puny seventy two. The bunker, just to the front was where Horton said the grenade was thrown from that hit LePeilbet. The position of that bunker meant I had to take it out because they could fire from it right up along the hogback. The NVA were firing steadily but not wildly, and trying to work around our flanks already. I knew they were well led by what I saw, well we were to.

This was the oft mentioned "gate" and we were positioned at the "event horizon." Taking just a few seconds, I checked third platoon's positioning and the linkup with the fourth. There was a storm of bullets, flying everywhere and small limbs and leaves raining down from the trees. I yelled to both platoon's; "conserve your ammo, shoot at the NVA, not just blow off your ammo." I rolled LePeilbet over again, he was still out but his bleeding had slowed, thanks to the medic's efforts. I started to take the bunker in front of us with an M-72 LAW but we were too close to it. I yelled in Horton's ear; "we are going to take that bunker in a maneuver left through that bomb crater!" I went on, "get several men and when I move, fan out to my left and cover me, I will hit the bunker. You take your men and hit those NVA on the left side." Beyond the bunker, directly in front there were additional bunkers and lots of NVA firing all down the finger from us. I yelled in Campbell's ear;"start firing burst of six rounds into that bunker. I am going to take Horton and several more and move left through that bomb crater. When you see me wave to you, move your fire to the right side of the finger." Campbell nodded his head and started firing into the bunker, which was a mound of dirt with a small aperture on our side, with the gooks firing from it. Horton had flea and airborne and nodded his head to me. I yelled to both platoon's "keep up the fire, concentrate to the center and right of the finger, and don't waste ammo." I yelled to Horton, "okay let's do it follow me and move to my left." We jumped up and moved into the bomb crater. I waved Horton to the left and yelled, "okay, cover me and hit those gooks!" Horton, flea and airborne didn't need to be told, as they were all shooters. I crawled to the edge of the crater and looked at Campbell and waved. Campbell was a cool gunner and quickly shifted his fire to the right. I jumped out of the crater and with AK rounds popping all around me, moved in on the NVA bunker.

I was no doubt, the only man on the hogback standing up when I got to the rear of the bunker. AK slugs were hitting the top of the bunker, and it seemed odd that I wasn't hit. An NVA soldier, leaned out of the rear aperture and tried to shoot me, and I pushed his AK aside, with my right forearm. I did the business, and rolled back to the side of the bunker by the bomb crater, where there was a big aperture with a bamboo mat rolled down over it. I unloaded the rest of my thirty round M-16 magazine through it. Even with all the noise, I heard them grunt as my M-16 slugs hit their bodies. There were four or five gooks in that bunker. Just to make sure they were dead, I crawled up on top of the bunker, I guess I was over exposed. I quickly loaded another magazine into my M-16 and fired it down the finger. Then with my left hand, I grabbed a grenade and started to pull the pin out with my right hand. I could hear Horton and the others firing heavily to my left. Just before I got the grenade pin out, something blew me off the top of the bunker. I was lying on my back and knew I was hit badly. I looked, and saw the two jagged broken ends of my right femur, the largest bone in the body, sticking out of my right leg.

I had glimpsed a small cloud of dust go up down the finger as I fell. I knew I had been hit with an RPG. The NVA that shot me must have had a heat warhead on his launcher. He just missed me, hitting instead a tree to my right. The explosion hit me, and Horton, the Flea and Summerlin were all hit by something, perhaps the RPG also. If the RPG warhead had been an antipersonnel warhead, I would probably have been killed. The femoral artery in my right leg was cauterized by the heat warhead. That kept it from bleeding, probably saving my life. I would have quickly bled to death, right then and there by that bunker, had that artery not been cauterized. Horton was hit badly in the trunk of his body and one arm. The Flea had a bad shoulder wound and I can't recall where Summerlin was hit. The troop's laid down a steady wall of fire to cover us. Sergeant Muck had come to the point of fourth platoon close to the bunker. I heard Muck yell, "okay guy's, you all know what we got to do!" I yelled to Horton and the other two, "start crawling back to the perimeter." Suddenly Pappy Rawls of fourth platoon, a tough veteran, ran out to me and threw me over his shoulder in the fireman's carry and brought me to the perimeter. Other troop's were carrying Horton and assisting Flea and Summerlin back to our perimeter. I had left my RTO with fourth platoon when I moved on the bunker. I quickly got twenty one on the radio and told him what was happening. Twenty one answered, "we are surrounded at the hilltop, can you get to us?" I asked for artillery and twenty one said; the observer was working on it. Well, big woo! I knew in an instant if we were going to survive this combat to the death, it was totally up to us.

There had been thirty five men total combined in third and fourth platoon's when we started down the slope. Now we had five men wounded, and the troop's had seen the three ranking leader's shot down before their very eyes. I checked LePeilbet and he was clutching his rifle tightly, but he was still unconscious. Horton was in great pain but still had his rifle and was able to shoot, likewise with the Flea. LePeilbet was a real tough stud and we were going to need him. The medic gave me a shot of morphine and said, "sergeant I can't believe it, your leg is not bleeding!" My rifle had been blown away from me, and I was hit in both hands bad, along with my leg. This was the real moment of truth, when all men's souls are laid bare. I was still lucid, and knew I had to get the troop's moving in the right direction, north back up the slope toward the remnant of the company. I knew somewhere out there was an NVA officer thinking they were going to overrun this trapped American unit. This was a desperate moment, and I sucked it up and knew I had to make it happen, or the NVA were going to take us out. I heard an FNG cry out, "we are going to die!" I yelled out, "stop that shit, we are not going to die today. Those out there in the brown uniforms are going to die today." I added, "we will die in the far future, in the cardiac or the cancer ward." Loucks laughed, and both order and discipline were restored. I yelled out to all the squad leaders in both platoon's, "okay, you squad leaders stay with your men I am in command and will issue my orders through Loucks."

Lying there, with my left ring finger shot almost off and my right wrist as big as a ping pong ball with a piece of steel in it, along with a horrific leg wound, I had to make a decision. Quickly I checked the situation the NVA fire kept rising and falling. That could mean their leader was moving his men around, which might mean he was getting ready to rush us. We had several factors that would help us. We went into the fight with twenty two magazines apiece and lots of M-60 ammunition. I never saw an NVA soldier with more than five magazines. We were in a good defensive formation on the hogback. That put us up higher than the enemy. We each had six grenade's apiece, better quality grenade's than the NVA had. I called Loucks, and yelled loudly to inform as many troops as possible, "gather up the wounded that can't walk here with me, and let's get them all lying on ponchos. Assign one man to pull each poncho and each wounded man will help all he can." I can't remember how many M-60 machine guns we had, either two or three. I had Loucks put fourth platoon behind the wounded facing downhill and third platoon leading uphill. That was easy, as the platoon's were deployed that way anyway. I set up a walking fighting perimeter, with the wounded in the middle, and I quickly distributed all of my nineteen magazines to the troop's. I was about to give the order to move, when the NVA started yelling things at us to get their courage up. I heard one yell in pigeon, "Americans all die now." That was a good indication that they were about to rush us.

I had Loucks put the machine guns on the side of the yelling. I saw Rollinger kill an NVA with a burst of six. Something kept tugging at my thoughts. I had Loucks move a gun back to the quiet side. Actually there was no quiet side as the battle uproar was deafening. Moving one M-60 back to the side where it had been was fortunate. Most of the NVA tried to attack from that side. I knew if we could go a short distance the steep drop on the sides of the hogback would favor us. Then the NVA jumped up to charge us and our M-16's and M-60's cut them down. However, there was one NVA officer incredibly brave, who came through our fire. He was bleeding from the mouth and had blood spots all over his front. He also had a smoking hand grenade in each hand. He was only ten or fifteen paces away, coming up the steep slope. I yelled at Loucks, and when he looked at me, I pointed at the NVA officer. Loucks dropped him in his tracks, but as he fell he managed to throw the grenade's in among us. I yelled, "down down!" and everyone was. I reached out with my crippled right hand, trying to get one that was close to me and throw it out. I could not reach it, and looked away not wanting to take it in my face. My RTO at my side must have been praying again. Both grenades went off with a loud pop like a nickel firecracker. I laughed and yelled "we are going to kick hell out of these son of a bitches! let's move it!" The grenade powder trains must have become wet in the monsoon. We had several more wounded by then, and it was hard to believe none had been killed yet. The firing was heavy and without a pause. I kept the walking perimeter moving and my men killing NVA but not shooting wildly. Loucks yelled to me that he saw gunship's toward the hilltop. I called twenty one and told him I was moving uphill and would come in from the south. Then I asked for an airstrike or artillery. He replied, "wait" whatever the hell that meant. My shot of morphine was wearing off but I fought the pain.

After we stopped the NVA attempt to rush us, we moved farther up the ridge and the sides became steeper. This worked in our favor for a time. We were holding the commanding terrain as we moved along the hogback with the wounded. The NVA, were having to shoot uphill and they were shooting high. They did manage to get some snipers in the trees on the hogback that we had to deal with. In one incident that stands out in my mind, Lieutenant LePeilbet came to and shot a sniper dead and he fell like a squirrel. I yelled, "good shot, Lt!" but he looked like he had passed out again. I think he had a piece of steel in his spine and morphine would not deaden it. The finger leading to the hilltop where first and second platoon's were fighting was not to steep. If the finger had been a lot steeper, the troops could not have managed to drag the wounded to the perimeter. That would have required me to make a very tough decision. I would have probably, had the wounded that could not walk including me, left in a small perimeter and fully armed. Then the troops could move quickly to the perimeter to bring back help. In no case, would I lose the lives of the other troops just to stay with us. That would not have worked anyway, because the troops, especially Loucks, simply would not leave us. It must have been around 1300, when we got to where the hill was high enough over the bamboo thicket, for us to see the hilltop. I could see that first and second platoon's and the command group were surrounded, but fighting hard. When we got to that point, I could see no air support or artillery at all. We had gunship support at the hill off and on. In our struggle to break through to the hilltop perimeter we had received no air or artillery support at all. I had called for it several times. Captain Hockett was aware of our long pointblank firefight.

When we came closer to the bamboo thicket, two NVA machine gun's opened up on us from the bamboo. They were firing grazing fire and we were pinned down on the narrow hogback. Grazing fire is defined, as being fire that doesn't rise above the waist of a man for 800 yards. When that happened, the NVA behind us put heavy pressure on the fourth platoon rear. Loucks lay down beside me, and said something to me with an air of resignation. He said, "Sarge, we are going to buy it this time. There is no way we can get those two gun's. There are ten or fifteen NVA with them dug in. They are shooting down our throats and if we try to rush them on this narrow hogback they will slaughter us." I said, "Loucks, have you checked the flanks? Is there no way we can maneuver around them?" Jerry replied, "No, Sarge, it's too steep." The advantage of terrain now worked against us. I was about to give the order to pull in tighter, and we would try to hold them off playing for time. Maybe something unexpected might happen. I was also beginning to worry about our ammo. Suddenly my RTO pushed the handset to my ear and I heard a cold distant voice say "eighty nine this is cobra lead, are you in trouble?" I replied quickly; "cobra, this is eighty nine I am in deep shit come quick." He came right back; "eighty nine, cobra lead give me a six."

A six digit coordinate identifies your position to the nearest hundred meters. I reached into the right cargo pocket on the right leg of my jungle fatigue pants. They had been rotted off just below the pocket, before I was hit. I was relieved to find the pocket with the POLIE JAR SEING map sheet still there. I jerked the map out of my pocket and quickly gave cobra lead our six Digit coordinate. He came right back; "eighty nine, cobra, I am nearby running 100 knots plus, right at tree top. Will be there soon, pop smoke!" I yelled to Jerry and he popped a purple smoke. I heard cobra say, "I identify purple" and I replied, "cobra eighty nine, that's us close around the smoke." Cobra lead said "where are they eighty nine?" I replied; "cobra eighty nine, they are in the bamboo just uphill to the north fifty meters." In a second He came back "eighty nine, cobra get your men flat here comes the shot." I was lying on my back and still had not seen cobra lead. Suddenly I looked at the bottom of the cobra right above us, and he fired two rockets and a mini gun. Loucks yelled "he got them all Sarge." I said "then let's move and keep firing, especially to the rear." I could feel the troop's emotions take a leap. I have called for and adjusted a lot of indirect fire and air strikes, but none ever made me feel as good as THAT air strike! Cobra lead roared off in glory, never to be seen by me again. When we moved through the burned shattered bamboo dead NVA were everywhere and the broken parts of the machine guns with them. When I was dragged through the bamboo, a sharp piece sticking up hit my leg wound and a terrific shot of pain went through me. I looked back down the finger, the undergrowth and trees were shot all to hell and dead NVA were everywhere. It was a picture right out of Dante's Inferno, "hell itself beyond the gate."

It was still a distance to the company remnant and the first and second platoon's were fighting very hard. I could see one of the new Lieutenant's moving through his platoon and shooting as he moved. In such close quarters combat it is necessary to keep coordinated with the other friendly troop's nearby. One thing I was always very careful of was to coordinate with the commander when I was coming in. I was always trying to avert any possibility of a friendly fire incident occurring. I called twenty one; "this is eighty nine and we are closing from the south. I am going to keep my fire to the flanks and rear so watch out for us." Twenty one came right back, "roger eighty nine, glad to see you, will send a link up." I yelled to Jerry; "fire flanks and rear. They are coming down to help us." I don't remember which platoon came to us with their lieutenant leading the way. My men were too tired to cheer, but it was a joyful linkup. In a few minutes we were in the perimeter. First and second platoon's had almost as many wounded as we did with one KIA. I will not identify him to preclude breaking some hearts afresh after all these years but it is sufficient to say, he was everything an American soldier should be. The linkup was certainly not the end of it, and the "Black Train" was still running. However it was very surprising to have only one KIA after a raging horrific firefight that had already lasted five or six hours and was worsening. When we reached the perimeter, I had sergeant Muck get third and fourth platoon's integrated into the company perimeter.

The third platoon squad leaders had been great. The leadership provided by Sergeant's Muck, Novotny and Scarver had been superb. The same could be said for the fourth platoon squad leaders and Sergeant Jerry Horton, who was a calm super brave leader. As for Jerry Loucks there was never an American soldier more deserving of the Medal of Honor. The skill and bravery of these super guys along with the fine young men we commanded, was going to be tested even more, as the afternoon wore away. In the initial confusion of the linkup, I was left lying out in the open. Some NVA sniper shot at me three times and I yelled out, "some NVA bastard needs to be shoveling shit in HANOI." Most of those NVA could not speak English, but they knew what a bastard was. Suddenly I felt someone land on top of me. It was a black medic who was brand new to the company. He yelled in my ear, "Sarge, I don't know what your doing out here. Put your arms around my neck and hold on and I will crawl over there behind that log." When he got me there, he looked at my leg and said;"I can't believe it. You are not bleeding!" He was another very fine African American soldier. Then Hockett crawled up after having linked up the perimeter and yelled; "white so nice to see you!" No time for levity as the situation was grim. We had so many wounded there were only fifty or less troop's still able to fire their weapons. In addition, they were rapidly running out of ammunition. The fire was heavy both incoming and outgoing. At that moment, the Brigade Commander made his brave effort to resupply us with ammunition. His command ship was hit hard, and the Sergeant Major killed. Nevertheless, they still managed to shove a few cases of ammunition out of the bird. The Battalion Commander, Colonel Buckner was flying low calling for resupply, reinforcement's, air strikes and whatever else he could do for us. The clearing had the NVA on the far side and that's why resupply was so difficult. Lieutenant LePeilbet, Jerry Horton and I were lying behind the log, and all we could do was give advice and encourage the troops.

Captain Hockett, in a show of leadership or desperation, lined up our remaining troop's on the ground and made an assault across the clearing. The attack forced the NVA to retreat. Then Hockett set up a new perimeter around the clearing and included the log inside it. There were wounded lying all around the log that were being treated by the medics. It must have been after 1700 at the hilltop by then. The NVA fire got heavier and it looked like they might counter attack. Hockett, Andrews and Porter lay down behind the log by LePeilbet, myself and Horton. I could see the strain in all their faces. At that time we had no supporting gunships, but the artillery observer had a battery of 155 MM (killing radius 100 meters) hitting close to where most of the NVA seemed to be. Captain Hockett, yelled above the hellish roar "men we are running out of ammunition. We have got to force the NVA back long enough for Buckner to send in those resupply choppers. I want to fire on our own position what do you say?" After a short thought, the platoon leaders said, "Yes." I had been through a friendly fire on my position before; I said, "Captain that's 155 are you positive about the ammunition count?" He said, "Yes," and I said okay. Hockett said,"shoot it to the artillery observer."

In a few moments, the artillery observer looking young and stressed yelled, "on the way!" Hockett and everyone yelled "down!" Actually this order was not needed as the fire was so heavy everyone was down already. The woods all around us seemed to tremble and blaze, as though we were in the pit of hell. There were tree limbs, some quite large and small pieces of wood raining down on us like a hail storm. The barrage probably caught the NVA by surprise and hopefully sent a bunch of the little bastards to hell. Throughout the immediate area there was dust and smoke almost blinding the troops. I heard the artillery observer say; "oh shit, our troops can't see!" I being a wise ass said; "don't sweat it! The dirt falleth on the just and the unjust." About that time Loucks hit the ground beside me and said, "just checking on you, Sarge." I said, "don't worry tough guy. Just kill more Gook's." I have no idea how many Loucks killed that day but he was a "one man army." Leaders like me, Horton, LePeilbet, Andrews and Porter's main job was to get our men in position, where they all can kill and kill quickly. Yes, we help out when the Troop's are doing their thing. The Company Commander does the same thing for the Company. This day without good leadership, A Company would not have survived. The NVA were too many and we were caught at the wrong time, in a recon in force. The day was growing late and the NVA were momentarily set back on their heels. Captain Hockett was getting us quickly reloaded with ammunition, water and combat rations. Unfortunately there were no reinforcements to be had. I will never forget, Loucks and George Ardonetto from first platoon, out there with their sleeves rolled up if they had any, carrying ammunition boxes to the troop's, under heavy fire.

Soon after the resupply Hockett still cool and calm but showing fatigue, said; "now we have to dust off the wounded before dark." I heard him tell Buckner on the radio, send in the dust offs." I think there was only four dust off's orbiting. Horton, LePeilbet and I were the most badly wounded. None of us wanted to go first, as we were Leader's. LePeilbet was finally conscious, and I asked him if he remembered shooting that sniper out of a tree, and he replied, "NO." Hockett said, "no arguments about it men, we only have a few dust off's right here at dark and you're going." The first dust-off was call sign three seven and fortunately it was flown by a very tough brave man by the name of Rinehart. The NVA, reappeared as he was making his approach from the west with the sun behind him. The clearing was such that chopper's could not land. All resupply had to have been thrown out to us. The wounded would have to be boosted up on the fingertips of brave men standing up. Dust off 37 had been to another company and already had wounded aboard. But Rinehart, bravely radioed he could take three more. He hovered over the clearing five or six feet high. Several very brave men stood up and held both Horton and I on their fingertips as the NVA opened up on that Red Cross with everything they had. Hockett had our guy's shooting as fast as they could, trying to cover the dust off. When it was my turn, a young blonde kid leaned out and grabbed my shirt and yelled, "Sarge, you got to help me if you can."

I reached with my damaged right hand and grabbed a seat support and pulled with my remaining strength. The medic dragged me in and on top of other badly wounded men. Horton was down there somewhere, in great pain. When they held me up on their fingertips I looked down at those brave men. Loucks was one of them and he yelled, "goodbye, Sarge!" I yelled, "You're the best, Jerry." Another third platoon troop and a very good brave man Gary Feldman, who was known as "country", was hit. This occurred as he was helping hold me up to the dust off and never relaxed his strength. I yelled, "goodbye A Company!" and several of the men even with all the shooting going on yelled, "good luck, Sarge!" Just before the exit another young troop and a good man, was boosted up into the dust off. He was only hit in the shoulder, which was bad enough but he yelled,"going home! I got the million dollar wound!" Then he sadly took three or four AK-47 rounds in the chest, falling over on me. He died lying on me with blood and guts everywhere in the bird. It was a dust off loaded with suffering humanity all who had given their best for the green machine and their country. I heard the copilot yell; "lets go!" I heard the AK-47 slugs knocking hell out of that dust off. Rinehart gave it everything he could to fly that damaged chopper out of there. We roared away from A Company's hill hitting the skids on the tree tops, nevertheless Rinehart kept control of the bird. Somewhere that day I had prayed to myself; "Lord, if you would just save me one more time." On the way to POLIE KLENG I started hurting real bad as the morphine had worn off. The chopper was lurching around in the sky, but Rinehart kept fighting to keep it in the air. I remember thinking, "don boy, you may die today anyway."

When Rinehart began his approach to POLIE KLENG, he started calling, "mayday! mayday! 37 hit bad going into POLIE KLENG." When we landed it seemed almost a crash landing but Rinehart had saved all of our lives. The crew, took us all off the chopper and treated our wound's and tried to resuscitate the troop hit in the chest, but it was no use. I will not put in his name for reasons before stated. Rinehart had already called for another bird to get us to a hospital. There had just been a mortar attack on the airstrip and there were holes in the PCP still smoking. A Special Forces officer brought down a platoon of CIDG's to give us cover while we waited. I heard the officer tell Rinehart; "they better get a move on with those Bird's." The NVA are going to hit us with a ground attack at any moment. When that happens we will pick these guys up and Di Di" (Vietnamese for hurry up), "for the bunker's." I lay there with my fate out of my hands and thought about Loucks and all the fine men who had fought for A Company that day. I knew it was going to be one hell of a night on that hill. Soon two Bird's arrived and we were on our way, I knew not where and did not care. That was the last of my killing in a horrific, pointblank, fought to a finish infantry war. I remember the bird unloading in front of the triage, at the hospital at the Fourth Division base Camp at camp ENARI.

— CHAPTER NINE —

FROM THE PIT

Oh Lord thou hast brought up my soul
From the grave, thou hast kept me alive,
That I should not go down to the pit.
PSALM 30: 3

On the chopper ride out of POLEI KLENG on the way to camp ENARI hospital we stopped at some medical facility for what reason I don't know. Perhaps it was to stabilize badly wounded men. I was in bad pain, but before they gave me a shot I was handed a cold Pepsi Cola. The doctor smiled and said, "take a pull of that Sarge." When I did, he quickly jerked my leg out by the ankle and put on a metal splint to keep the ends of the femur apart. Then they gave me a shot of morphine,I think it may have been the third one. This must have been 2000 or later, and then we were reloaded on the chopper and flew on to the triage at camp ENARI hospital. Hell, I think it was the hospital at the Fourth Division base camp. I was in bad shape after the hellish day. They carried Horton, the Flea and me into the tent they used as a triage. It was dark in there lit only by a candle. The next tent was lit and I saw Rinehart's medic the blonde headed kid in there with a quart of Jack Daniels in his hand. That told me Rinehart and his crew had made it safely through another day. I don't know how the kid knew I was in the dark tent but he came in and said, "Sarge, if it is medically okay I will give you a shot of this Jack." I said; "young man, you and your crew have done many good things this day so don't sweat it."

A doctor and nurse started going down the line of litters with a flashlight and clipboard. At the first two, the doctor said, "good, we can fix both of these guys just fine," Horton may have been one of them. On down the line they came. At one litter the doctor said,"this one is already gone. Get his name off his tags and religious preference." Moving on to another litter, he said; "really bad shape, let's rush him in to the OR right now." When they got to me, the doctor checked and said, "Sarge, that's a bad leg wound but we will fix it and both hands as best we can. Your vitals are just fine, lay back and have a Pepsi and we will get you in to the OR after midnight." I lay there in the darkness thinking about the hill where A Company or what was left of it, was fighting to survive. I knew they would win out if humanly possible. After all, Captain Hockett, Lieutenant's Andrews and Porter and Jerry Loucks were there, and they had a great bunch of guys that would hold together until hell froze over. I dozed off, remembering that the evil thereof was enough for the day.

When I woke up I was in a full body cast and it was March 13, 1969. I was in a ward with a lot of other guys, I don't remember how many. Sergeant Horton was nearby but we really were not close enough to talk. The doctor who operated on me came by and said, "Sarge, I did the best I could. I don't know how good your leg will be. You probably will not be on crutches or cane after six months." He went on, "as far as your left hand ring finger, I reattached it and had to use a skin graft. You will never be able to use it, but it will be there. I could not do much with your right wrist but in time you will be able to write, but your penmanship will be ugly. The wound under your left eye is not dangerous to your eye, but steel is going to come out for years and will be stressful." (AUTHORS NOTE: Today is July 12, 2012 and I drove my F150 165 miles today. When I stopped and got out, I had to hold on to the side of the truck for three or four minutes, before I could put my right foot down.) Shortly after the doctor left a Major from Battalion operations, 1st Battalion, 8th Infantry came by to see me. He said, "Sergeant white, we did a recon of the battle site, especially that south finger where your platoon and fourth platoon got into the NVA base area. We were in a chopper escorted by several gunship's. We flew at tree top high and were a little tense. I guess the gunship's kept the NVA from shooting at us, if they are still there. You know of course, the enemy always makes determined attempts to carry off their dead, so we won't know how many they lost. We counted fifty two dead NVA that we could see from the top of the triple canopy."

There was an ugly incident after the Major left, a nurse showed up with one of those pony tails that came down to below her waist. She was a 1st Lieutenant, standing beside my bed she said; "Oh, you poor boys! those damn lifer's took you back to that PLEI TRAP place again. They are horrible." Suddenly a doctor burst in. He yelled;"you damn bitch, I have told you before about this shit." He continued, you get your stupid ignorant ass out of here and never come back." Well what the hell, maybe I am horrible, at least a bunch of NVA think so. I am sure some of the badly wounded troops in the ward were upset by all the uproar. Things were tense in the ward and then the Flea showed up. He had one arm in a sling and a huge bandage on it, but was walking. He had a big milkshake in one hand and that wiseass look on his face, that he always had when he was going to harass someone. He said;

"I don't know about you sergeant's, you get yourselves wounded where you can't get around, and can't eat and drink the good stuff." Then he disappeared, but was soon back, pushing a tray table with two cheeseburgers and two chocolate milkshakes for me and Horton. Because of where Horton was hit, I don't think he could handle the cheeseburger but he hit the milkshake hard. After all that, an older grey haired man came in and asked for me. He introduced himself as being from MACV, in the after action report section. I thought maybe CIA, and he wanted to know the details of the battle. We talked for about an hour, especially about my impression of the NVA's capabilities.

The day was getting a little long for me. I was glad and still amazed, that A Company only had two killed, and two more killed from the tracers, and the brigade sergeant major made five. I lost count of the wounded, but it was too many. I knew whatever remained of A Company, they were fighting and I hoped all were okay. Late in the afternoon, I felt like hell but was cheered up, when suddenly Lieutenant LePeilbet hobbled up, bent over and in pain. He told me, the doctor said he needed to move around. The doctor's had removed pieces of steel, from his spine. He was very lucky to be able to walk and would recover. He said," he was being reassigned to MACV, as his six months in the field, were past anyway." In NAM, the MACV policy was for officer's, to only have six months combat duty as the army had more officer's, than they had combat slots. The aim, was to get as many as possible combat experience. The tour in NAM, for the troop's was twelve months and then home and discharge, unless they reenlisted. The career NCO CORP, in the army and marine infantry, were in NAM in the bush their entire tour. They went back, over and over, until killed or too badly wounded to stay in the infantry. The NCO casualty rate, was what created the need for the shake and bake sergeants, many who did well. I tried several times, to get Jerry Loucks promoted but was told, he had too many previous breeches of authority and was insubordinate. In the army of that time, an NCO could not recommend a man for a decoration, he could only write a supporting letter. Hell, if I could, I would have recommended Loucks for the Medal of Honor. Lieutenant LePeilbet told me he had written me up for the DSC, and Horton for the Silver Star. We both got Silver Stars and LePeilbet the DSC. If I could have made recommendations for medals, I would have written up that African American medic who covered me with his body. I was just glad to have recovered enough, for the 1970 duck hunting season at Ft Riley.

That first hospital day in the body cast was hell. It was a few days before I could eat much. I was put on Darvon, a super aspirin that second day, and it was probably the same with Horton. The care in the army hospital at ENARI was certainly sufficient, but not superb by any means. After a week or so, I was flown to the hospital at CAM RANH Bay, and the care was much better. The army was short of doctors and all kinds of medical personnel. Most doctors whose education was subsidized by the government, chose to go where it was safer and easier duty, such as the navy and air force. At CAM RANH Bay, I had a Colonel for a nurse who was a red head about forty or so. She was very nice and took good care of me. The South Vietnamese army (ARVN), was responsible for security at CAM RANH Bay. I don't know who in hell made that decision. I was flown on to Japan in a few days. Sometime after I left a VC sapper team broke through the ARVN security, and got into the hospital. They murdered a number of nurses and wounded. The marine's, flew in a marine rifle company of hard guy's, they quickly wiped out the VC sapper's.

The next day and many thereafter were painful, nerve wracking and most certainly depressing. During my long recovery, I saw many things that do not reflect credit on the United States. The week or more at the hospital at ENARI were of course the most painful. When I was flown to CAM RANH Bay hospital, it was to get me ready for a long flight to Japan. I spent a few days, at the air force hospital at YAKOTA and had my own TV and a corpsman by my bed at all times. The care in the air force hospital was far superior to the army hospital's I experienced. I finally heard from my sweet wife. First she had been told by the Red Cross that I had been killed in action. Then that I was still alive, but had lost my right arm. After the delightful time, of watching Japanese TV and the Japanese Baseball games, I was flown to the army hospital at Yokohama. The chopper that took me to Yokohama was the most dilapidated piece of crap, I ever saw. After all I had survived; to get killed in a chopper crash in Japan would be the height of irony. The chopper did however take me by Mount Fujiyama, snow cap and all. The Yokohama Hospital was the worst army medical facility I have ever seen. The building was like the old army prefab barracks with asbestos and all. It was heated by coal and was cold and cheerless. We had an African American sergeant who was the only corpsman for our entire ward, of approximately forty or so beds. He referred to himself as soul brother number one. We also had an old kindly Japanese lady that washed our feet. One day, SB #1 was blowing about his sexual success of the night before, in the red light district of Yokohama. The old lady was washing my feet. She looked up, and winked and said in pigeon; "he #ten bullshit."

I am sure many wounded combat vets had similar hospital experiences to mine. In the Yokohama ward, there were a number of critical cases mixed in with troop's who were already on their way to recovery. There was a young troop in the bed to my right, who had a terrible experience each day. He had been hit in his right leg, below the knee and the bones were in small pieces. The infection in his leg had to be cured, or his leg would be amputated. We only had two Doctor's and two nurse's for the entire ward plus sb#1. One afternoon the kid saw the doctor coming with a large pan and a large syringe. The kid knew what it was and started shaking and crying. To see a man cry in NAM made me angry, but I felt sorry for this young troop. A nurse laid down on him to keep him as still as they could while the doctor flushed out the wound. It smelled like rotted flesh, I don't know what came of the poor kid. Then a night or so later, I heard the troop in the bed across from me get the death rattle. I yelled loudly and cursed loudly trying to get a doctor or nurse to rush to our ward, but they were too late. There was a soldier, hanging up in a leather contraption just outside the door to our ward. A nurse turned him around every hour and he was most certainly dead with a horrific head wound. One day his grandparent's came to the hospital to see him. The old lady lost it and ran into our ward screaming and cursing several of the troop's broke down.

I would say the Army let itself get pushed around by those grandparent's there probably was a congressman involved. The patient had obviously been brain dead for some time. The grandparent's caused the Army medical unit to keep his heart beating. The old woman should have known better than to cause many of the wounded to get upset, by running into a ward full of badly wounded men. The Doctor's were certainly not to blame and the two old folks finally were told to make the trip. I was in traction in an attempt to pull the two ends of my femur closer together. They gave me an XRAY every few days to determine if I was healing. The War, the wounds, the daily tragedy of it all on top of this obviously decrepit hospital were a heavy load. Then one day a Doctor came to my bed with what looked like a wood drill in his hand. Suddenly a nurse laid down on me without a word being said. I did not get any kind of shot or pill for pain. Without saying a word, the Doctor cut and drilled a hole through my leg and femur end, about two inches above my knee. I was utterly amazed, there was no pain. Someone reading this narrative might find some of the events I relate, very hard to believe. I promised in the first chapter that this narrative would be absolutely factual and no bullshit. As God is my witness,these are the facts. When the Black Train runs, it always leaves pain, sorrow, death and destruction, in its wake. I had taken my war to the limit and the results were sometimes shocking. Soon I got the word, another chopper ride back to YAKOTA air force base was coming up. You guessed it, on the same worn out chopper. At least I saw Mount Fujiyama again.

When I got to YAKOTA, I got the same great treatment and food. I was immediately told, I would be flown to the United States the next day. The bird was another C141 and we were flying through Elmendorf air force base in Alaska, then to Scott air force base in Illinois. Before the wounded were loaded they gave us all something to make us sleep. There was a Doctor on board and several flight nurses. There were all types of emergency equipment on board. I remember we were flying at night and several times a nurse checked me. I was in a very hard uncomfortable body cast, and my femur ends were still over an inch apart. When we landed at Elmendorf, probably to refuel, the door was opened and the chilled Alaskan air blew in. The cold air seemed so clean and refreshing. The Officers Wives Club got on board with milkshakes and sandwiches for everyone. I had so much medication in me I threw up and my windpipe became blocked. The Doctor and nurses worked quickly to make my breathing easier. I was sick the rest of the way to Scott air force base. The lobby of the hospital was crowded with wounded men in pain and the air force medical staff was working hard. So far I have avoided a very unpleasant truth; wounded men with the added stress of travel, usually become unable to void their bowels or urinate. The situation at Scott was very hard on both the wounded and the medical staff. Wounded combat veteran's have a lot tougher time than civilians in a hospital at home.

The scene at the Scott hospital lobby and receiving was not happy. I looked around at shocked families who were unprepared for the sight of badly wounded men. Men who were mostly in their twenties who looked forty. We were all including yours truly sick from war, wounds, travel and the stress of it all. Many including me were dirty and smelly from blood, pus, drainage and the inability to bathe. Men in body casts or heavily bandaged, with bullet wounds in their legs and arms, cannot care for themselves. All were in pain, blood and pus running out of bandages. It was a pile of suffering humanity and stunk from it. Stay with me reader, there is still a lot of harm from the long Black Train ride ahead. Men don't go to the pit and return the same men. I lay there on my litter and corpsman that was an air force master sergeant tried to help me. Later on, I had a good bed even though they could not cut me out of the body cast, until I got to my recovery hospital. Some will be a little shocked to learn the Army's method of removing a wounded troop from a body cast was with a chain saw. The saw only a little smaller than the ones used in logging. Sometime in the evening, after I was fed I was informed I would be flown to Ft Riley, Kansas the next morning to Irwin Army Hospital. That is the first time I have typed "Irwin Army Hospital" in forty years and I can feel the old stressful rage working in me. I tried to watch TV that night, but was so tense and sore from the many days in that body cast that a doctor gave me a sedative to knock me out. The next morning I and several others were taken to the tarmac to board the flight, which transported the wounded to hospital's around the country.

The inside of the aircraft was painted with various peaceful scenes, I guess some head doctor thought that would have a calming effect on men, many of whom had recently been killers. It was a smooth short ride with good looking flight nurses on board. It must have been about 1000 on someday in April 1969 when we landed at the civilian airstrip at Manhattan Kansas. I learned later on that the Fort Riley Airstrip would not take a large jet. The jet taxied way off to the other side of the field, well away from the tower or any other hangers and buildings. When the aircraft stopped, we sat there a few minutes with the engines running. Then my litter was carried off and set down on the side of the strip, near some trees. Then they took off a young Indian kid who was hit several times in the chest and stomach. The kid was unconscious, very pale and looked BAD, Black train Bad. Then a flight nurse got off and walked toward me with tears running through her mascara. I looked at her and thought, THE GRUNTS ARE ABOUT TO GET FUCKED. This would be a good time not to read this paragraph to children. The nurse bent down and knelt beside me and said;"sergeant, the Fort Riley ambulance meets us here every day but today for some reason they are late. We have called them and they assure us the ambulance must be very close." She went on, "your vitals are fine and he is okay, we must hurry on to San Antonio to Brooke Army Hospital as we have critical burn cases on board." She got back on board and away they went. WELCOME HOME FROM NAM.

WELL WELL WELL, 531 days in NAM had made me a very tough, violent, and cynical man who could laugh at the unlaughable.

If that had not been the case I would not be alive today. Remember, I said it would all be facts and most facts are not pleasant. We lay there awhile, maybe fifteen or twenty minutes. It was a nice warm, sunny Kansas spring day,and a dove flew by. I thought to myself, this must be what most people call peace; if so, I don't need any of it. Suddenly the Indian kid started choking and fighting to breath. Oh yes, I had heard it many times, the DEATH rattle. I tried to reach him with my bandaged right hand, but they had put him down too far from me. Then, I yelled at the top of my lungs, a terrible scream hoping to cause him to jump and clear his windpipe. The death rattle grew louder, luckily I found a rock and flung it at him and was lucky enough to hit him in the side. He jerked and it seemed to clear his windpipe and he settled down a little. I listened to him and thought the death rattle was gone, at least for now. I lay back in my body cast, in pain and misery and felt the rage began to grow and I began to curse. I cursed Lyndon Johnson, Hubert Humphrey, Richard Nixon and Spiro Agnew and every American who had sent us through that hell on earth to the inferno. Then, I cursed life itself and every wrong I thought I had received in my life. I cursed every bad day in my life and most of all those American war protesters. If the communist had ever overcome America, they would have shot those traitorous bastards before they got around to guys like me. I cursed Jane Fonda and the Chicago Seven or five or whatever in hell they were. I cursed the Ivy League school cowards and every so called liberal who had ever lived. I cursed the Weathermen and the Berkeley and Madison, Wisconsin traitors. I finally went almost unconscious with froth and spit dripping from my mouth.

Finally the army ambulance showed up with two scared looking privates in it. It was a miracle I had not had a stroke and I was so exhausted, I just glared at them. No, it does not seem funny now if you were an infantryman in NAM you would understand. When we got to Irwin Army Hospital's lobby, the Indian kid's mother and father were there to meet him. They were very nice looking people who looked like Native Americans, not these white interlopers with very little Indian blood. When his mother saw him she screamed and almost fainted and her husband had to grab her. I was by myself on a gurney off to the side. I pushed myself up on my elbows and yelled loudly, "lady, lady, come over here! I want to tell you what your Nation, your Army, and your Government almost did to your boy!" The hospital Sergeant Major was standing nearby and whispered to a corpsman, "get that sonofabitch upstairs fast!" yes indeed welcome home from the NAM. I lay for several hours at the far end of a dimly lit lonely ward. Lying there alone, with no Doctor, Nurses, or medication but that's all right because I was a real tough boy. Finally as I knew it was late, I started yelling and cursing and believe it or not a Nurse showed up. Yes indeed the American people were welcoming home their boy's from the NAM.

The Nurse, who came to check me out proved to be far too nice to be subjected to such filthy garbage as was coming out of my mouth. I am ninety per cent to blame the American people can have the other ten per cent. She said; "my lord who are you and how long have you been back here?" She was probably in her forties and a Lieutenant Colonel. Trying to suppress my anger, I told her just enough that she understood that here was a wounded combat veteran in need of assistance. She looked at my records and said; "try to be calm, I will be right back." In a short time she was back with some pills, and a big hamburger and milkshake. I took the pills, and ate the hamburger and drank the shake of course. I immediately felt the pain start to go and a deep lassitude start to set in. She leaned over and whispered in my ear, "Sergeant, if you have any personal honor at all, you will never tell a living soul I gave you medication without a Doctor's order." She went on, "I have enough time to make full Colonel before I retire, but if what I have just done became known I would be lucky to retire a Major." I said; "lady and you are a real lady, man can't sweat the NAM and you sure don't have to sweat this." I never told a living soul, except my wife ten years or more later. I didn't notice her name badge but saw her walking down the ward weeks later. I was cleaned up, and she did not notice me but she sure as hell did not need to worry about that incident. When I thought about her, I had the feeling she was an angel. The next morning after the warm welcome home, I was feeling much better as I knew they would get me out of that body cast and help me clean up.

On toward the middle of the morning, a corpsman showed up at my bed and took me on a gurney downstairs to a room with what looked like a hot tub in it. He left and a young specialist came in with what looked like a chain saw, but was smaller. I thought to myself, this looks like a bad deal for grunts. The young troop fired up the saw and started trying to cut the body cast off of me. He got scared and started shaking and crying, and yours truly was not feeling all that chipper. Then an older Doctor, a Major, came in and said, "kill that saw." thank the good lord for Major's. He told the young troop,"it's okay son, I will take care of this." A nurse came in and the Major told her to get a nerve pill for the specialist, and looking at me he added, "get a shot of morphine for the sergeant." Seems funny as all hell now but it was not amusing at the time. That was the last shot of morphine I have had in my 75 year life, but it was needed. After I relaxed the doctor cut the body cast off of me and the nurse helped me get cleaned up. The Doctor came back in and introduced himself. He was all business but if it had not been for him, I would have never been able to walk again. He was just doing his military obligation but was an orthopedic specialist, and was getting a great deal of experience in a short time, since Irwin Army was the orthopedic center. When I got back to the ward a corpsman brought me a phone and I called my sweet wife Hope. Since I was a platoon sergeant and wounded, I got quarters quickly. That made it possible for Hope to bring our two children and move to Fort Riley from Oklahoma. The corpsman who brought me the phone was a good Christian, and after I could limp without a cane he took me on my first pheasant hunt.

The days passed slowly at the orthopedic ward at Irwin Army Hospital but not without several disgusting incidents. Troop's looking at long hospital stays are assigned to the Medical Holding Company which is part of the post headquarters unit. The medical holding company had a Captain for a company commander. He was young and seemed like a good officer and had a wife and little children. As the long years of Vietnam passed by, the discipline of the Army eroded. There was hardly any drug use in the bush when I was there, but the base camps had really bad drug problems. This led to dangerous incidents with hand grenades and racial problems at the base camps. There was a definite implosion of discipline and competent performance of duty. We went into Vietnam with a very fine Army and came out with an Army whose combat performance was dangerously reduced. One day soon after I arrived at the hospital a black soldier high on drugs, broke thousands of dollars worth of stained glass windows. The worst was yet to come in the barracks for outpatient troops, a white sergeant told a black soldier to empty a trash can. I don't remember exact details, but the black troop wound up in the company orderly room with a pistol and shot the Captain dead. The first sergeant walked into the orderly room just after it happened and courageously disarmed the murderer. I don't remember the general court martial sentence, but it should have been death.

Incidents like this, led to heavily armed military police on every ward and in all parking lots 24/7. Not long after, my wife Hope and our two children arrived there. My bed had been moved out in the hall so my room could be cleaned. I was lying there about half asleep, when suddenly I saw an angel with a child's hand in each of hers floating down the hall toward me. It was one of the happiest days of my life. Hope was twenty seven then and really pretty; UH UH haf caf, THAT'S not to say she isn't now. She was in a lovely dress and high heels and seemed to float down the hallway to me. After we got settled down, I would not let her come to the hospital at night. Drugs have done awful things to our country and are still tearing this country apart. Hope has always been a worker and was soon working every day for the Red Cross. She is one of those ladies that always have a sympathetic ear and good advice for troubled friends. While at the Red Cross, she met the wife of the assistant post commander who was a General Officer. They became super close friends sharing all their secrets. I had never taken Hope into the Army's social system and she never thought about the social distance, most officers had been trained to believe existed between officers and enlisted. When the General found out about his wives close friendship with the wife of a platoon sergeant he demanded that she break it off. Hope was really hurt by the situation, and the General's wife was crying when she told Hope they could not be friends anymore and rushed out of our quarters sobbing. I of course was still in the hospital and Hope's eyes were red when she told me about it. The situation pissed me off since my wife had been hurt, but there was nothing I could do about it. Well hell, what a switch from the long Black Train to a soap opera.

April 1969 gave way to May and I had been in bed almost sixty days. At least now I was clean and in traction with my right leg but could move the rest of my body freely. In NAM TET' 69 had come and gone with the usual result. The NVA was falling back over the border after heavy losses, of course leaving enclaves of sizable bodies of infantry and artillery deeply dug in and heavily camouflaged. The 101st Airborne was still operating in the AShau valley against a large NVA force. During the month of May they found them in force at AP BIA Mountain, hill 937 now known as, Hamburger Hill. The westerly side of the hill went across the Laotian Border. The 101st leadership ever mindful of the NVA hill trap maneuver hit them with several battalions and sufficient reserves. Heavy artillery fire and airstrike's were also used. The NVA was dug in deep and it was the kind of battle they liked with the border right behind them. If the shit got too deep they could fall back to safety. The battle cost the 101st over 300 casualties including both killed and wounded; the NVA left several hundred dead on the hill when the 101st carried the hill by assault. The media was quick to name hill 937 "Hamburger Hill." In Washington, Senator Edward Kennedy had harsh criticism for the commander of the operation, for not just using the B52's. Politicians in Washington never seem to understand that if you want to win and they did not, the infantry has to finish it. The Colonel who directed the battle said to the media, "my orders were to find the enemy and fight them. I found them at hill 937 and that was where we fought them." Aerial bombing cannot win a war alone bombing is a part of the combined arms team.

Laying there in that hospital was both boring and frustrating and I had a feeling of being useless. The War was going full tilt and I was just lying there. At least I had a good looking nurse, her name was Captain Carter. There were two beds in each room and one day, she was in the room at the other bed with her back to me. I crumpled up a piece of paper and threw it under my bed. She saw it and said,"damn, sergeant white, you did that on purpose." I replied, "I did what?" She frowned and crawled under my bed to get the paper. When she was completely under, I pushed the metal safety panel down and she could not get out. She started yelling for the corpsman to get her out. I got my ass chewed out of course, and yes a mature man should not do crap like that but it shows the extent of my boredom. After she stopped trying to yell at me she almost cried from embarrassment and that made me feel lowdown. The hospital at Fort Riley was a cleaner, modern and much nicer building than any hospital I had been in yet. There were just barely enough Doctor's and Nurse's to operate the facility. I was lucky in that I had the Major, an orthopedic specialist whose name I wish I could remember. By mid May, the x-rays showed my femur ends were growing closer together. The Doctor had them giving me milkshakes with every meal for the calcium. The Army was bringing back a Brigade of the Big Red One to Fort Riley from NAM. I guess the withdrawal was starting to take place leading to Vietnamization. The Doctor told me that I might not make a full recovery.

I continued to heal looking forward to Hope's every day visit. After the armed military police were stationed throughout the hospital and the parking areas, I heard no more of violence in the area. The hospital was a dull routine, although I did experience one unsavory incident. Late one night a Nurse who was on duty came into my room. I had seen her before and there was something about her I did not like. The other guy in my room was sleeping quietly on the other side of the room. She saw that I was awake and slipped her hand underneath my covers and rubbed my left leg. She said,"sergeant is there anything I can do for you?" I said; "lady, there is not a damn thing you can do for me." Well don't everyone laugh, like all infantry platoon sergeants I am no moral giant but there are some things beyond decency. She quickly hit the door and I never said anything about it to anyone. The only medication I received after

April was one Darvon a day. One night some nurse, maybe the sexaholic, messed up all the prescriptions on the ward. I knew what was brought to me was not my usual, especially as I had not been getting anything at night. Knowing there was a mistake I didn't take any of it. Then I had to lay awake all night as there was a wild uproar of yelling, laughter and singing until daylight. I was a little troubled by what I saw on my right leg x-rays. The ends of the femur were getting close but my leg was full of shrapnel. There were several pieces that were as large as the head of a one half inch bolt. I could count as many as fifty five. My right wrist was healed up but was a little stiff. My left ring finger was unusable and still painful. I was never able to wear a wedding band after healing without the skin graft bleeding. I had shrapnel in small pieces come out under my left eye for twenty years.

I was released from the hospital on Memorial Day of 1969, 79 days after being hit. The x-ray that morning showed the two femur ends connected by a thin sliver of bone, the size of a pencil lead. I told the Major there was no way I could get up without the sliver breaking. I had heard of patients getting up too soon and their leg breaking again at bedside. The Major laughed and said there was little likelihood of the bone breaking. He said that sliver seen on the x-ray was far stronger than I could imagine. When I swung my right leg very slowly over the side of the bed, it seemed like a huge amount of blood rushed down to my foot. My leg felt like it weighed 100 pounds and would pull the femur apart. The doctor laughed and said, "Sarge, I know what you're thinking. Sit there for five minutes and things will get more normal." Hope came in soon after to take me home to our quarters. One of the rehab specialists came in about that time and showed me the proper way to use the crutches. They took me to the lobby in a wheelchair and Hope picked me up at the door. We had a 1968 Pontiac Lemans that was a fine car and I learned to drive using my left foot. I was then an outpatient coming into to rehab five times a week.

Memorial Day weekend 1969 came and went and I was happy to be home with my family. There will probably be Veteran's who read my narrative and are familiar with Fort Riley. My quarters were at the corner of Jackson and Custer Hill road. We were on Jackson facing south and down the hill from the Custer Hill elementary school. We had two level quarters as that was all that was available when Hope got there. To go upstairs, I had to set down on the bottom step and using both hands and my left leg propel myself up and down stairs. We took the kids swimming in Manhattan one day and I did not get in the water as my wounds were not completely healed up. I was sitting on a reclining chair in the warm sun and a little girl said; "mommy, look at that man's leg and pointed." I was a little embarrassed and went to the dressing room and dressed. Getting around on crutches was a chore, but I had developed an exercise program for myself. Every day after rehab I walked two miles in the quarter's area on the crutches. I had to work out to make a full recovery. My normal weight was in the mid 150s and when I got out of the hospital, I weighed 195. I went on a diet Hope came up with and lost thirty pounds in a month but still needed to lose ten more. I got off the crutches and to a cane in mid September. Then in the first week of October I got off the cane. I had a real bad limp at first and was in moderate pain. I had gone to Oklahoma and went dove hunting on the cane, and almost fell when I took a shot. Duck season came in late October at Fort Riley and there is a great public hunting area where the Republican River comes in to the west end of Lake Milford. There were a lot of flooded corn fields there with thousands of Mallards. I bought some decoys and already had a Remington twelve guage and went hunting by myself. I fell down wading to put out the decoys and had to use my gun like a base ball bat to get up. Okay time to get back in the Army and the doctor said; "what's the hurry haven't you done enough?" I had a permanent three profile so there would be no more infantry for me or that's the way it was supposed to be. I talked the Doctor into restoring me to duty status at the end of December.

Since I was a combat veteran, and had been an instructor at Texas A&M, I was assigned to the fifth army NCO academy as an instructor, in January of 1970. I taught map reading and small unit infantry tactics. I had my own office and it was across the street from the cavalry museum and down the street from General Custer's house, which was still used as quarters. Then the Army decided to upgrade the NCO corp. I was the only NCO at the academy that had college hour's, of which I had sixty. So guess who got to teach the exciting public speaking classes. Luckily at that time the Army found a young draftee who had just finished college with BA in English, if memory serves me well. His name was Randy Anderson from Minnesota and as an added bonus he liked to hunt ducks and was a right wing fanatic. We worked together on the speech classes. I was a good Bull Shitter but would have never made it without private Anderson, otherwise known as Super A. When no one else was around Anderson referred to me as Super Chief. What in hell would Jerry Loucks think about that? He or Sergeant Horton would have probably said, "Sarge, it just don't sound right."

The year 1970 passed easily and peacefully for me for the most part. However I was watching TV at home and the news featured an anti war demonstration. One section that really stood out was a swine with a rag around his head, probably thinking he looked like a freedom fighter and yelling; "GET YOUR GUNS". I yelled at the top of my lungs, "I wish you scum would get your guns." Then I was yelling, "We have been killing the wrong people." It's a good thing I did not have my shotgun loaded and by my side, as I might have shot the TV. I managed to jog very slowly, a mile in combat boots in January. It hurt like hell, but I went on from there. There was an old sergeant at the academy who was a real good guy but unhappily was dying of heart disease. He had a female black & white pointer not quite a year old named Lucy. He knew I hunted and I had told him once that my father had been a dog trainer. He wanted me to take Lucy so she would have a good home. I did, and she made the best quail dog I ever had in a lifetime of hunting. The first night we had her at our quarters she cried all night. I thought Hope was going to cry too. While 1970 was not a bad year, I had a hard decade there in the 70s. During my time at Riley, we danced and partied a lot at the NCO club. Many might take issue with this statement but I said I would speak the truth. During the entire time after the War to my retirement on August 30, 1978, I did not hear one career NCO say one word about PTSD. In the chapter to come I will get back to that. In the summer of 1970, the sergeant who controlled of the RVN POR school retired. The POR School was the Vietnam preparation course for troops on their way and was attached to the NCO academy. I was assigned against my wishes and took over the school. I gave it my very best to give the best instruction and best information about personal action's a young man had to be prepared for in NAM. I also had included a field problem on patrolling and the ambush and counter ambush in the course. There was only two weeks for each group. In NAM, I saw several FNG's who when under their first enemy fire could not reload their M-16's. I made sure those young soldiers could.

In April, 1970, I was awarded the Silver Star for my actions on March 12th, 1969. I had been recommended for the Distinguished Service Cross but received the Silver Star instead. Hell, if I had been a second Lieutenant I might have got the MOH. Just talking to hear myself talk, the Army in my opinion was not as even handed, on medals and awards to enlisted men as to officers. That also is debatable; I was supposed to be awarded the Silver Star by the Major General that commanded Fort Riley at his office. The General was so drunk his aide had to make the award. Well Vietnam was very hard on the US Army. My father was 75 at the time, and with his girlfriend had driven up to Riley from Ardmore, Oklahoma for the ceremony. Out east of Wichita on the Kansas Turnpike he got in the wrong lane and was going east in the west bound lane. It must have taken half the Kansas Highway Patrol to get him stopped. He was still pissed at the ceremony. One of the Patrol Officers had said to him, "SIR, ARE YOU LEAVING KANSAS SOON?"

When 1971 came around I still had a late evening limp and dropped things with my hands and put up with some degree of pain. Normally when you get a permanent three profile it precludes you from serving in combat arms, especially in the infantry. In February 1971 I had been restored to duty thirteen months. Suddenly and from out of the blue, I came up on levy Infantry Korea. This just indicates how short the Army was of senior infantry sergeant's. I knew what the terrain was in Korea and knew there was no way I could keep up with a rifle company in those hills, in summer heat or winter snow. I was also concerned I might reinjure my right leg and never recover completely. I put in a request to be removed from the levy citing my profile, my injuries and combat record plus two hardship tours in a row. The answer came in a telephone call from a Colonel in the assignments section, Department of the Army. He was cursing and said; "forget it, sergeant, you're going." I am over ten percent Cherokee and at the time Senator Fred Harris from Oklahoma was a big guy in the Cherokee Nation. I gave old Fred a call and a letter. I was off the levy in less than two weeks. If the Colonel had not cursed and yelled at me I would have just gone to Korea. The Colonel called again, and this time called Sergeant White a "God Damned Sonofabitch". I had no idea what the Colonel's service record was, but sergeant white had the Combat Infantry Badge, Silver Star, Bronze Star with Oak Leaf Cluster, Purple Heart with Oak Leaf Cluster, that's two each, the Vietnam Cross of Gallantry (unit citation) and the Meritorious Service Medal and all the goody-goody stuff. Besides those were fighting words and also a civil rights violation. I said, "Colonel, you're getting in deep in the civil rights area." He cursed me again and said, "Next levy you're on it!" and slammed the phone down.

I did not call Fred again. However, not long after the incident the new all volunteer army was announced. The Army needed recruiters badly and wanted combat soldiers if they could get them. Well, well, I had finished the career course and with family and all, reported into the Oklahoma City Recruiting District Headquarters in the American General Building on northwest 6th and Robinson, in June, 1971. The American General Building was one block north of a building construction site. The new building was going to be named the Murrah Building and was a Federal Building. In a few pages I will get back to the Murrah Building, as I finish my army career in the chapter to come. I was a natural and fit right in becoming the top new recruiter in the southwest region in 1971 and 1972. My area in the beginning was Logan County with Guthrie as the county seat, just north of Oklahoma City Metro. We had recruiters who were afraid to be on the street in uniform. I never backed up from any of the vile bastards, who wanted to yell insults and call names at those who had served our country.

Sometimes I felt like I had found another war at home. Recruiting was a very stressful occupation and I usually worked at it at least six full days a week. All that had happened to me in my army life was leading to one hell of a finish to my army career.

— Chapter Ten —

Aftermath

In the Nation that is not
Nothing stands that stood before
There revenges are not forgot
And the hater hates the more
-A.E. Houseman

I recruited from June 1971 until I retired on August 30, 1978. I actually had twenty years active on August 1st, 1978 but had learned too much about the Army personnel center, so I stayed the extra month to make sure I was credited with twenty years. I learned a lot about salesmanship and prospecting from recruiting. In addition, I learned a great deal about selling myself and a product. In my life after the Army, I used all these factors in a twenty one year real estate career, as a broker. The seven years and two months in recruiting command were filled with tremendous stress, violent anger, lots of laughs and making contacts in the Oklahoma City area that helped me in later years. When I started in Logan County, since I was a rural recruiter, I received a 1970 Ford to drive. The Army paid for the gasoline and also my medical bills, if Tinker air force base hospital was not convenient. The Government also leased a townhouse for me and my family, that was nice. One thing I used to my advantage as a recruiter and real estate broker was as an after dinner speaker, at all the local business and charitable organizations. My first year recruiting was anything but dull. I recruited fifty six high school graduates, the first year. The Army was out for their definition of quality, having forgotten General Patton's dictum. Patton liked the jailbird's better than the school boy's, for fighting men. I also put together a slide program about The Battle of Little Big Horn and George Armstrong Custer that helped me get into all the high schools. Oklahoma being Indian country, I had to be careful in my language and my facts about the Indian wars. Sometimes parents would come in and listen to me. Service recruiting has always been under the watchful eye of the media, who were looking for illegal enlistments and immoral activity. I can say, without reservation that I never put a felon in the Army, or worked to clean one up. I did see a few activities that could not pass muster where lawful recruiting was concerned. When I became a station commander and an area supervisor, I never, knowingly allowed illegal activities to take place. I can hear the old veteran's laughing now. I did see an old recruiter, not under my supervision make a passable birth certificate with a DA form

72 and a fifty cent piece on the AFEES stairs. This tale will get more interesting as I move along.

When I started recruiting, the Army was just trying to work the kinks out of the new system. This program was going to guarantee an enlistee a school, and a job or an assignment in a career field. Things were a little rocky at first, however time worked in our favor and most enlistment contracts were honored. The enlistments were for two, three, or four years. There were enlistment bonuses, of $1500 or $2500 for combat arms with a guaranteed duty assignment for a year. I have been out of the army thirty four years, so I hope my memory serves me well. In my assigned 1970 ford, I drove probably from one to two hundred miles each day. Many night's I was exhausted when I got home. Being a rural recruiter, I usually would bring my applicants to the AFEES and if they didn't go that day I had to take them home. AFEES (Armed forces entrance, examination station). Recruiters pay and benefits was a little more than a sergeant in a unit, but the only real perk was having your family with you. The 1970's as I wrote earlier was a tough decade for me. One of the first incidents that gave me a laugh later happened at the corner of north Pennsylvania and the northwest highway in Oklahoma City. I had stopped for a red light and had my window down. A college type with his windows down pulled up beside me and yelled, are you guys still killing babies over there? I calmly looked at him and replied;"HELL yes, we got fifty this morning!" He was stunned and looked a little sickly as he drove off. I almost got arrested on recruiting duty more than a few times. If the other recruiters wanted to take their shit, that was their business, but I didn't back up. I owed it to guys with names like Loucks, Horton, Pierce, Muck, and Novotny and so many more that I don't have room to type. I had to defend our personal honor. We had 59,000 that failed to make it back, and I owed it to them most of all.

Many the mornings in the 1970's as I stood in front of the mirror brushing my short haircut I looked down at my ribbons and CIB and said. "ok top soldier, don't hurt anyone today." I found out right quick that the American people didn't care jack shit about their own servicemen and woman. If I had ten dollars for every man or woman that shot me the finger, I would be a very rich dude. I liked to see the surprise on their faces, when I gave back much worse. I never got much flack from downtown since I was putting people in the Army. One day in my ford I stopped for a stop sign and a woman ran into my back bumper. She hit me so hard my neck was jerked and I was stunned. She walked up to my window and said, "Hell, you're not hurt" and roared off. I could not find my pen quick enough to get her tag number. When I first came to Oklahoma City all the clubs had nude dancers and I do mean NUDE. The first or second day, I was getting some training concerning AFEES processing, prior to going to work in my assigned area. Some of the recruiters who had been around awhile said, "white, let's go get a beer after duty hours." I have never drank much but to be friendly, I said, "okay." We went to a place named the "valley of the dolls" that the old timers referred to as the "valley of the dogs". Every woman in the place was stark naked, even the bartenders. Well it was the valley of the dog's all right.

Time marches on and in 1973 I was brought into Oklahoma City to be in charge of the North Penn Plaza recruiting station. A large chunk of the area recruited by North Penn was the most high income area of the Metro area. The Army at this time was afraid to use the word "quota". Instead we had "objectives". If a recruiter missed his objective a few times he was out. I made my personal Quota twenty seven months in a row and then with the quota only two short and still a week left, I had a bad kidney stone and was in the hospital for five days. I received a call from the Colonel saying;"what in hell was the matter with you this month?" The pressure on everyone in recruiting command was enormous, including all the officers as well as enlisted. We at one time had one of the most abusive Colonel's, I saw in the Army. He could insult you and not know he had. Referring to me, he said often in my hearing, "don boy's his name and lying, stealing, and cheating is his game." One day I had enough of that and said, "well sir, I think my record might suggest that fighting infantry wars is my game." The headquarters went silent, until the Colonel slapped himself on his leg and said, "By God,

White, you're right!" I don't know if I made him feel like an idiot or he was too dumb to know it. When I was outside and on the way to my car, I breathed a sigh of relief, having bearded the lion in his den and got away with it. I was still a Sergeant First Class e-7, and my family would have been hurt if I were to be reduced in rank. Every recruiter in the state walked on eggshells around that Colonel.

By 1973, my leg had healed and I could walk and run without pain. However as the years have passed, I have started having a lot of trouble with my leg and all my wounds. Oklahoma had missed badly the state objective for almost a year, and the chain of command made the recruiters lives, beyond stress. In a meeting with the area supervisor one day, the supervisor formerly in the signal corps, threatened to send anyone who could not make quota to the infantry. My big mouth was about to overload my hummingbird ass and I stood up and said; "Hell, send me I've been in the Infantry before." I felt a little bad about it later on as it was a cheap shot on my part. I was still one of the top producers in the entire region and knew I wasn't about to get sent anywhere. The advertising for the entire US Army recruiting command was contracted to a top Madison avenue advertising corporation named, NW Ayers. The US taxpayer was paying these guy's millions every year to handle our advertising. One day, after a meeting in which most of the recruiters complained about not getting any walk in's from the newspaper ads, I decided to check it out. North Penn, which was my station, didn't get walk ins anyway because we were in the high income area. I took the Daily Oklahoman and went in my office and with my feet on my desk read the ads. Hell, it hit me in a flash only people who already have been trained, look for work in the classifieds. Young people who join the Service's need training and are also LOOKING for work. The Army advertising should have been on the help wanted page. Big woo! A mere Sergeant had caught the suits with their ass hanging out, now I was going to take advantage of it.

I put my mind to it and wrote a five line help wanted ad that promised work, training and the GI Bill. All of these points were the simple truth, and in the simplest way told a young person where they could find what they needed. Of course, it was a recruiting ad for the Army with my name, station address, and phone number. Then myself, and the five sergeant's I supervised put up ten dollars apiece to pay for it. I did not want the downtown headquarters to know about it. I hustled the ad out to the Daily Oklahoman and paid to have it put in the help wanted section for the coming Saturday and Sunday. The Oklahoman had by far the state's biggest circulation. The sop, for Oklahoma recruiting command assigned each station a certain area to recruit in, and we were supposed to keep our prospecting in that area. Well, I was only advertising in the newspaper that was in my area, RIGHT? My station objective normally ran between 24 and 30 a month. The large recruiting stations in the state never made their quotas, unless a miracle happened. I was going to create a miracle. We usually missed station objective by three or four every month, even though I usually made my personal objective. I never said a word to headquarters or NW Ayers representative downtown, and told my recruiters to keep shut about it, period. The enlistments started pouring in from all over Oklahoma City metro and occasionally from out in the state. That month we needed thirty and put in thirty seven and held several, for the following month. My goodness, we were all six heroes and an officer was coming from region to interview me. Keeping a straight face which wasn't easy, I told him what he wanted to hear.

My answer was that we simply followed the rules of prospecting, selling, overcoming objections and closing. The NW Ayers rep downtown that did not like me anyway, tore up the classifieds in the Oklahoman, looking for my AD. The suit's STILL didn't get it and I kept the world's greatest soliciting operation operating. I don't remember how many months in a row we were the Oklahoma& world champ army recruiters. Finally, one of my men got pissed about something and ratted me out. When I heard I fired his ass, but it was too late. I was not surprised when the operations officer downtown called me to come down. I did not feel guilty about doing what I had done to make my station super, and told him so of course in a respectful manner. I also showed NW Ayers classified Ad and compared it to my simple help wanted AD. Toward the end of the conversation the Colonel came in and sat down behind me.

I had violated the sop and taken enlistment's from all the other areas as well as my own. The Major, leaned back with a big smile on his face and said, "it's great to see a sergeant who can think, but you have to share the Ad with all the other Oklahoma City stations on a week by week basis." In the end, I still had one of the highest production station's and NW Ayers had egg on their face. When I walked out of operations, I heard the Colonel guffaw and say, "like I always said;" don boy's his name and lying, stealing, and cheating is his game." OH well I just used kiss, keep it simple stupid.

Well, so much for recruiting high jinks. I was always straight forward with my enlistee. In recruiting command, where trouble was always just down the street, I had to look out for self and my men. Oklahoma City always fostered a patriotic reputation, but had plenty of young men who avoided the draft and hated the military to cover their shame. The front window of the station was shot out six times at night. They used either a twenty two rifle or a very powerful pellet gun. We also had to have our rank by our names in the phone book. I guess the powers that be were silly enough, to think young prospects would pick the recruiters out of the phone book, and call them at home to join up. Well you know the answer to that. We got all kinds of threatening calls after midnight. At least once every few day's I would be threatened or cursed. My kids were nervous about it and never told anyone at school that daddy was in the Army and especially, that dad was a NAM vet. The Vietnam War is like a huge tiger, always following you just a few steps behind and if you slip up, it will catch you. Many the night after midnight, I have told some sob, come on down bastard I would love to hurt you. Once at the state capital I was being harassed before I told the bastard, "Let's get it on". A highway patrolman told me to get the hell out of the building, saying nothing to the other guy. I leaned over and put my face by his pistol and looked up and smiled. That told him the only difference between us was I didn't have a gun. He had a slightly surprised look on his face when I left. I was a crazy sob in the 1970's and was lucky to get away with that one. Nobody could have lived through the combat I did and not be changed for the worse, in some way. There were so many incidents of harassment for being a NAM vet I can't remember them all.

One of the recruiters who worked for me was named Bowman. He was from Mississippi and had been badly injured in a chopper crash in NAM. He was going to his apartment one night after duty. He was alone; his wife was still in Mississippi. He was riding his Harley and lost control and hit a telephone pole. Somehow his right arm was cut off and he lay there in shock bleeding to death. Some Good Samaritan, in a pickup came by and picked him up and rushed him to the Baptist hospital emergency room. His arm was gone but they saved his life. We never found out who saved him. His wife was coming in by air from Jackson Mississippi, and I was there to pick her up in my army car. I picked her up and started for the hospital and told her about it as I drove. She was a very sweet nice young lady and she began to cry. I was going north on a four lane street toward the hospital. Some young punks about nineteen or twenty years old pulled up by me, and started yelling baby killing army shit. Instantly I went over the cliff and started screaming at them and followed them home. They jumped out and ran in the house. I stood in the front yard, cursing them and daring them to come out. I was out of my mind, until I saw she had buried her face in her hands. I jumped in the car and rushed her to the hospital. I felt so ashamed, until she said, "sergeant, don't worry about it, I know about the NAM." Hah, the Colonel said, "good job, white," when we arrived.

It sometimes seems like unpleasant happenings come in bunches. That afternoon I worked at the office until eighteen thirty, cold calling off my high school list. Everyone had gone and I locked the door and ran by the hospital to see Bowman. I stopped at the door to his room and seeing that he and his wife were in each other's arms and she was crying, I quietly slipped away. In a few weeks the Army gave him a medical discharge and he went home to Mississippi. This was a sad case that may have ended well. I found out through the local recruiter that within a week after he got home, the VA hired him at the hospital. So he had his medical retirement, VA disability and a job at the Veterans hospital. His wife had a job also, I heard her say something about it.

When I got to my car I was really feeling beat from the sadness and problems of the day. When I got in the car, I leaned back in my seat and said, "the evil thereof was enough for the day." But hell, the day wasn't over yet. Coming out of the Baptist hospital parking lot I turned out the North West highway towards home. About a mile or so down the road, I noticed a Lincoln continental was tailgating me and weaving around on the street. I was going a mile or two over the limit; it wasn't like I was going too slowly. The light was yellow at the next cross road and a policeman had someone stopped in the left turn lane. So I stopped as the yellow turned red. The guy behind me had a woman in the car with him and yelled, "don't stop, you army sonafabitch!"

This dumb bastard was drunk and hadn't noticed the cop. I got out of my car crazy mad and rushed back to his car. He quickly rolled up his windows and his woman panicked, begging him to shut up or so it seemed. I hit his window with my fist and yelled get out you dirty son I am going to hurt you. The COP, not even noticing that he was looking at a cinch DWI arrest says to me, "sergeant, get in that car and get out of here and I won't tell you again." I glared at him but said nothing and got in my car and drove off when the light changed. There was a golf course a mile down the road and I had pulled over waiting on the continental. When I saw him coming I stepped out in the road yelling but he jerked around me and roared off. I don't know how in hell I lived through the Seventy's. It was summertime and still daylight as I wearily turned into the drive of the townhouse area where I lived. I had to walk by the swimming pool on the way to my townhouse. As I walked beside the pool, a little girl was fighting the water in the middle and going down. I jerked off my shirt with my badges and ribbons and got rid of my billfold, and hit the water and pulled her out. Her mother came screaming out of a nearby doorway yelling; what are you doing to my little girl? Luckily for me, there were two women who were walking to the pool who saw everything and said; "lady, this sergeant just saved your little girls life she was going down for the third time." That little girl is forty years old now and lives in London. Well, one hell of a day ended with a good finish. I know I look like a good guy and hero in all this but remember, I am not telling you about my foul-ups.

After all these years I can still remember an uplifting moment in the middle of a snow and ice storm. I and three other recruiters in overcoats went around the corner from the office to a café and had coffee. I was driving and on the way back to the office I was in the right lane and a car pulled up beside us. The driving conditions were really bad but that old American motors junk that in town recruiters drove for some reason handled the ice and snow okay. The car besides us had four or five college boys in it, and they rolled down the windows and started the usual filth. There were no other cars nearby due to the road conditions. Suddenly the punk's car high centered and was stuck big time. There was no one behind us so I stopped and we jumped out. They rolled up their windows and locked the doors. While we were cursing them and daring them to get out we started rocking their car back and forth sideways. This went on for a few minutes and we really had it rocking. They were obviously scared and hunkered down in their seats. Finally a car came from behind in their lane and we pushed them clear and they roared away. We laughed ourselves silly and jumped back in the car and headed to the office. Recruiting went along with no real changes until Nixon signed the executive order stopping the draft. That made the Army and Marines all volunteer for sure. Recruiting got tougher after there was no longer a draft. One afternoon I was sitting in my office, which was located at the side of the plaza break area. The Snacky snack man came in the side door. He said; "Sarge, the clothing store next door is closed. Those old ladies lost seventy five cents in the machine and want it back. Will you watch for them and take it to them when they come in?" I said, "sure, not a problem." In a few minutes I saw them come in. I took the seventy five cents to them and said, "here is your change from the Snacky snack machine." One old lady turned around and said;"listen snacky snack man, you better get that damn machine fixed." Well, so much for medals, ribbons, and uniforms in the end you're just a Snacky Snack man.

In our complex was an Air Force and Marine office along with ours.

The air force had a female recruiter with a great body and legs. The guys being disgusting soldiers like yours truly, always ran to the window every time she walked out to her car. One day several of my men told me, she had been telling prospective recruits that if they joined the Army they would only learn to dig holes. The guys wanted to know if I could stop it in some way. Never one to pass up a challenge I gave it some thought. There was a small town and school fifty two miles northwest of the metro. I knew the air force recruited the rural area from their in town office's. I remembered seeing her in Logan County when I recruited there. I figured it was probable that was still in her area. I pulled out the Marshall Oklahoma High School list and picked out a name from the list that would be hardest to get to. I called the air force office and got her on the line. Using my southern accent I told her I was this kid and wanted to join the air force today. I told her I lived two miles north and one west of Marshall, knowing the blacktop ran out before it got there.

My recruiter's had heard my dialogue with her and we were lined up at the window to see what would happen. It was about one pm in the afternoon when she came out moving fast going for her car. When she roared out of the parking lot heading north, the guys cracked up and hit the floor. It must have been after six pm and we were working late when she came back in. Her car was covered in mud there was some even on top. When she got out of the car, we didn't run to the window. She was tired and dirty with mud on her uniform. She walked halfway to her office and stopped suddenly, looking at our office. After a moment she went on to her office, and we didn't hear anything more about digging holes. She knew if she accused us of setting her up we would just deny it. She would be broadcasting how foolish she was, without being sure it was me. I had another interesting incident with the Ardmore army recruiter. He was a really big guy with a gorilla reputation. I was always a small guy of just below average height and weighed 155. One of my best friends and hunting buddy in Ardmore sent his son to me in the city to join the Army. I was really surprised when he walked in the door and asked for me. Him being one of my best friend's sons I naturally enlisted him, and got him exactly what he wanted. Under those circumstances

I did not feel I was violating the standard operating procedure. One afternoon shortly afterward, I get a call from the Ardmore recruiter, just raving about how he was going to rough me up. I told him to come on up and we would see about that. I knew that this could be a real bad experience, but you never know about those small guys. That's one thing about the NAM when you had the black death in your hands you were anyone's equal. We were having a state sales conference at a south side motel the next week and I knew he would be there. On the drive down my guy's were cracking jokes about the next middleweight champ. When I pulled into the parking lot, there he was just getting out of his car. In those times there were a lot of hitchhikers on the roads. He pulled a girl out of his car by her arm. She looked to be late teens maybe twenty at most. She had a decent body but was filthy and had a backpack. He roughly pulled her over to the door of a room. When he pushed her inside, I heard him say in a bad way, "bitch, you better be in that bed when I get back." WOW, as God is my witness it's all true. I went into the conference room and whispered into the Sergeant Major's ear, there was a bad criminal action taking place at room number so and so. I told him, he and the Colonel needed to check it out right now. The Sergeant Major said who is it? I told him and added a few details. In just moments he and the Colonel and the executive officer left the room. In a little while, I saw the Ardmore recruiter drive out of the parking lot without the girl. The Colonel and Major came back into the conference room. In a little while a civilian in a suit came in and asked for the Colonel, and there was a lady in slacks with badge and pistol with him. They talked outside and a little later I saw the girl leave in a car with the policewoman. I knew the girl was going to be okay, and probably sergeant white also.

During the mid 1970's I was transferred to a position at the downtown American general building in the AFEES /armed forces entrance examination station/ as the senior Army guidance counselor. Hmmmm, what on earth is that? I was the senior closer for the entire state of Oklahoma with two other closers working for me. Some would call that the Super T.O.man to give it a car business slant. My job was to take army applicants as they came to the AFEES and get them tested, through a physical and if qualified for the army get them sold on a job and ship them as soon as possible. This was a difficult high pressure position, and in addition to the sale and close, I had to threaten them with death, hell and the grave if they were concealing a moral or physical disqualification. If they were, send them home to their recruiter. It was a job that could keep you up at night. I usually left home at six am at the latest and left the AFEES to drive home at the earliest seven pm. There were two other noteworthy happenings in my army life in the mid 1970's. The St Louis District Recruiting Commander killed himself. A sergeant there, conveyed to some of our people that he got one threatening ass chewing to many from the Region Commander. He was heard to say; "they will not threaten me again." Then he walked in his office and shot himself. I got that second hand but there is a good chance that something really bad happened up there. He was a Vietnam Veteran of course, and did that affect him? There was also the finishing of the Murrah Building one block south on 5th street. The army recruiting headquarters for Oklahoma moved in on the fourth floor. Two years later, when I was the Oklahoma City and northwest Oklahoma supervisor, my office was on the fourth floor. The office looked out over fifth street, where that scum parked the U-Haul Truck in April 1995.

I first came into contact with computers at the guidance counselors office, and had a good book for operating and learned fast. The longer I was in the Army, the more pissed and bitter I got about the anti army crowd. The lack of any guts on the part of anyone, in the Defense Department or Department of the Army to stand up for the NAM veteran's, really got me angry. In my later years in the Army, I NEVER made illegal enlistments. I always played to beat the system, like with my newspaper ad that worked the entire state, until I got caught. I quickly realized at the T. O. office, if you had exotic jobs to sell like air traffic control, x-ray technician, computer repair, etc. you could get more enlistments. I would be waiting at my computer at seven am, when the recruiting command job selection program came on line. The best career oriented training school slots for the exotic job's, were only two or three per day for the entire Army. I would quickly log on, and make false reservations in names such as Abraham A. Lincoln, George A. Custer, Clark K. Superman, even Captain Marvel. I was angry and cynical, almost daring the powers that be to catch me. When I had an applicant fully qualified that wanted to be in air traffic control for instance, I would quickly cancel the false reservation and make a new reservation for my man. My system worked well for a long time, but I had to stay late every night to cancel any unused reservations.

Going around subverting the Army's systems was really just small time stuff and not really something to be proud of, it bordered on immorality anyway. I did however increase the State Of Oklahoma army enlistment total by seven or eight a week. In the 1970's the Army undoubtedly regarded and rightly so, the recruiting process as crucial. After all the defense of the nation, to an extent depended on it. Nixon having stopped the draft by executive order, it would have been almost impossible for a later President, to have restarted it. There would have been mobs in the streets, all claiming to be fighting for freedom. The Vietnam War was a moment of truth where all men's souls were laid bare, and the majority of college age youth in the 1960's behaved selfishly and cowardly, in many cases. The coward's who went and remained in Canada to this day even have a monument to themselves as courageous freedom fighters. The Vietnam War, as I said earlier, had more justification than any so called war since, due to the remorseless march of communism across Europe and ASIA. Well what the heck, at the Guidance Counselors office the beat went on through 1975 and 1976 and the stress level of sergeant white and crew, grew and grew. One day I caught an applicant with an open felony charge trying to get in. He was from eastern Oklahoma and the way he talked and presented himself it was obvious the recruiter knew it. I sent him home with both a meal and bus ticket, and said nothing to operations. The recruiter must have been too dumb to breathe. He called the operations officer who was a Captain, and said," I kept a perfectly good man from joining.' The Captain called me and yelled; "are you trying to keep us from making our objective?" His stress level was so high he didn't even think. In another hour or so, a felon slipped by us and didn't cough up the disqualification until the AFEES Colonel was about to swear him in. The same Captain called and screamed; "are you not even checking them?" I just laughed and in a few moments he did also.

Sometime in the summer of 1976, Oklahoma was being investigated for fourteen illegal enlistment's extending over the last eight months. I had to be questioned and make a statement as nobody went into the Army from Oklahoma unless I signed off on them. Hell, I had screened them all with the uniform code of military justice and all other requirements in army regulations. I was really tense and worn out and was sure as hell not scared. A Major from the recruiting command headquarters adjutant general's office, walked in. Then we had to be behind closed doors for him to investigate me and my men. I had to tell him over and over again, pertaining to each case that all proper procedures had been followed thoroughly. Then show him our copies of the paperwork, where each enlistee had signed a statement that he was not concealing anything. He kept on dogging me about the investigation. By 1976 I knew army recruiting completely, and I knew our office was as honest as any in the country. I finally blew up and said to his face, "Major, stick this army in your ass." He stopped, and we were both quiet for a few moments and then he smiled and said, "okay sergeant, I was there too as an advisor to the ARVN Rangers. Don't worry about any of this Sarge, but you need another job before you lose your health."

Every so often we had an incident at the office that was noteworthy. On day we had an applicant from Oklahoma City's north side qualify to go Army, and I had him sitting out in the waiting room. I don't remember if I was going to process him or one of my closers was. Suddenly, I heard a strange noise that made me feel I should look into it. I walked out into the waiting room and he was gone. I walked out into the hall, and there he was with his right forearm pressed up against an attractive ladies throat, actually holding her in the air pressed against the wall. He could have killed her, if I or someone else had not come along. I grabbed him by the throat and said, "let her go, you bastard!" and threw him aside. She was probably in her late forties and looked like money. She started crying and said; "sergeant please get him in the Army. He is twenty and has failed at everything he has ever tried to do." He started cursing her in the foulest manner. She was his mother and was just trying to get him to be a man. I told him to shut the hell up and get back into the waiting room and sit down. I actually had no judicial authority over him as long as he had not sworn in. She begged me to find him something while I was thinking we don't need this trash. I looked at his test scores and physical and he was qualified and had good scores. I asked him what he would like to do in the Army, knowing full well he didn't want any Army. He finally managed to say "anything." I felt sorry for his mother or I would have sent him infantry Korea. I knew he would never make it in our infantry, besides we didn't need him. I sent him for a medical tech job to leave that day before he hurt someone in his family. I was surprised when he swore in at AFEES. When 1630 came around, I stepped to the window where I could see the bus to the airport. He was in line to get on when he bolted down the street and vanished in a cloud of dust. His mother was standing there sobbing. With a smile on my face, I sat down at my desk with his file in hand. Then I called the Provost Marshall at Fort Sill to report an AWOL.

It must have been in the summer of 1976 and I had four very tough looking African American young men sitting in the waiting room. They had all qualified and told me they would go infantry if they could leave today. I was too tired and stressed to wonder if there was some ulterior motive for the hurry. My phone rang and low and behold it was Oklahoma City Police Homicide. The man on the other end identified himself as the watch commander and asked if I had four young black men and named them. I replied; "yes they are sitting in my waiting room." He said, "Is your office room XX on the third floor of the American General building?" I replied in the affirmative, and he said, "don't do anything to alarm them, the SWAT team will be there very shortly." I was sitting there thinking about my life and if I had wanted a life that was not dull. Then I saw a bad looking dude take a peak around the corner of the front door. In seconds, six heavily armed men had them face down on the floor handcuffed and reading them their rights. Wow another exciting day in the Army.

There was always a large number of prior service wanting to reenlist. One would think any man wanting to go back in the Army would know what to expect. On one occasion in 1976, I enlisted a prior service troop that wanted Airborne and back in his previous job skill (MOS). I don't even remember what part of the state this one came from. Well of course it happened on a stressful busy day. I get a phone call and it is this prior service troop. He is in town in south side Oklahoma City and he tells me, he is driving downtown to kill me. How stupid, I had so many other recruiting problems I didn't even pay it any mind. I laughed, and told him; "you do remember where I am don't you?" I also said,"would you like me to send a car to get you?" He slammed the phone down and of course I got another call from him later. I laughed louder that time and said;"shall I send a car to get you?" On the third or fourth call I said; "listen asshole, killing and violence are not strangers to me. Since I have an office to run, get your ass down here or go to hell." I never heard from him again. If you had any type of leadership at the enlisted level in recruiting you ran into those types of situations frequently. NW Ayers advertising as if they had not wasted enough tax payers money already, came up with a new bright idea. They wanted to put up a large picture ad at various places on the Oklahoma City freeway system, showing one of the top recruiters in class a uniform (army green) with ribbons, badges and all. They would run his name and duty telephone number across the bottom of the ad with a big question, "HAVE YOU SEEN THIS MAN?" After I heard about it I laughed and forgot about it. Then one afternoon not long after, I got a telephone call from one of our best recruiters and my friend Will Williams. Williams said, "Hey Don, I was driving down I-40 and saw the new AD and almost lost control of my car". Before I could say anything, Williams roaring with laughter said, "It was you, Chingo! It was you!" Oh well, we all know why the government is so far in debt and we have for years.

Someone who may not have known what they were talking about said CHINGO was Korean for friend. Not long after that light note, I got a call from a worried recruiter who had a recruit at Fort Jackson, South Carolina. The young troop called home and told his mom and dad, he hadn't been paid in the four months he had been in the army. Of course his parents were raising hell. Will Williams was a Vietnam Vet and an African American who really knew his Army. Will was also as very smart man, with hundreds of friends throughout the Army. I got the kids name, SSN number and active duty date, and called Williams. I said, "Will I need you to get this problem fixed quickly." Will said; "lay it on me Chingo!" and I put him in the picture. Will laughed and said; "guess what? The Fort Jackson Sergeant Major is a brother and one of my best friends. Let me go Chingo, and I will move on it." The time of day was just after noon. It was just after four pm when the recruiter called me back sounding at the top of his game. He yelled, "sergeant White the troop's mom just called and she was happy. The boy just called and said;" the post Sergeant Major came and picked me up in his jeep and I got all my money."

Williams was one of those guys who sometimes made recruiting endurable. After his handling of the pay problem, I suggested a beer at the Valley of the Dogs, Will was too smart for that and said, "Uh think I better pass." Will was driving a brand new Chrysler Imperial; the car was white and loaded with power. It was in the time of the fifty five mph speed limit on the highway. We were going pheasant hunting in Nebraska in the Chrysler. Will was running eighty on the Kansas Turnpike. A big eighteen wheeler went by heading south, Will picked up the CB handset and said, "breaker one nine for a Smokey Report, this is the Oklahoma City soldier boy." There was a bridge over the turnpike and guess what, Smokey was parked on it as we flashed underneath. The next thing we heard was, "this is Smokey Oklahoma City Soldier Boy and you better slow that big white heap down." We raced off slowing down, and Will stayed off the CB. It was in the fall of 1976, that I got an interesting call from region late one afternoon. The region operations section monitored all enlistment school reservation's on the system. That was one reason I expected to get caught with my reservation school system, but had not since I started in 1975. I was not violating a direct regulation. I guess no one had ever thought of someone having a system like mine. The region operations sergeant was on the other end of the phone. I had a reservation faked to hold an exotic school assignment in the name Usless S. Grant. The sergeant said; "there is a problem with one of your assignments, sergeant white." I was astounded when he went on in a calm businesslike tone of voice, "you have an enlistee named Grant going on active duty on November 25th that's Thanksgiving Day." I replied, "oh hell, must be a typo Not to worry, I am on it." The school was a sought after aviation school. Within the next hour, I cancelled it and very quickly enlisted a qualified young enlistee with a November active duty date, and never heard another word about it.

The above is one of the reasons I stayed one month on active duty, beyond twenty years. In the seven years and two months I recruited, I learned far more about the army than in my service before. During my entire time in recruiting, I always had the entire MOS structure and pay scale and TO&E assignment structure of the entire Army, at my finger tips. I learned that there were lots of troops of all ranks that either did not know their job's or did not care. For those who are readers but not veterans the term MOS stands for military occupational specialty. For Instance, MOS 11b was light weapons infantry and 11c was heavy weapons infantry. The stateside army never seemed to have drug problems like the Vietnam rear echelon had. You saw lots of sergeant's and officer's, with alcohol problems. I still remember that in 1978 the base pay of a four star General was $36,000 per year. Since recruiting command had no first sergeant's in the field, when I was promoted E-8 in 1977 I was a master sergeant and retired at that rank. If I had taken that transfer to the infantry in Korea the colonel tried to get me into, I would have been promoted First Sergeant.

I had written earlier about that tiger running along behind every NAM vet, and sometimes the tiger catches up. Sometimes life just catches up. Many young people just don't understand that it takes courage to live. Sometimes it takes more courage than other times. In November 1976, I was thirty nine years old needing three more months to be forty. I was driving home from the guidance counselor's office, having stayed to seven pm to fix the computer and shipping list. I was going north on grand avenue and was almost to Baptist Hospital. Suddenly, I felt terrible and felt like my nerves and respiration were doing strange things. I pulled into the Baptist Hospital Emergency entrance and parked and went in. The long years of stress, of making decisions in dire emergency situations, like the hogback ridge at PLEI TRAP and just NAM in general plus recruiting had caught me. The hundred's or thousand's of bombs and shells that had gone off near me plus fighting and moving in the rain and heat had caught me. The sheer physical strain of jumping out of choppers with that huge rucksack and weapon had caught me. Then the strain of three bad wound's and almost losing my right leg went beyond the limit. The years of knowing that many Americans hated me and what I stood for, all those things came home and almost struck me down.

I was lying on a bed far better and cleaner than the triage at the field hospital in NAM. I knew that something was seriously wrong with me besides my Vietnam hangover. Then a young Doctor came in and checked my vitals. He said; "Sergeant you have not had a heart attack, at least not yet. Your heart is beating very unevenly. It is irregular and something is causing it." He said; "I am not going to hold you overnight but am going to make you an appointment for tomorrow at the heart clinic on the back side of the hospital." Then he asked me if I did anything strenuous at night. I told him I usually ran two miles every night. He said don't do it tonight, just go home and rest. He gave me a card with an appointment time on it and the phone number, seems like it was about one pm. I went home and tried to relax with Hope close by trying to help if possible. Well folks, such happenings are lonely happenings with a person having to depend on others to help you through it. It actually seemed strange with no brave capable men at my command, no M-16 with a thirty round magazine to bail me out, just sitting there waiting for the other shoe to fall. Only thirty nine years old and I sure did not expect to have heart trouble that young. Oklahoma recruiting command, had just had a new recruiter in his thirties have a very dangerous heart attack and was medically retired. That night I tried not to think about it, especially as I could not take a definite action to overcome my problem. I felt and nearly was helpless. The trip to the pit and the strain of the homecoming was taking me beyond.

The next morning, I left home about 0600 driving for the American general building with a very irregular heartbeat. Every few seconds it would give one very hard beat in my throat. I felt like someone who death had passed by so many times, who had been after all so vulnerable. I remember going down northwest 10th, east toward downtown and working hard to control my anxiety. I had left a very worried wife at home and the day was not a good one. When I got to the AFEES, I stopped in to see the Doctor who was a good friend. He checked me over and said almost to a word what I had heard the previous night, "You have not had a heart attack but you need to find out what's going on and get it fixed soon." Since the operations officer was my normal supervisor, I called him and gave him the facts, and told him also about the one pm appointment. He said," sergeant white leave whoever you think in charge and come over here right now." Operations had already moved into the infamous Murrah Building, one block south. On the way I walked by the famous tree that withstood the 1995 blast. When I got there, the Captain had me sit down in a comfortable swivel chair, and told me that at eleven thirty the operations sergeant would take me in an army car to the heart clinic. The sergeant was a Vietnam Vet and a very good guy. He got me there at twelve thirty and I checked in. A heart Doctor who is since deceased checked me over. He said; "you might not have a serious problem. This may be stress related and your blood pressure is 150/100." No one remembers now but that had been considered normal blood pressure for many years. In any event they gave me a stress test with the treadmill, which was inconclusive as my heart was irregular any way. I was set up to check into the hospital the next morning for a heart catheterization.

I checked in on time after a bad night. I was taken into the OR and a young doctor introduced himself to me. Just the guy I needed, his name was Ron White and he was an ex NAM marine. So we have Ron White, giving a heart catheterization to Don White. It seemed like it was over in seconds. When I was fully awake in recovery, Doctor White came in and said, "no sweat, GI." He went on, "your heart including valves is strong and perfectly normal, and you do not have any blockage." While he was telling me this he had the picture on a screen. Then he added, "see that little crook in that artery? That might give you some trouble someday." Then Doctor White said, "Sarge, all this is stress related. You need another job." Many years later on February 19th, 2005, Doctor Ron White put a stint where that crook was, and I was ready for another waterfowl season. In 1976 the Army jumped in when I thought I was ready to go back to duty. An ambulance was sent from the Ft Sill Hospital to get me. I don't know how that came about, but the ride was a lot better than the ride from the air field at Manhattan Kansas, to Irwin Army at Ft Riley. The Fort Sill hospital was fine, even though some poor soul died in the room across the hall. It sounded like he was dying of emphysema, and it was a bad scene. There have been too many bad scenes in my life.

At the hospital in Ft Sill the same test was given with the same result. The difference was that a medical report was sent to the Oklahoma City District Recruiting Commander that I had stress problems relating to the War and recruiting. It was possible for me to have a heart attack. The Doctor recommended my transfer to a less stressful job. I felt somewhat bad about that as my belief system was always built around whatever the scene, I could handle it. They held me for observation two more days at Sill and then released me. Hope was waiting for me to call, so she could drive down and get me. The Chingo, Will Williams called to see if I was good for another million miles, and said he had to come to Lawton to the recruiting station and he could pick me up. Same old Will, a better man I never met, we had lunch with the Lawton recruiters and laughs all around. I was at home in the early evening. The Fort Sill doctor put me on a blood pressure prescription and such has continued to this day. It was now December 1976 and I had twenty month's to go actually just nineteen to get twenty years active duty. The next morning, as soon as the day began I got a call to come over and see the new Colonel. I reported in and felt okay with this Colonel. He was Airborne Infantry,

CIB and Silver Star and a NAM Vet of course. To this day, I am glad he came in to command the Oklahoma district recruiting command as we had NAM, the CIB and the Silver Star in common. I had been promoted to master sergeant in 1977.I think my deep anger against the anti war protesters, now turned anti military. The entire frustration of the War and stressful recruiting would soon cause my alligator mouth to overload my hummingbird ass. The new Colonel said, "white I have seen your production record, and I want you to take over the Oklahoma City and northwest Oklahoma area as supervisor." The area had a Captain named Matthews as commander, so I would be his assistant.

Captain Matthews was a NAM vet and a very fine Christian man. I actually stopped cursing so much around him. He always supported decisions, I made about recruiting methods in the area. Speaking of area, I drove every other week from Oklahoma City through northwest Oklahoma, all the way to the panhandle and up to Liberal Kansas. Then I went back to Guymon, Oklahoma before coming back down the Northwest Passage through Woodward to Oklahoma City. My job was to help all recruiters who had problems with production in our area, and to train the new guys. It's been a long time, but seems like we had either four or five recruiting stations in Oklahoma City metro plus Norman. I had a nice office in the Murrah Building, on the fourth floor as I wrote before. My window looked right out over 5th Street where that swine parked the truck on April 19th 1995, just outside the nursery and social security office. I guess if there was anybody that could be described as a real expert at selling the Army, I guess I came as close as anyone else. One of the highlights of 1977 was when I was teaching a class on closing at North Penn Plaza and noticed several men, hurry out of the bank across the street. I understood, when seven or eight police cars showed up.

Since the Oklahoma City metro and northwest Oklahoma had the most recruiters and population, we normally had the largest quota each month. Our quota normally ran from 120 to 200 and I don't think we ever made it until the Army started taking category four's, recruits who scored less than 31 on the test. The Army also opened a large number of jobs to women that had always been men only. During those years, women were barred from combat arms. Today female activist groups are pushing hard to get women in the infantry, and that would be a terrible mistake. Nature has not equipped women in the generality, with the physical body and the emotions, to handle the hardships and emotional intensity, of severe close quarters infantry combat. I would use as an analogy, my very words concerning the hellish nature of combat in the NAM. Today the Army has far more woman in it than in the years I served, and the middle east operations are represented by activist's, as proof that woman can function well, even in the infantry. These operations were conducted by our 21st century military and there is no doubt, they are very brave and of high quality. However, these operations were against third world armies sitting in the open, as the finest air force ever created turned them into nothingness. If not against third world forces, they were against terrorist, who were not well armed or trained and were no match for our troop's. I stated early in my narrative, between late fall 1965 and the end of the summer 1969 we consistently had killed in action from 100 to over 800 per week in NAM. The week of Woodstock, that example of filth and peace activism, we lost killed in action, 109 American fighting men. There are many things requiring great intelligence and sound common sense that women are far better at then men, but infantry war is not one of them.

While I was running all over northwest Oklahoma trying to help recruiters get their production up, I noticed an event that happened at the guidance counselor's office that was noteworthy. There was an applicant processed with a Masters degree in education, who made less than thirty one on the entrance exam. Since I was a supervisor, I had a copy of the screening test. I took it home, and had my fifteen year old son take the test, and he made eighty five. Captain Matthews only made one trip with me to northwest Oklahoma and Liberal Kansas. We were driving back on Highway three, known as the Northwest passage. We were easterly bound, running at seventy miles per hour with me behind the wheel. We left Watonga in Blaine County and were heading toward Kingfisher when we were run off the road by a drunk. I pulled off the road to the right by at least twenty yards. Captain Matthews said, "What's going on?" I answered, "You will see in second."

The driver was most certainly drunk and passed us as we sat well off the shoulder. He was looking straight down the highway all hunched down. Captain Matthews was astounded that someone could be so drunk they would drive on the wrong side of the road. In my duty position, I saw a lot of Oklahoma and by having a recruiter friend at Guymon Oklahoma, I got in on some great pheasant and waterfowl hunting. There was one incident where I undeservedly got away with a huge traffic ticket. I had been down west of Lawton on recruiting business and as the day was advanced, I was speeding, going east back to I44 to return to the metro. The speed limit was still fifty five and I was doing seventy five, on a two lane blacktop road. I ran through a speed trap and the Highway Patrol stopped me. He came up to my window and I handed him my driver's license. It was a US Government vehicle, no liability insurance was required. He said, "well sergeant you must be in a hurry to get home." He looked in the window and saw my CIB. He said, "I was in the Army a few years ago, sergeant." I thought, damn he would have to be prior service and probably does not like sergeant's. He said, "Hell man, I was there too and also in the infantry." Then he said; "tell you what sergeant, I have already torn this ticket so I have to write it. Let me have your driver's license. Then he told me, "don't be in a hurry to pay this. I will talk to the Judge; just call the number on this card in five days." We talked a little while, and then shook hands and I headed for the metro. When five days had passed, I called the number and a super nice lady answered;"why sergeant white, I just mailed you your driver's license. The judge looked at your case and found you not guilty." Well certainly I was guilty but hell, even a NAM Veteran, ought to get a lucky break sometimes. The year was 1977 and I imagine the NAM Vet Highway Patrolman is long retired, I hope he is enjoying life.

Well enough recruiting high jinks and bullshit. I was getting close to the end of my long relationship with the Army of the United States. I had met a retired air force sergeant who was a real estate broker in the metro, and was also a builder. We hit it off pretty well and he talked me into thinking about real estate as a second career. As the months past and August 1978 was getting closer, I told the personnel sergeant to get my retirement papers ready. When May 1978 came, both myself and my wife Hope had real estate license's and I also had sixty days accrued leave. The Region Commander, who was a one star General heard I was going to retire. The General was in Oklahoma City on business at the headquarters, in the Murrah Building. I was in my office on the fourth floor, and he came over to see me. I of course rendered him the proper military courtesy and we sat down to talk. He said; "sergeant, your record here is tops and we can't afford to lose you." I had the Recruiting Gold Badge with two sapphire stars for having been a top ten army recruiter on production. He went on to say, "If you will reenlist I guarantee to make you a Sergeant Major in two months."

Well no doubt the General could do what he promised and it would be an honor. I looked at the pay chart from 1978. I would only get seventy five dollars per month more. I had told him, "I would think it over and I did". When I first went to the War, I was a true believer. The years of demonstrations and bigger lies from the protestor's than our own government lied, was a bridge too far. To stop the Communist sweep over the planet that had already put fifteen or more nations in their camp, was a worthy cause. However you don't stop aggression both military and political, by fighting with your hands behind your back. You only waste human life, by allowing your enemy sanctuary. You don't win hearts and minds, when your allies are the same people who were on the French side, in the first Indochina war. Most Vietnamese farming people probably saw us as a less brutal version of the French who preceded us. The old Communist tactic of fighting while negotiating, did not work well for Johnson or Nixon. Another big thing that sickened me was to have quit the War with 1600 men unaccounted for. The American Nation in doing that committed the crime of murder against these brave men. There is no telling how many of the 1600 were alive and prisoners and died a slow death of torture, starvation and disease. The North Vietnamese negotiator in Paris, Le Duc To always maintained unto death that he told Kissinger when he handed him the list of prisoners held by the North Vietnamese;" that these are all we have." He also swore that he told Kissinger "as for the rest you will have to talk to the Laotians." To be fair to Kissinger, he has always maintained that Le Duc To, said nothing of the sort. I am an American and I will side with Kissinger, but there is something really wrong there.

The direction the Army was taking was not something I liked either. There were some young women given direct commissions right out of college. Yes they had to go through officer advanced courses and all that, but they had no experience of leadership. I had seen enough policy statements that caused me to think, the senior officers of the Army thought, we NAM veterans were damaged goods. I never saw it in writing but late at night in my office, reading the crap that came down from the pentagon, just sickened me. I saw glowing reports about advanced courses, that were going to build a new Army. Well the Army had deep problems of discipline, the things I saw at Irwin Army Hospital at Fort Riley were deeply disturbing. Most of all was the murder of the Captain commanding the Medical Holding Company. In one incident at Fort Riley, the Commanding General was going to inspect the engineer Battalion and the troops walked away from their Officers and sergeant's and formed a peace symbol. I also remember seeing a truckload of troops in the front leaning rest position beside Kansas sixteen, on post. They had given the Commanding General the finger. The General was standing there with armed military police. This was the same General who was drunk, when I was awarded the Silver Star.

I felt like I had given the Army my best. Because of the leftover emotional impact of NAM, I just didn't have a good feeling about myself or the Army anymore. Somewhere about the first of June, an incident occurred that made up my mind for me. We had a young, twenty two year old female Captain come into the unit. I don't even remember what her job was but she had an additional duty as the supply officer. One day I was coming into the metro from the north and stopped at the North Penn Plaza recruiting station, to talk to a recruiter. When I started to leave, the Station Commander asked me if I was going downtown. I said, "yes," and he asked me to pick up a packet of pencils and drop them off to him.

I said, "no problem" and made the trip to the Murrah Building. When I had done some paperwork in my office I stopped by the supply office. I and the supply sergeant were on a first name basis but he was not in the office. I picked up a packet of pencils and left the sergeant a note, with the stock number and said if he needed me to, I would come back and sign a requisition. I was about to step out of the main office door when I heard a shrill voice saying, "SERGEANT WHITE." I stopped and looked around; it was the new female Captain. She probably had been in the army six months more or less. I was standing there a Master Sergeant with almost twenty years service. I was wearing the Combat Infantry Badge, Silver Star, Bronze Star with Oak leaf, Purple Heart with Oak leaf, Viet Cross of Gallantry, Meritorious Service Medal and a gold Recruiting badge with two sapphire stars. She thought she was going to chew me out. This twenty two year old kid thought she was going to cut me down, in front of the entire office staff including some civilians. When she began yelling at me in a child's voice, I felt the NAM and all the years of stress, wash over me. When she ran out of breath, after she finished raving about me taking a packet of pencils without signing a requisition, I said, "are you finished?"

The room was totally quiet. I was losing the battle to control myself when I said; "young lady, you can take this Army and shove it up your ass." That was thirty four years ago and still makes me mad to remember, and write about it. She was standing there with her mouth open wearing her little good conduct medal and her national defense service medal, and I made the trip. When I was down the hall nearing the elevators, I heard the entire office erupt in a roar of laughter. When I got in my car I sat and thought for a moment, wondering how it would feel to retire at pay grade seven instead of pay grade eight. Nevertheless, there is right and there is wrong, and I have done lots of wrongs. This incident said to me, that if a highly decorated loyal combat soldier can be talked to like that by a nice little girl, it is an Army that does not need me. When I got to the north Pennsylvania avenue station with the pencils, the Sergeant Major was waiting for me on the phone. The Sergeant Major told me the Colonel said;"that if it was not for that

Silver Star I would be court-martialed, but it better not happen again." I replied, "okay Sergeant Major I will be right back down there to put in my retirement papers." THAT'S why I left the Army.

There will come a time in every soldier's life to stop being a soldier, at least in securing the wealth, health and livelihood of his family. I had sixty days accrued leave at the end of June 1978, and took thirty beginning on July 31, 1978. The Army would have to pay me the other thirty days, on my retirement day. So on the first day of July 1978, I had thirty days left in uniform. The NAM was the crucial happening of my Army career and for that matter, of my life. I was still the area supervisor of the Oklahoma northwest area as my time began to run out. We got in a new Colonel at a time when the states recruiting production was falling. It was also early in July that the Sergeant Major, either got sick or went on leave. I was the ranking enlisted man in the state after the Sergeant Major, so I became acting Sergeant Major for my last thirty days. I sure was an acting this or that a lot in my career. The Colonel being new was really feeling the pressure and I tried to help him all I could. It was a mission where you could never do enough. It was just like a realtor, no matter how many you sell, it is never enough. I seldom saw our female Captain after the incident and to honest about it I being a professional soldier, kept to the company of other professional's. We had a civil service operative working at the headquarters named Steve ######, he was a good man and had been in the Special Forces during the war. ###### wore a black beard and was in and out, he was supposed to be working in public relations. ###### never talked much, always seemed to have a good story if you asked him where he had been. He was well educated and very intelligent. One day in July, I was wrestling with paperwork in the Sergeant Majors office. ###### came in the office and said, "I hear you're retiring. I can't believe a man like you would leave the Army." I said, "well there is a time and place for all things." He replied; "you didn't know it but some guys I know have seen your records. They are in the corporate security business and are always on the lookout for experienced combat vets." He went on, "here is a card with their phone number on it, call it at any time day or night. When someone answers give them your name and they will say, we will get back to you." I laughed and said, "well I thought you guys had to work overseas by law." He stood there quietly fighting to keep from smiling, and then said, "it's a legit job."

Legit job all right, it was in the time the CIA was supporting the Contra Rebels in Central America and cannon fodder was needed. Years later I read a book ###### wrote named "The Devils Secret Name". He was always a supporter of the central highlands Montagnard organization named FULRO. They sought independence from the Communist Government in Ho Chi Minh City (Saigon) and Hanoi. They were a good group and fighting for the right cause, but the Communist forces were too many and too well armed. ###### wrote several books with Vietnam overtones. The Montagnards were special friends and operatives of our CIA and Special Forces. They were just another group of freedom fighting people thrown under the bus by the democrat's, when they cut off aid to Southeast Asia.

Sometime about three years or more afterward I had a great real estate business going and one night got a call. The caller identified himself as Tom and wanted to know if I was a Vietnam Vet named Don White. I told him I was, and asked him if I could help him in some way. Tom wanted to invite Hope and I to a Vietnam Veterans party at an address in North Oklahoma City. Hell, they already knew Hope's name. Hope and I partied a lot then, so I said we might stop by. I knew it was probably not a normal Vietnam Vet party. We were going dancing that night but went by the address where Tom said the party was. I knocked on the door and a huge African American man answered the door. Before I said a word he said, "Sergeant White and Hope, come right in." Well there was great food and free drinks all in great supply. Hope and I just moved right in and had a Jack Daniels and coke and a sandwich apiece. A man I had never seen before came up to me and introduced himself as Colonel somebody ,and said he wanted to talk to me in a few minutes, and he was glad I came as I was their kind of guy. I guess that their kind was this crowd, of big hard looking guys all drinking and telling Special Forces war stories. I looked around and didn't see

and it occurred to me, he might have shaved his beard off and I would not recognize him. Hope said with a smile, "having fun yet?" I said;"these guys have CIA all over them. Let's make the trip back to our real estate lives." I have never been sorry.

Well back to my last days in the Army of the United States. I got a call from the new Colonel a week or so after my terminal leave started. The Colonel said he needed me back down at the recruiting headquarters, and that if I was willing he could get me hired as a GS-11. We had been selling real estate for several weeks and were off to a blazing start. I asked, "Colonel what is the pay for a GS-11?" as I did not know much about civil service. The Colonel did not know much about civil service either as he said he did not know. I told him I would think about it, I did think about it for three or four seconds. A few days after that I got my separation documents in the mail, be at building so and so at 0900 on August 30, 1978. I was on time in my tropical worsteds and with all ribbons, badges, and medals as per instructions. I needed a haircut by army standards but would have looked great by NAM standards. The first thing I had to do was take a retirement physical, which seemed to go okay until I got to the mental health part of it. I went in and sat down by the shrink's desk without being asked. He was a Captain and had my records spread out before him. He looked up and said, "sergeant white, I see you have been in some exceedingly violent combat." I was quiet for a few seconds and then said; "well Doctor, lots of troops have." He said, "I bet you have lots of bad dreams." I have only had one bad war dream since my War ended and none before that. Being an arrogant bastard, I said, "Oh yes doctor, have you seen that movie where David Soul chases this horrible looking vampire all across America?" I went on, "I have had terrible dreams ever since I saw it." He said,"okay, wise guy," and stamped my records 10% PTSD. My total was 60% service connected.

That awarding of 10% PTSD was the first time, I had heard of PTSD in the nine years since my last day of fighting in Vietnam. Well every painter to his own brush, but I have seen as much combat as any man, and I was a very successful real estate broker for twenty one years after

I left the Army. In the period of my life from March 12, 1969 until August 30th, 1978, I was a professional soldier who never heard other Vietnam Veteran professional's mention PTSD. During my real estate career I also completed three university degrees including a Bachelor of Science in Marketing. However I have great difficulty sleeping and often think about the War at three or four o'clock in the morning, but no bad dreams. If I have PTSD, maybe the sleeping problems or the anger management problems in the 1970s are it. In any event I have five battle wounds that account for most of my disability. I am fully aware that I am as normal as anyone could be who experienced a great deal of close quarters infantry combat. My wife has always maintained that since the War, I am much angrier and violently inclined, than before Vietnam. Well I am not a mental hygiene specialist and it's not for me to say. I know this for sure, men in the infantry who fought in Vietnam, went through an extremely stressful horrific trial by combat. They could not be expected to be totally mild and rational afterward. The ever dwindling number of Vietnam Combat Veteran's in our country, have been treated badly by their non veteran fellow citizens. The Vietnam War, destroyed many a loving couples married life and the happiness and love of life for many of the survivor's.

On my retirement day from the army, I mainly just wanted to get free from the Government. I still had some loyalty to the Army but nothing like before the War. The retirement processing itself after the physical was a boring process of signing papers. The civil service clerk, who processed me certainly did not care about me or his job, he just wanted to get through. I myself had my mind on a lucrative real estate deal I had working in Oklahoma City and wanted to get back to town. I remember standing in formation and marching in many retirement parades in the 25th Division in Hawaii, before the war. I certainly was not interested in anything like that for me. I would not want to have put the troops through the hassle of a parade. When the paperwork was finished, I had to go to finance to get my final army pay. I had my thirty days of accrued leave to be paid for as well as my last active duty month. The Army Finance Center at Fort Sill, of course had it all fouled up and it took an hour to get through that. When I finished at finance, it was back across the street to sign out for the last time and I also had to initial a form covering the entire paperwork hassle, and get my copies. When it was all over at last I stepped out on the porch and took a deep breath. On the walk to my car my recruiting Gold Badge fell off my shirt and I left it. I had my hat off and passed a Major without saluting. He stopped and made a noise but I kept on walking. I should have been polite to him. I stopped on interstate 44 and looked back at the post wondering why I felt nothing. Then when looking at my pay sheet I saw they had shorted me twenty dollars, I headed for Oklahoma City.

— CHAPTER 11 —

A TIME AND SEASON

To everything there is a season,
And a time to every purpose under the heaven;
A time to be born and a time to die;
A time to plant, and a time to pluck up that which is planted;
A time to kill, and a time to heal;
a time to break down, and a time to build up;
ECCLESIASTES 3:1-3

This chapter will mark the end of my narrative, of my actions, thoughts, decisions and orders given in the last great infantry war. Before I began the summation of this work, I will do a "where are they now section." To further remark on the bravery and courage of many of those who went to the pit with me. First however, I have decided to name several of the principals who I did not name, in the story of my time with the 1st Battalion, 27th infantry, 25th Division. In the hellish combat on November 3rd, 1966 at the Michelin Rubber Plantation, after the charley company commander was killed, the Battalion commander Major Guy S. Meloy Jr. flew to the remnant of Charlie Company to take command. In a terrible moment of death and fury, he rallied the troops and led Charlie Company to survival and victory. Major Meloy was awarded the Distinguished Service Cross for his great leadership. Today retired General Meloy lives in Texas and is still a great American soldier. My first company commander in Vietnam with Charlie Company was Captain Ardeen Foss, the nephew of the famous WW11 fighter ace Joe Foss. Captain Foss at all times was calm and deliberate in the taking of life and death decisions. TheCaptain was a brave man and exhibited superb leadership at all times. Today retired Colonel Foss lives on in Colorado. The First Sergeant leading Charlie Company up the trail by the DAU TEING airstrip was Samuel K. Soloman. First Sergeant Soloman died in heroic action trying to rescue badly wounded men caught in the kill zone of the ambush. The First Sergeant was a native of Oahu, Hawaii and a school is named in his honor there. Today alive and well in Iowa is Dick Seibel who was the company commander's radio telephone operator and survived the hellish kill zone. SP4 Seibel with great courage and calmness was pinned down in the buffalo grass all night. It was Sp4 Seibel who rescued two wounded men and called in several airstrikes. SSG Rueben Tomlinson was the survivor from weapons platoon who told me the story and a brave and loyal American fighting man.

These five brave men are the only 27th Infantry Wolfhound veteran's who I knew where they were from and whose names I could easily remember. There are so many very brave men of the Wolfhounds who

I have had no contact with since the War that I could not name. The American people should know that the American combat troops from all branches of service in Vietnam were brave and courageous. They were all deserving of the good will of all the American people. The troops who served in the base camps have received much unjustified criticism. Most were hardworking and true; a troop could be killed at any moment in the perimeter. Since 1999 due to the efforts in the beginning of former 4th platoon sergeant Jerry Horton, I have had close contact with many of the brave survivors of A company. They fought against many times their number at PLEI TRAP on March 12th 1969. The March 12th A Company Commander Captain Charles Hockett lives in California. He is a most deserving American officer who gave sound leadership to A Company in a very bad close quarters combat. Lieutenant Andy LePeilbet one of the finest officers I ever came in contact with is a realtor in Reno Nevada. Lieutenant John Andrews 1st platoon leader was a brave and very fine officer and is alive and well in New Jersey. Lieutenant now Retired Commander US Navy Tom Porter formerly one of the few Navy Officers to ever have the CIB and the brave and capable leader of the second platoon, is a doctor in Houston Texas. So many times a young officer would be rushed into a command position in NAM without proper preparation due to the high rate of junior officer casualties. A company was very lucky to have these four on hand on March 12th, 1969.

Of the A company enlisted men no man could say enough. I wish it were possible for me to name every single one both alive and dead. I can only remember those I have known since 1999 in our reunion group. Every enlisted man with us that day can only be described as brave beyond the call of duty. I hope and pray I don't forget to name someone I know from the reunion group and wish I could name all. Staff Sergeant Jerry Horton is a Silver Star Winner and a very brave man with great leadership qualities. In NAM he did an E-7 platoon sergeants job with skill and daring, and is alive and well. Jerry is a commercial company selling realtor in Florida in the winter and a north woods fisherman in the summer. He also has a Doctorate in Computer Science and has developed and sold his own software company. I wish I could work miracles and bring back to life my terrific and super brave point man Jerry Loucks. Jerry died of a heart attack seven or eight years back and I could hardly bear the news. Jerry had the well deserved Distinguished Service Cross and if enlisted men could recommend a Medal of Honor, I would certainly have fought to get it awarded to him. I believe every living survivor from A Company would second the recommendation. Normally a career platoon sergeant and a rebel like Jerry would not work well together. However our minds and combat experience had some strange connection. We both seemed to always be able to anticipate the thoughts and tactical notions of each other. There will never be another Jerry Loucks.

David Muck from Michigan is alive and well, and like all Vietnam Veterans I know, has had a successful life with a fine family. Dave is retired now and surprisingly does not look a great deal older than in 1969. Sergeant Muck was a top soldier and a brave and loyal friend. Frank Novotny from Minnesota was also a third platoon squad leader and a very good tough sergeant. He is like so many, a brave and capable soldier and good family man. The last Third Platoon squad leader was Henry Scarver who died in 1999 of a rare disease. Sergeant Scarver was a very brave and superb leader and a fine man, America will always need such men. Randy Pierce, the Flea of fourth platoon was often the fourth platoon point and was exactly that on March 12th. Randy works for the TVA and is alive and well and is a tough veteran of some serious combat. George Sams otherwise known as Snook is still with us and living in Illinois. George has, like most A Company vets hung tough in some very bad scenes. John Campbell was the fourth platoon machine gunner who now is living in Oregon and when I last saw him looked hardly older than on March 12, 1969. The tough shooter from the Tracer LRP team is Randy Chrietzberg. He is alive and well in California and was awarded deservedly the Distinguished Service Cross. Ken McCormick is also from California. He still has his moustache and is a very successful businessman in the San Diego area, with a super family. In NAM he was a very good man to have around. Greg Rollinger is still alive and well in Minnesota and was a very good machine gunner with third platoon. When I was being pulled in a poncho after being hit, I will always remember Rollinger beside me, firing that M-60 in short burst, over and over. Gary Feldman is farming beside the Mississippi River in Illinois. Gary was a super troop and stood up in heavy fire, helping hold me up so the medic could drag me into Dust off 37 and was painfully wounded in one hand doing it. My good friend Pappy Rawls is the very tough experienced trooper from fourth platoon who carried me back into the perimeter after I was hit and probably saved my life. Pappy looks younger now than in 1969 and lives just north of Little Rock, Arkansas. Mike Rinehart was Dust off 37 who flew to wherever mercy was needed no matter how heavy the fire. Dust off 37, brave and fearless is now living in Florida, retired. He probably saved the lives of myself and Horton. Paul "Airborne" Summerlin won the Silver Star in the fourth platoon and was one of Horton and LePeilbet's best men, sadly died of cancer a few years ago. I have tried to make sure I have included everyone mentioned in my narrative; I hope I have not left anyone out. These men and indeed all the men I served with in NAM came out of the great heart of America. They with great courage faced the gut wrenching moment of truth that is close quarters infantry combat. Perhaps they are best described by some poetry written by Rudyard Kipling about the British infantry in the nineteenth century. He wrote; "THOSE WHO CARRIED THE HILL WITH THE BAYONET AND CANNOT BE KNOWN." I have always known when I return in thought to that hellish place men called NAM, I was lucky to have at my side these brave and resolute men. The American people did not deserve to be served in combat by such men, and I will carry to my grave the memory of them all. They were all so young and reckless and determined to do their duty no matter what.

As the years go rolling by, another A Company man who I wrote of was Rich "Spider" MELI. Spider left us in December 1968 while we were still dug in at firebase twenty five northwest of BEN Het. Spider lived for years in Staten Island and worked on a tugboat in New York Harbor and is now retired in south Florida. Spider was in fourth platoon when I was platoon sergeant. He holds the distinction of never giving his platoon sergeant a pull on his bottle of Jack Daniels kept carefully hidden in his bunker. Spider insist that I once made him dig an "8 by 8" hole ,but Gosh why on earth would I do that? In any event Spider is one hell of a guitar player. During the war great efforts were made by the Johnson administration to make our effort a truly allied one through SEATO and NATO. The Australians having seen what unchecked aggression could do in WW11 came to our side. I don't remember how large their troop commitment wa but it is generally agreed that they fought well. New Zealand and Thailand plus the Philippines also sent small detachments. The South Koreans sent an infantry division that hated Communists and also fought well. When their division arrived home after the pullout, millions of South Korean civilians met their ships with wild cheering and celebration. The greeting for the South Korean troops is in sharp contrast to the one at Travis Air Force base where it has long been said, that American protesters broke through the main gate. They got all the way to the tarmac where they threw sandwich bags full of feces, at our wounded being unloaded from air force Medevac flights. Considering my many confrontations in supposedly patriotic Oklahoma City, I would say the story is probably true. Company A LT Tom Porter says, when he was unloaded at LAX coming home, that a girl protester hit him with a sign. If Doctor Porter said it I believe it.

I noticed a lot of difference between the 25th Division in 1966 and the Fourth Division in 1969. While the troops in both units were both brave and capable, the 25th Division units were much larger and closer to TO&E strength. That may be because the 25th had just come straight from Hawaii in 1966 and the Fourth had already been in country in 1969 for several years. In 1966 the feeling was the War was still young and we were impossible to beat. Down there in 111CORP in 1966 there was mostly flat terrain and the difficulties the rubber plantations caused, plus the booby traps and huge tunnel systems, made for tough fighting. However to fight in the 11CORP central highlands with the triple canopy overhead and the hills near straight up and down, made demands on the human spirit almost beyond belief. When I got to the fourth division, I was surprised at how much less fire and air support there was available.

In 1966 we were always supported by artillery, mortar and air support immediate on request. The 1st Battalion 27th infantry, when I was there had a colorful FAC (forward air controller) code named, Jack the Fac. He always arrived over the battle site with a hearty, "NEVER FEAR JACK IS HERE." At DAU TIENG on November 3rd 1966, I saw a 105MM battery from the eighth artillery fire one thousand rounds in a short time. On all ambushes, NDP's and patrol bases I was always able to register defensive concentrations in 1966. I was seldom able to get them shot in, while with the fourth division.

When General Abrams took command from Westmorland of MACV in the summer of 1968, the tactical deployment of the infantry divisions in Vietnam was altered. This was done to use General Abram's plan. General Abrams wanted a redeployment of US forces to assist ARVN more directly, in winning "hearts and minds." The bulk of US divisions were withdrawn from the border areas back closer to the new life hamlet areas, to help ARVN control and protect the people. I outlined this in an earlier chapter but it became serious in TET'69. The Marines held the I CORP QUANG TRI northern area, from the coast to LANG VAI. On the north end of the western Border, the 101 airborne had a brigade operating in the AShau valley border area. Then to the south, the fourth division deployed along the western border in small units. The fourth division by this time in the War was seriously under strength. The companys in the 1st Battalion 8th infantry had approximately seventy to eighty men per company which was just over fifty per cent of TO&E. I was, a mere sergeant but based on my experience, it seemed that artillery, mortar and air support was not easy to get, especially in TET, 69. Gone were the thunderous artillery barrages of 1966 and the super deadly air strikes. The fourth division was so short of choppers that we had the previously mentioned incident in VC Valley of no food for twenty four hours. When TET' 69 began we only had several movements by air and then with just one or two choppers. That could be done safely with a small company only if the landing zone was cold. When TET' 69 began in March until my last action on March 12th, I only got one artillery fire mission that was fired. Fortunately we had several timely gunship air strikes that enabled us to overcome difficult situations. The NVA had entered South Vietnam in the tri border area with forces much larger than ours.

My understanding of the tactical operations sop was when the NVA moved into South Vietnam, the fourth division found them and attacked them. We would receive heavy reinforcement's from the interior, if needed. Our company was alone and usually spread out in a platoon sized patrol mode after leaving POLIE KLENG on March 3rd. A Company only occasionally regrouped until March 6th. On March 6th, 1969 we went into the DAK HODRAI and DAK ROTIL area and were obviously in near contact with a large NVA force. The NVA were heavily armed with both artillery and anti aircraft guns. Alfa Company was obviously dangerously overextended, and that was no doubt true of the other 8th infantry companies in operation Wayne Grey. We fought well and overcame all difficult situations. If any American units from the village protection forces in the interior had shown up, we would have no doubt crushed the enemy. In conversation with my buddies in our reunion group, the unwounded survivors of March 12'th, tell me they fought on for days in one small contact after another. They even came under NVA artillery fire on one hill, where they lost a KIA. When TET' 69 ended the NVA withdrew to Cambodia and Laos without accomplishing anything. A tired, battle weary but undefeated fourth division maintained its control of the tri border area. In Lewis Sorley's book "A Better War"(4), General Abrams tells his staff that the fourth division was overestimating enemy strength in TET' 69. Well that's certainly open to debate from a grunts position in operation Wayne Grey.

Looking back to March 12'th, 1969 to the hog back ridge leading south from a hill overlooking the DAK ROTIL Creek. It seems a miracle that we only had three killed the entire day and that includes the brigade sergeant major. There were however some very real factors in play. ONE: We walked into the north end of a large NVA resupply and deployment area. The NVA bunker area was north of CHU HING and east of POLEI JAR SEANG. We caught the NVA totally by surprise. TWO: we were deployed up the finger and on higher ground than the majority of the enemy. THREE: at the point we struck them we encountered only lower ranking troops with their Leader's further downhill, thus it took them longer to get organized. FOUR: Because I quickly locked my platoon in an oblong perimeter to the rear of fourth platoon we could attack from a concentrated base of fire. FIVE: Our troops were carrying twenty two magazines and six hand grenades a piece, with far more M-60 ammunition than the basic load. SIX: the NVA, no doubt had their usual six or seven magazines per man and their grenades were inferior munitions to ours. SEVEN: The battle area where third and fourth platoons made initial contact was small in size. The NVA, having a much larger force than us had difficulty bringing a large mass of troops against us at any one time, without shooting each other. EIGHT: The sides of the ridge were steep giving us an initial advantage. NINE: The size of our force fit the hogback making it easier for me to make a fire and maneuver fallback, towards the hilltop. TEN: There was ample underbrush and trees to give us good cover to fight a hedgehog defensive fight. ELEVEN: Captain Hockett at the hilltop was initially out of the first moments of combat and had time to form a perimeter, and call for anything that battalion could send. TWELVE: When I gave the order to cover and fall back, I used fourth platoon as base of fire. When third platoon was back up the ridge fifty meters I stopped them and had them fire on the sides of the ridge, and then moved fourth platoon back to us. It would have been a deadly mistake to have moved fourth platoon through the third platoon, presenting the NVA with a massed target. I did the same fall back maneuver,all the way to the linkup.

Since I was almost without my right leg, if Jerry Loucks had been hit early in the combat we would have been in an even worse situation. Third and fourth platoon squad leaders had all they could handle with their squads and Loucks was a terrific fighting man and also relayed my orders. I kept hoping Lieutenant LePeilbet would come fully awake, as he was a real stud leader. However every time LePeilbet came to he went back under, I guess due to the pain. One more thing that saved us was the brave and daring chopper run in of the brigade commander, to throw out a resupply of ammunition to Hockett on the hilltop. First and second platoons were fighting like hell on the hilltop and that no doubt drew enemy troops around to the north and west sides of the hill. That relieved some of the pressure on us. The most important factor was the sudden arrival of the Cobra gunship in time for me to put him on the NVA machine gun position in the bamboo. Those factors kept our unit from having more killed in action or be overrun.

The VC and NVA had launched four offensives since January 1968. They started with the TET'68 very large offensive all over the country expecting the people to rally to their cause. Instead the people clung to the Saigon Government and the Americans. The VC had been sent in ahead of the NVA and was almost wiped out. The NVA suffered huge casualties, but still launched two more big offensive actions during 1968. Both later NVA offensive's were smashed with heavy casualties. Next year they had TET'69, which resulted in much the same result, with the only difference being the NVA did not succeed in attacking the large population centers. Then in September 1969, a lesson plan was captured that gave instructions of the details of implementing resolution nine," A BETTER WAR"(4) by Lewis Sorley chapter 10 page 154. In November of 1969 the "resolution nine" was captured by the 199th light infantry brigade. "A BETTER WAR chapter 10"(4) The Communist had put out a general sop of tactics to be followed by their units each year. For instance in "resolution eight" for 1968 etc General GIAP could have used resolution eight for toilet paper after TET' 68. Resolution nine in total, instructed the VC remnant to go back to small unit guerilla warfare, where they started in the late 1950's. The resolution also ordered the breaking down of the NVA in country, to small units and hit and run tactics. Many large NVA units were pulled out to Cambodia and Laos. This was a tacit admission by the Hanoi leadership that they could not beat the Americans. It did not matter what our morale, discipline and drug problems were in late 1969. The resolution went on to state that, small units would seek to inflict casualties on the Americans and the Hanoi leadership would appeal to the American left wing to force us out of the war. The anti war protesters and celebrities, as well as

Vietnam Veterans against the War, were expected to force Nixon to start the withdrawal.

I suspect that a large number of Vietnam Veterans against the War had never been in the armed forces. However, it must be admitted that many were most certainly Vietnam Veteran's and even combat veterans'. This was the kind of shameful thing that led to a withdrawal of our forces with 1600 men unaccounted for. Nixon and Kissinger had a difficult time getting our prisoners of war back, when it was obvious to the whole world that we were not united. Thousands and thousands of brave young men had fought long and hard, to buy time for South Vietnam and hold back the tide of Communism. Yes this is a free country and all can say what they want, but would we at least keep faith with our prisoners of war? No negotiation can be a complete success if the other side knows your people are not united. That may have been the first time in history, that an enemy rallied a large group of American's against their own armed forces. I spent the 1970's in a terrible rage. I knew that a large number of our guys were being mistreated in places like the Hanoi Hilton and many American's did not care. When Nixon stopped the draft by executive order, many commentators in the news media said the demonstrations became much smaller. How awful it must have been for so many American mothers and fathers to know their son was a POW in North Vietnam or Laos. Especially as so many Americans did not care.

In my last years in the Army after the stoppage of the draft, I had a pretty good part of recruiting the all volunteer army in Oklahoma. I think the caliber and quality of the new soldiers was great. Since the start of the all volunteer army, it has become fashionable at the Defense Department to make crude remarks about our Vietnam combat troops. There have been remarks about the draftee army. I think there were as many volunteers as draftees, and in courageous fighting ability it was impossible to tell them apart. I never knew which of my men were drafted and which ones had joined. Today's armed forces are obviously brave and skilful, but they have never faced the close quarters violent combat to the death, that was so trying of men's courage in NAM. In both the Korean War and Vietnam, the American armed forces faced real gut checks in battles fought under extreme weather conditions and in very difficult terrain. I am glad that superior technology, has kept today's forces from having to experience the hell that was Korea and Nam. We certainly should be proud of today's armed forces but it is sobering to know that only ½ of one percent of military age youth join the service. We have to recognize that to be sent away from family and home over and over again, is very trying on the morale of our armed forces on active duty. Yet they have borne the sacrifice with courage and fortitude and have fought magnificently. Time marches on, and I have come to the end of my story of my journey to the hell of NAM, and back. On my journey, I and many more fought in a hellish combat far away from family and home. Those who returned faced a surprisingly large number of American's who wanted only to shame and vilify us. So many refused to acknowledge our courage and combat achievements. When I started this narrative, I promised a story of facts no matter how grim and I have delivered. Since I have now used up the Biblical three score and ten and few more if by strength, I know that my long road is near the end. Soon I will cross the river and if there is a hereafter perhaps I will see Jerry Loucks and many other brave men I knew along the way.

This marks the end of my testament of violence, stress and courage.

—Donald R. White, formerly platoon sergeant
United States Infantry

This Book is dedicated to anyone who has ever known and loved an American fighting man.

WHITE
U.S.AR

THE AUTHOR

This narrative is a nonfiction account of the author's 531 days in the US Army infantry in the Vietnam War and his personal life in the aftermath. Retired US Army Master Sergeant Donald R. White was born in Ardmore, Oklahoma on February 23rd, 1937. He entered the US Army August 1, 1958. Master Sergeant White served the first twelve years and ten months of his army career in the infantry. He was wounded on three separate occasions on five places on his body. On March 12, 1969 his right leg was shot almost off above the knee. This wound caused the reassignment of sergeant white from the us infantry to the us army recruiting command in June 1971. Sergeant White retired from the Army on August 30, 1978 and is a highly experienced and decorated infantry veteran. He has written this narrative from a clear memory and the assistance of the actual Vietnam maps on which he operated. This narrative is factual and does not omit the details of the sheer hell that close combat in Vietnam entailed.

The emotional impact of point blank infantry combat is the feeling of riding on a long Black Train to hell. This is a book for Adults only and children should not be exposed to it. The hellish infantry combat in Vietnam is detailed in the balance of this book. The last of the narrative concerns sergeant white's time spent in US army recruiting and the graphic threats and insults he and many like him faced from the American people. Sergeant White has now been retired from the US Army for thirty four years and currently resides in Oklahoma City. As recent as the summer of 2008, the word NAZI was placed in his front yard by the use of a defoliant as effective as Agent Orange.

After his US Army career, sergeant white was a real estate broker in Oklahoma City for twenty one years until October 1999 when he retired for health reasons. He has three university degrees including a Bachelor of Science in Marketing and two associate degrees. He is now seventy five years of age and wishes to leave a true narrative of the hellish nature of the deadly combat, that the attempt to halt the rise of Communism in South East Asia entailed. The mission of the US Armed Force's was simply to buy time for the South Vietnamese to build their own military forces.

Master Sergeant White has been decorated with the medals and badges listed below:

- Combat Infantry Badge
- Silver Star Medal
- Bronze Star with Oak Leaf
- Meritorious Service Medal
- Vietnam Cross of Gallantry
- Purple Heart with Oak Leaf
- Vietnam Service Medal
- Vietnam Campaign Medal
- National Defense Service Medal
- Gold Recruiter Badge with two Sapphire Stars
- Expert Infantry Badge

REFERENCES

STREET WITHOUT JOY & HELL IN A VERY SMALL PLACE by Bernard Fall. Both of these very authoritative and well researched books were concerning the first Indochina War between the Communist Vietminh and the French Union Forces. The War raged from 1946 until May 1954. The French, using mostly mercenaries from the French empire with French officers and noncommissioned officers were attempting to REIMPOSE their rule over Indochina. The Vietminh led by Ho Chi minh were fighting to establish an independent communist state. STREET WITHOUT JOY was a history of the entire war. HELL IN A VERY SMALL PLACE is almost a daily history of the Battle of DIEN BINH PHU. The French opposed almost the entire Viet Minh battle force of between 30,000 and 50,000 men with eleven battalions in the chamber pot valley of DIEN BINH PHU. Only the French airborne and foreign legion Battalion's were thought of as elite. The other units were mercenaries from all over the empire and did not support France. These two books were my first reference books (1).

MEN AGAINST FIRE by General S.L.A. Marshall was a very well researched book about War in general and had interesting comparisons of statistics. These concerned infantry combat actions and most of all, percentages of American combat troops who actually fired their personal weapons. Reference book two (2)

CITIZEN SOLDIERS by Stephen Ambrose is a great factual story of the actions and service of the US Army in world war two. This book looks at the great service given our country by those brave fighting men who joined or were drafted into the US Army in the second world war. There is also emphasis on the service of reserve and National Guard units. The professional US army was not excluded. I was surprised when I read that only eleven per cent of WW11 American infantry fired their weapons. This fact emerged from a survey by Department of the Army after the war. Reference book three (3)

A BETTER WAR by Lewis Sorley was written with great research and skill at the High Command level at MACV during our Vietnam War. There are many quotations of conversations and words actually said by our top Generals and South Vietnamese officers of comparable rank. There are complete explanations of orders given and the strategic and tactical intentions of our senior officers and diplomats, including the CIA leadership. I was surprised and gratified by the Authors statement that by 1971, most authorities worldwide said the war was won by us. Reference Book Four (4).

SHAKE & BAKE SERGEANTS by Jerry Horton was a very detailed story of infantry sergeants in Vietnam. The shake and bake sergeant's came from an NCO advanced course at Fort Benning Georgia. The program was designed to replace the large number of career noncommissioned officers killed and wounded in the US Army in Vietnam. The young soldiers were just a short time in the Army and were all specially selected. I found most if not all to be brave and capable and certainly some of America's best. The story is at the individual level and concerns A Company, Ist, Battalion 8th United States Infantry. The story is a very good one and reveals the thoughts, attitudes and horrors these brave young men and their troops went thru. This true story also includes myself and the details of our war together. Reference book five (5)

NAM by Leo J. Daugherty and Gregory L. Mattson is called a photographic history. Certainly it has many great and sometimes shocking photos. There is also a very large and specific description presented, of the Vietnam War's toughest battles and a complete record of the trends and major events in NAM. This book superbly accounts for the horrific almost daily happenings in South Vietnam. I derived much factual information from it. Reference book six (6)

GLOSSARY

AMMO-Abbreviation for Ammunition

ARVN-Abbreviation for Army Republic South Vietnam

ARTY-Abbreviation for artillery

AFEES-Armed Forces entrance and examination station

ANTI-PERSONNEL-any ammunition manufactured to kill people

BIRD-Abbreviation for Helicopters or fixed wing aircraft

BODY ARMOR- Thick heavy protection used today, to keep American armed services personnel as safe as possible from small arms fire, or indirect fire, bombs and booby traps.

Breechblock-The closing mechanism normally found in Artillery to close the Breech and allow the weapon to fire also found in naval guns

CAMP ENARI-Fourth Infantry Division base camp near PLEIKU

CP-Abbreviation for Command Post

CH-47-Large two engine helicopter normally used to ferry both troops and equipment named CHINOOK

CIDG-Civilian irregular defense group, mercenaries recruited and controlled by the US Special Forces normally from among the hill tribes in the central highlands or border areas. Many recruited from the MONTAGNARDS, MOUNG etc.

CRATS- C-rations or combat rations some just barely eatable from the Korean War.

CONVENTIOPNAL WAR- War fought with regular forces on fixed lines. There are safe areas in the rear and with terrain objectives leading to control of an enemy nation, population centers and infrastructure

COUNTER GUERRILLA INSURGENCY-War fought by specially trained troops to defeat the insurgency by killing the guerillas and defending the population centers and infrastructure and winning the people to the US side

COMMAND GROUP- Unit command organization normally consisting of unit commander, fire support personnel, radio telephone operators for the unit commander and the unit top sergeant

DAISY CHAIN-Pattern normally flown by armed helicopters to cover infantry troops leaving helicopters in a landing zone.

DAISY CUTTER BOMB- Bomb used by air support to clear a landing zone on a hilltop that is covered by trees and underbrush.

DEAR JOHN LETTER- Letter from young woman to break off a relationship either marriage or fiancé or girlfriend with a soldier fighting for his country

DEROS-Date expected to return from overseas, in NAM go back home

DSC- Distinguished service cross, second highest medal given US Army personnel for gallantry in action.

FAC- Forward air controller flying small single engine aircraft to answer calls for air support and adjust the bombs on the enemy

FNG-Fucking new guys who would become battle hardened veterans if they learn the ropes and survive awhile. We have all been FNGS at some time or place in our lives.

FULRO-Montagnard organization formed to fight Vietnamese oppression.

GUERILLA WAR- War started to achieve political control usually by a small group operating with small unit tactics, to spread fear and make an established government unpopular with the local people. Many guerillas could be called terrorists; they are all fighting for a political result.

HALAZONE-Fowl tasting pill to use in Vietnam water to make the water safe for US troops to drink

H&I FIRE-Long range artillery fire used randomly against likely areas that the Vietcong or North Vietnamese might be using. This fire was normally fired into free fire zones where the Vietnamese civilians had been removed. Great care was taken to keep H&I fire away from civilians.

HOOK- Large heavy utility helicopter to move heavy loads or troops. The CH47 Chinook was normally referred to as a hook. The Hook would usually pick up a load underneath with a hook.

INTEL REPORT- Intelligence report normally from the CIA or Vietnamese Intelligence or US armed services intelligence. The Special Forces along with the CIA and South Vietnamese generated much useful intelligence.

JAG- US Army Judge advocate general's office, mission to try or defend US armed forces personnel, accused of breaking the US military law or the laws of a country the US armed forces were operating in.

JERRY CANS OR GERRY CANS-WW11 term sometimes used in NAM to describe cans that water or fuel could be carried in.

JOLLY GREEN GIANT- Term used to describe the CH54 Sky Crane helicopter that could carry extremely heavy loads such as a field hospital. The CH54 when seen in the air reminded one of a giant dragon fly. The CH54 units were sometimes referred to as the jolly greens, perhaps because of the lyrics of a song in the United States that included the words THINK ABOUT A JOLLY GREEN GIANT.

KHE SANH- Site of the famous battle fought in Tet'68 where the US marines defended their position against a huge force of NVA that outnumbered the marines many times. The base had an airstrip and was in the north end of ICorp near the BEN HIA river. The marines endured a great deal of NVA artillery and repulsed infantry attacks against the surrounding marine hill positions.

KIA-Killed in action

KS-Abbreviation for a grid square on the Nam maps measured IN approximately 1000 meters from corner to corner or can be thought of as a kilometer. Pronounced as KAYS.

LANG VEI-Special Forces camp in NW corner QUANG TRI province. The camp was situated five miles (8 km) west of KHE Sanh. The night of February 7th,'1969 the NVA attacked in large numbers, out numbering the twenty five Special Forces advisors and their 500 MONTAGNARD troops many times to one. The NVA also had five Soviet PT76 Tanks. This happened after a day of heavy artillery bombardment. The camp was overrun with the Special Forces and their mercenaries going down fighting hard. One PT76 Tank was destroyed and swarms of NVA were killed by the camps M-60 machine guns and M-16 rifles. Most of the Special Forces fought their way into the jungle and were rescued by helicopter later. There were seven Special Forces KIA and 200 MONTAGNARDS.

LOG CHANNEL- The radio frequency for ordering resupply of Food, Water, Ammo etc logistics.

LONG BLACK TRAIN-Reference to the violent close quarters horror that the NAM infantry war became and the steady increase in death and ghastly horror.

LOACH-Heavily armed light observation helicopter, hovered slowly right on top of the trees.

LOH-Abbreviation for Light Observation helicopter mostly used for reconnaissance.

LP- Listening post referred to by the French, as SONNETS, door bells, we used them to give us as early a warning as possible.

LNO- Abbreviation for liaison officer.

LT-Short for Lieutenant, we had both 2nd Lieutenant's and the more experienced 1st Lieutenant's.

LZ- Abbreviation for Landing Zone normally for Helicopters.

LRP-Abbreviation for Long range patrol unit, late in war some units changed name to rangers.

MACV-Abbreviation for Military assistance command Vietnam. Headquarters for American Forces commander and staff.

MEDEVAC- Normally thought as a dust off rescue helicopter for the wounded.

MONTAGNARD-Central Highlands tribes that served Special Forces loyally as mercenaries.

M-60- American 7.62 Machine Gun weighed twenty-three pounds and in open field had a maximum effective range of 1100 meters. Sometimes referred to as the pig by its handlers.

M72 LAW- Light anti tank weapon recoilless and was great against bunkers.

NATO-North Atlantic Treaty Organization set up by us with European allies to oppose Communist aggression in Europe originally.

NCO- Noncommissioned officer, US army enlisted ranks E-5 through E-9 originally organized in Roman Legions to assist the officers, Centurions etc.

NVA- North Vietnamese Army- conventional Communist Army from North Vietnam to assist the Vietcong and oppose US & ARVN.

NAMSPEAK US infantry jargon used by the troops in the War. Grunt-US infantry soldier/ sorry about that, there it is, referred to catastrophic horrors the grunts could do nothing about. Man can't sweat the NAM, to do so increased your odds of getting killed. WAG-Wild ass guess: only NCO'S qualified to us SWAG-Scientific wild ass guess: only officers qualified to use.1000 yard stare, referred to tough veterans who had seen beyond such as White, Loucks, LePeilbet, Horton, etc

OPS Abbreviation for operations, referring to specific missions.

PIG-Nickname of us M-6o Machine Gun, heavy and had high cyclic rate of fire eating up much ammo quickly, thus a PIG.

POW-Prisoners of War.

PUFF- Abbreviation for Puff The Magic Dragon, C130 four engine gunship with many machine guns, Gatling guns and sometimes rockets with infrared sighting for night action. Thus the grunts predilection for 1950s, 1960s cartoon names. When the NVA heard puff above they knew it was time to go.

RALLY POINT- Point or terrain feature selected by patrol leader for patrol to regroup if scattered by action.

RED LEG- Nickname or abbreviation for US artillery.

ROK- Abbreviation for Republic of Korea Army.

RTO- Abbreviation for Radio Telephone Operator moving with each infantry leader.

RUCKSACK- Large bag carried on back of infantry soldiers to carry food, extra water, ammunition, sometimes clothing. Sometimes poncho liners were carried to wrap up in, possibly sleeping gear, malaria pills or Halazone, to carry whatever might help a grunt in his daily travail.

SEATO- Abbreviation for South East Asia treaty organization of which members were to oppose communism and help in the War, Thailand, Burma, Australia etc

SITREP- Situation report to inform chain of command of current situation.

SMOKE- Smoke grenades to signal helicopters of position or mark enemy position, Red, Purple, Blue etc

SLICKS- Utility helicopter, the UH1B Huey troop carrier or supply carrier was normally referred to as a slick with the doors off. This helicopter was developed by Bell helicopter at Fort Worth, Texas.

STAND TO- First light and time to get the troops awake and alert.

SKIRMISHERS- Lateral formation for infantry unit to bring all troops side by side on line and facing same direction where all could fire at enemy and search the underbrush for the baddies.

SRPS- Short range patrols, usually a reconnaissance patrol of three or four men led by sergeant-e-5.

TET- Vietnamese lunar New Year holiday, a time to relax forget wars and big ugly men from far away. A time to be with family normally occurring in late January or February and sometimes extending into March.

TO&E- US Army tables of organization and equipment specifying the number of personnel and weaponry a unit should have.

TROOPS- Infantry jargon for the men, the soldiers, the way most infantry leaders referred to those they commanded.

SKYSOLDIERS- Nickname for the tough capable 173rd Airborne, one of the US Army's best units.

SILVER STAR— Third highest medal given by US Armed Forces for gallantry in action.

RPG- Communist rifle propelled grenade with both heat and antipersonnel warheads for vehicles, tanks, and personnel.

USAF- United States air Force

USN- United States Navy

USA- United States army

USMC- United States Marine Corp

VC- Vietcong, National liberation front, ARVN slang for the Communist Guerillas

VC VALLEY- Famous deadly low valley on each side of DAK AYUNH River just west of MANG YANG pass, favorite enemy cache area.

WAIT A MINUTE BUSH- The South East Asia version of the good old American Briar.

The main artillery pieces used by the American forces in NAM were 105 MM howitzers, light easy to move around with hooks, rapid firing with a fifty meter killing radius. The 155 MM howitzer, larger than the 105 with a 100 meter killing radius. The 175 MM howitzer with a huge killing radius that could shoot long range, most H&I missions fired with this weapon. The 175 could fire into North Vietnam from QUANG TRI or from the west South Vietnamese border fire into Cambodia or Laos.

PHOTOGRAPHS

THE UNITED STATES OF AMERICA

TO ALL WHO SHALL SEE THESE PRESENTS, GREETING:

THIS IS TO CERTIFY THAT
THE PRESIDENT OF THE UNITED STATES OF AMERICA
AUTHORIZED BY ACT OF CONGRESS JULY 9, 1918
HAS AWARDED

THE SILVER STAR

TO

[illegible]

FOR
GALLANTRY IN ACTION

[illegible]

GIVEN UNDER MY HAND IN THE CITY OF WASHINGTON
THIS [illegible] DAY OF [illegible] [illegible]

Official award of the Silver Star to Platoon Sergeant Donald R. White.

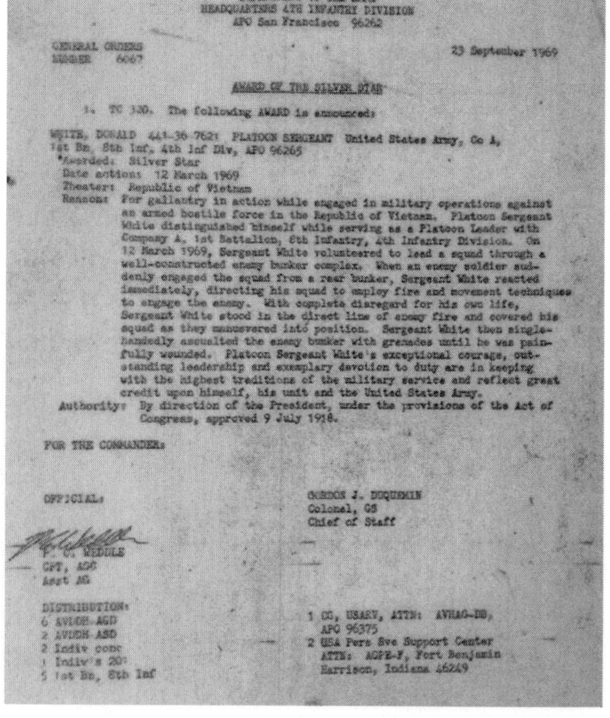

DEPARTMENT OF THE ARMY
HEADQUARTERS 4TH INFANTRY DIVISION
APO San Francisco 96262

GENERAL ORDERS
NUMBER 6067

23 September 1969

AWARD OF THE SILVER STAR

1. TC 320. The following AWARD is announced:

WHITE, DONALD 441-36-7621 PLATOON SERGEANT United States Army, Co A, 1st Bn, 8th Inf, 4th Inf Div, APO 96265
Awarded: Silver Star
Date action: 12 March 1969
Theater: Republic of Vietnam
Reason: For gallantry in action while engaged in military operations against an armed hostile force in the Republic of Vietnam. Platoon Sergeant White distinguished himself while serving as a Platoon Leader with Company A, 1st Battalion, 8th Infantry, 4th Infantry Division. On 12 March 1969, Sergeant White volunteered to lead a squad through a well-constructed enemy bunker complex. When an enemy soldier suddenly engaged the squad from a rear bunker, Sergeant White reacted immediately, directing his squad to employ fire and movement techniques to engage the enemy. With complete disregard for his own life, Sergeant White stood in the direct line of enemy fire and covered his squad as they maneuvered into position. Sergeant White then single-handedly assaulted the enemy bunker with grenades until he was painfully wounded. Platoon Sergeant White's exceptional courage, outstanding leadership and exemplary devotion to duty are in keeping with the highest traditions of the military service and reflect great credit upon himself, his unit and the United States Army.
Authority: By direction of the President, under the provisions of the Act of Congress, approved 9 July 1918.

FOR THE COMMANDER:

OFFICIAL:

GORDON J. DUQUEMIN
Colonel, GS
Chief of Staff

F. C. WEDDLE
CPT, AGC
Asst AG

DISTRIBUTION:
6 AVDDH-AGD
2 AVDDH-ASD
2 Indiv conc
1 Indiv's 201
5 1st Bn, 8th Inf

1 CG, USARV, ATTN: AVHAG-DB, APO 96375
2 USA Pers Svc Support Center ATTN: AGPE-F, Fort Benjamin Harrison, Indiana 46249

The general order of the award and actions meriting the Silver Star to Platoon Sergeant White.

SP4 White just after guard Mount at the 1st Battalion 27th Infantry Quadrangle at Schofield Barracks, Hawaii in June 1960. My rank at that time Specialist 4th class.

Platoon Sergeant White, age 28, at the Cu Chi combat base in January 1966. This picture taken in the time we were setting up the Cu Chi combat base.

In September 1966 at the Trang Bang perimeter in the 4.2 Mortar position when White was 4.2 Platoon Sergeant.

SGT White and the assigned 4.2 Platoon forward observers at the 4.2 mortar position at Cu Chi in 1966.

September 1966 at the Trang Bang position just down the road from where the picture of the Napalm burned little girl was taken. Many Americans never knew it was a South Vietnamese Skyraider Air Strike called by an ARVN Officer and Flown by a South Vietnamese pilot.

1966 at Cu Chi just before I came home in January 1967. Mortar attacks common at Cu Chi at this time.

Triple canopy forest of the Central Highlands at the east side Bunker position at Firebase 25 in late November 1968. One can see the dark and somber undergrowth where death and danger was always lurking.

This is Pappy Rawls of the 4th Platoon, a very tough brave troop who probably saved my life on March 12, 1969. Picture was taken at Firebase 25 in late 1968. This combat soldier was very experienced and respected.

At Firebase 25 in November 1968 after I had brought my Patrol back through the wire and bunker line. This was the patrol moving east to recon a trail north of Ben Het. Since I can't name them all at this late date its best not to name any. They were like so many thousands of others: brave and loyal to their uncaring country. I am third from left notice my ill fitting and ragged uniform.

This is Martha Raye a star of stage and screen with her assistant standing to the left. I didn't have a shirt on and grabbed a flack jacket for the picture. To the right is LT Andy LePeilbet a very competent officer and a very brave young man.

“The Flea” Randy Pierce, the 4th Platoon point man on March 12, 1969 and a young reckless warrior of great courage.

November 1968 firebase 25 before Horton came to us. I am talking to the squad leaders and LT Lepeilbet is standing behind me with his hands in his pockets. Our makeshift shower is behind us and to the right can be seen the Barrel of one of the 105MM Howitzers assigned to the Firebase.

Dak Hodrai Creek in the Plei Trap area. This was an extremely dangerous area in tet"69. The terrain was very tough and filled with NVA soldiers. However one troop has seized a quiet moment to try fishing

Very difficult terrain with a 60 to 70 pound rucksack on your back in the Central Highlands.

The edge of a blasted undergrowth area hit by an airstrike. This in action just east of Laotian border 1969.

NVA or VC Bunkers are hard to spot. Such concealment made them deadly traps to walk up on.

Patrol coming in through the wire at Firebase 25 from A company late 1968

Just another view of hell in the Central Highlands in 1969. This was terrain that tried the condition, determination of even the best US Infantry.

Sergeant White guides in an LOH with a rescued dangling troop from a lost Short range patrol. Notice my hardened fatigue shirt with solidified dirt embedded.

Tunnel mouth where the bad guys tried to evade death or capture.

The Flea with the reason why we had to take rabies shots in his hand at the Dak To combat base December 1968.

Bugs Moran and Flea with a package from home at Firebase 25 1968.

This is the hill position where the CH47 got shot down by an NVA with an AK47 hitting the rear engine just I was guiding it in on my smoke grenade.

Rollinger with his M60 on the left corner of track on Highway14 just north of bullet riddled Kontum City early 1969.

Polei Kleng waiting for the pickup. Smoke and fire from heavy airstrikes just to the west, March 3, 1969.

Greg Rollinger Third Platoon machine gunner in position beside Dak Hodrai creek. Much violence and fighting near this spot with heavy NVA casualties.

Dak Ayun river in VC Valley. Near hill 700 where we crossed the river and I climbed the hill.

An NVA machine gunner is just about to give these troops a reason to get out of the water.

Jerry Horton 4th Platoon Sergeant just before Tet 69. A very tough soldier and a strong and capable leader.

Jerry Loucks: a true American Hero and my point man whom I would go to hell with and have.

Jerry Loucks again with stripes he so richly deserved all in the service of an uncaring American public.

Jerry Loucks waiting on R&R at camp Enari. There was never a better, braver or more deadly American combat soldier than this man.

Knoll nw FB 25
where A company had
no security

Two troops: the rough
veteran Pappy Rawls
at left and Spider Meli
at right.

Troops eating
Thanksgiving dinner
back side of FB 25,
November 1968

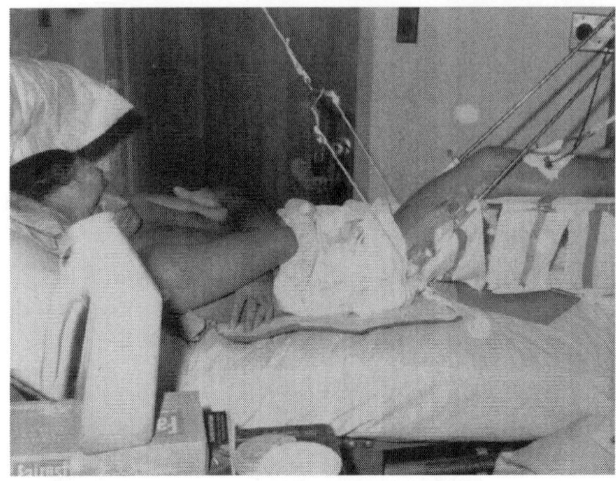

In traction at Irwin Army Hospital in the spring of 1969.

Mike Rinehart, the daring, reckless and super brave Dustoff 37 pilot whose courage and ability was responsible for myself and others to survive March 12, 1969.

Jerry Loucks, with Sgt White behind, lead the 3rd Platoon A Company, 1st Battalion 8th United States Infantry up the hill northeast of Kontum City where an NVA shot down a CH-47 Chinook with an AK-47, January 1969.

March 8th, 1969 company moving in single file at hill 744 just above point where Ho Chi Minh trail branch enters Kontum province South Vietnam.

Made in the USA
San Bernardino, CA
20 October 2014